PLAYING THE ENEMY

John Carlin grew up in Argentina and the UK and spent 1989-95 in South Africa as the *Independent*'s correspondent there. He has also lived in Nicaragua, Mexico and Washington, writing for *The Times*, the *Observer* and the *Sunday Times*, the *New York Times*, among other papers and working for the BBC. He now lives in Barcelona, where he write for *El Pais*. *Playing the Enemy* is being made in to a major film, starring Morgan Freeman and Matt Damon, and directed by Clint Eastwood.

PLAYING
THE ENEMY

NELSON MANDELA AND THE
GAME THAT MADE A NATION

JOHN CARLIN

ATLANTIC BOOKS
LONDON

First published in the United States of America in 2008 by
The Penguin Press, an imprint of imprint of Penguin Group (USA)
Inc., 375 Hudson Street, New York, NY 10014–3657.

First published in Great Britain in 2008 by Atlantic Books,
an imprint of Grove Atlantic Ltd.

3 5 7 9 10 8 6 4 2

A CIP catalogue record for this book is available from the
British Library.

978 1 84354 869 0

Printed in Great Britain by MPG Books Ltd, Bodmin, Cornwall

Atlantic Books
An imprint of Grove Atlantic Ltd
Ormond House
26–27 Boswell Street
London WC1N 3JZ

www.atlantic-books.co.uk

FOR MY SON, JAMES NELSON

CONTENTS

A section of photographs follows page 114.

"Don't address their brains.
Address their hearts."

— Nelson Mandela

PLAYING THE ENEMY

INTRODUCTION

The first person to whom I proposed doing this book was Nelson Mandela. We met in the living room of his home in Johannesburg in August 2001, two years after he'd retired from the South African presidency. After some sunny banter, at which he excels, and some shared reminiscences about the edgy years of political transition in South Africa, on which I had reported for a British newspaper, I made my pitch.

Starting off by laying out the broad themes, I put it to him that all societies everywhere aspire, whether they know it or not, to Utopias of some sort. Politicians trade on people's hopes that heaven on earth is attainable. Since it is not, the lives of nations, like the lives of individuals, are a perpetual struggle in pursuit of dreams. In Mandela's case, the dream that had sustained him during his twenty-seven years in prison was one he shared with Martin Luther King Jr.: that one day people in his country would be judged not by the colour of their skin but by the content of their character.

As I spoke, Mandela sat inscrutable as a sphinx, as he always does when the conversation turns serious and he is the listener. You're not sure, as you blather on, whether he's paying attention or lost in his own thoughts. But when I quoted King, he nodded with a sharp, lips-pursed, downward jolt of the chin.

Encouraged, I said that the book I meant to write concerned South Africa's peaceful transfer of power from white rule to majority rule, from apartheid to democracy; that the book's span would be ten years, starting with the first political contact he had with the government in 1985 (I got a hint of a nod at that too), while he was still in prison. As for the theme, it was one that would be relevant everywhere conflicts arise from the incomprehension and distrust that goes hand in hand with the species' congenital tribalism. I meant "tribalism" in the widest sense of the word, as applied to race, religion, nationalism, or politics. George Orwell defined it as that "habit of assuming that human beings can be classified like insects and that whole blocks of millions or tens of millions of people can be confidently labelled 'good' or 'bad'." Nowhere since the fall of Nazism had this dehumanizing habit been institutionalized more thoroughly than in South Africa. Mandela himself had described apartheid as a "moral genocide" – not death camps, but the insidious extermination of a people's self-respect.

For that reason, apartheid was the only political system in the world that at the height of the Cold War many countries – the United States, the Soviet Union, Albania, China, France, North Korea, Spain, Cuba – agreed was, by the United Nations definition, "a crime against humanity". Yet from this epic injustice an epic reconciliation arose.

I pointed out to Mandela that in my journalism work I had met many people striving to make peace in the Middle East, in Latin America, in Africa, in Asia: for these people South Africa was an ideal to which they all aspired. In the "conflict resolution" industry, burgeoning since the end of the Cold War, when local conflicts started erupting all over the globe, the handbook for how to achieve peace by political means was South Africa's "negotiated revolution", as someone once called it. No country had ever shepherded itself from tyranny to democracy more ably, and humanely. Much had been written, I acknowledged, about the nuts and bolts of "the South African miracle". But what was missing, to my mind, was a book about the human factor, about the miraculousness of the miracle. I envisioned an unapologetically positive story that displayed the human animal at its best; a book with a flesh-and-blood hero at its centre; a book about a country whose black majority should have been bellowing for revenge but instead, following Mandela's example, gave the world a lesson in enlightened forgiveness. My book would include an ample cast of characters, black and white, whose stories would convey the living face of South Africa's great ceremony of redemption. But also, at a time in history when you looked around the world's leaders and most of those you saw were moral midgets (the sphinx did not flinch at this), my book would be about him. It wouldn't be a biography, but a story that shone a light on his political genius, on the talent he deployed in winning people to his cause through an appeal to their finer qualities; in drawing out, in Abraham Lincoln's phrase, the better angels of their nature.

I said I meant to frame the book around the drama of a particular sporting event. Sport was a powerful mobilizer of mass emotions and shaper of political perceptions. (Another nod, short and sharp.) I gave as examples the Berlin Olympics of 1936, which Hitler used to promote the idea of Aryan superiority, though the black American athlete Jesse Owens upset those plans badly by winning four gold medals; Jackie Robinson, the first black man to play major league baseball, helping set in motion the necessary change of consciousness that would lead to big social changes in America.

I then reminded Mandela of a phrase he had used a year or two earlier when handing over a lifetime achievement award to the Brazilian soccer star Pelé. He had said, and I read from some notes I had brought, "Sport has the power to change the world. It has the power to inspire, the power to unite people that little else has. . . . It is more powerful than governments in breaking down racial barriers."

Finally coming to the point, I told Mandela what the narrative heart of my book would be, why it was that I would need his support. I told him that there had been one sporting occasion that outdid all the ones I had just mentioned, one where all the themes I had been touching on during this conversation had converged; one that had evoked magically the "symphony of brotherhood" of Martin Luther King's dreams; one event where all Mandela had striven and suffered for during his life converged. I was referring to the final of the—

Suddenly, his smile lit up the room and, joining his huge hands in happy recognition, he finished the sentence for me: ". . . the 1995 Rugby World Cup!" My own smile confirmed his guess, and he added, "Yes. Yes. Absolutely! I understand exactly the book you have in mind," he said, in full voice, as if he were not eighty-two but forty years younger. "John, you have my blessing. You have it wholeheartedly."

In high spirits, we shook hands, bade each other farewell, and agreed we'd arrange another meeting soon. In that second interview, with the tape recorder running, he explained how he had first formed an idea of the political power of sport while in prison; how he had used the 1995 Rugby World Cup as an instrument in the grand strategic purpose he set for himself during his five years as South Africa's first democratically elected president: to reconcile blacks and whites and create the conditions for a lasting peace in a country that barely five years earlier, when he was released from prison, had contained all the conditions for civil war. He told me, often with a chuckle or two, about the trouble he had persuading his own people to back the rugby team, and he spoke with esteem and affection about François Pienaar, the big blond son of apartheid who was the captain of the South African team, the Springboks, and the team manager, another mountainous Afrikaner, Morné du Plessis, whom Mandela described, in a courtly, old-fashioned British way he has, as "an excellent chap".

After Mandela and I spoke that day, all sorts of people agreed to talk to me for the book. I had already accumulated much of the raw material for my story during the six eventful years I worked in South Africa, 1989 to 1995, as bureau chief of the London *Independent*, and I had been going back to South Africa over the next ten years on journalistic missions. But I started seeing people specifically with this book in mind only after I had talked to Mandela, beginning with a star of that championship Springbok team named Hennie le Roux. You don't expect to emerge feeling warm and sentimental after interviewing a rugby player. But that was what happened to me, because Le Roux had been so moved as he spoke about Mandela and the role he, a decent enough but politically unversed Afrikaner, had found himself playing in his country's national life. We spent about two hours together in an otherwise empty office floor, as dusk fell, and three or four times he had to stop in mid-sentence, choking back sobs.

The interview with Le Roux set the tone for the dozens of others I did for this book. In many cases there was a moment when the eyes of my interlocutor moistened, especially when it was someone from the rugby crowd. And, in all cases – whether it was Archbishop Desmond Tutu, or the far-right Afrikaner nationalist General Constand Viljoen, or his left-leaning twin brother, Braam – they relived the times we discussed in a buoyant mood that bordered at times on euphoria.

More than once people remarked that the book I was going to write felt like a fable, or a parable, or a fairy story. It was a funny thing to say for those who had been the real-life protagonists of a blood-and-guts political tale, but it was true. That it was set in Africa and involved a game of rugby was almost incidental. Had it been set in China and the drama built around a water buffalo race, the tale might have been as enduringly exemplary. For it fulfilled the two basic conditions of a successful fairy story: it was a good yarn and it held a lesson for the ages.

Two other thoughts struck me when I took stock of all the material I had accumulated for this book. First, the political genius of Mandela. Stripped to its essentials, politics is about persuading people, winning them over. All politicians are professional seducers. They woo people for a living. And if they are clever and good at what they do, if they have a talent for striking the popular chord, they will prosper. Lincoln had it, Roosevelt had it, Churchill had it, de Gaulle had it, Kennedy had it, Martin Luther King had it, Reagan had it, Clinton and Blair had it. So did Arafat. And so, for that matter, did Hitler. They all won over their people to their cause. Where Mandela – the anti-Hitler – had an edge over the lot of them, where he was unique, was in the scope of his ambition. Having won over his own people – in itself no mean feat, for they were a disparate bunch, drawn from all manner of creeds, colours, and tribes – he then went out and won over the enemy. How he did that – how he won over people who had applauded his imprisonment, who had wanted him dead, who planned to go to war against him – is chiefly what this book is about.

The second thought I caught myself having was that, beyond a history, beyond even a fairy tale, this might also turn out to be an unwitting addition to the vast canon of self-help books offering people models for how to prosper in their daily lives. Mandela mastered, more than anyone else alive (and, quite possibly, dead), the art of making friends and influencing people. No matter whether they started out on the extreme left or the extreme right, whether they initially feared, hated, or admired Mandela, everyone I interviewed had come to feel renewed and improved by his example. All of them, in talking about him, seemed to shine. This book seeks, humbly, to reflect a little of Mandela's light.

CHAPTER I
BREAKFAST IN HOUGHTON

June 24, 1995

He awoke, as he always did, at 4:30 in the morning; he got up, got dressed, folded his pyjamas, and made his bed. All his life he had been a revolutionary, and now he was president of a large country, but nothing would make Nelson Mandela break with the rituals established during his twenty-seven years in prison.

Not when he was at someone else's home, not when he was staying in a luxury hotel, not even after he had spent the night at Buckingham Palace or the White House. Unnaturally unaffected by jet lag – no matter whether he was in Washington, London, or New Delhi – he would wake up unfailingly by 4:30, and then make his bed. Room cleaners the world over would react with stupefaction on discovering that the visiting dignitary had done half their job for them. None more so than the lady assigned to his hotel suite on a visit to Shanghai. She was shocked by Mandela's individualist bedroom manners. Alerted by his staff to the chambermaid's distress, Mandela invited her to his room, apologized, and explained that making his bed was like brushing his teeth, it was something he simply could not restrain himself from doing.

He was similarly wedded to an exercise routine he'd begun even before prison, in the forties and fifties when he was a lawyer, revolutionary, and amateur boxer. In those days he would run for an hour before sunrise, from his small brick home in Soweto to Johannesburg and back. In 1964 he went to prison on Robben Island, off the coast of Cape Town, remaining inside a tiny cell for eighteen years. There, for lack of a better alternative, he would run in place. Every morning, again, for one hour. In 1982 he was transferred to a prison on the mainland where he shared a cell with his closest friend, Walter Sisulu, and three other veterans of South Africa's anti-apartheid struggle. The cell was big, about the size of half a tennis court, allowing him to run short, tight laps. The problem was that the others were still in bed when he would set off on these indoor half-marathons. They used to complain bitterly at being pummelled out of their sleep every morning by their otherwise esteemed comrade's relentlessly vigorous sexagenarian thump-thump.

After his release from prison aged seventy-one, in February 1990, he eased up a little. Instead of running, he now walked, but briskly, and still every morning, still for one hour, before daybreak. These walks usually took place in the neighbourhood of Houghton, Johannesburg, where he moved in April 1992 after the collapse of his marriage to his second wife, Winnie. Two years later he became president and had two grand residences at his disposal, one in Pretoria and one in Cape Town, but he felt more comfortable at his place in Houghton, a refuge in the affluent, and until recently whites-only, northern suburbs of Africa's richest metropolis. An inhabitant of Los Angeles would be struck by the similarities between Beverly Hills and Houghton. The whites had looked after themselves well during Mandela's long absence in jail, and now he felt that he had earned a little of the good life too. He enjoyed

Houghton's quiet stateliness, the leafy airiness of his morning walks, the chats with the white neighbours, whose birthday parties and other ceremonial gatherings he would sometimes attend. Early on in his presidency a thirteen-year-old Jewish boy dropped by Mandela's home and handed the policeman at the gate an invitation to his bar mitzvah. The parents were astonished to receive a phone call from Mandela himself a few days later asking for directions to their home. They were even more astonished when he showed up at the door, tall and beaming, on their son's big day. Mandela felt welcomed and comfortable in a community where during most of his life he could only have lived had he been what in white South Africa they used to call, irrespective of age, a "garden boy". He grew fond of Houghton and continued to live there throughout his presidency, sleeping at his official mansions only when duty required it.

On this particular Southern Hemisphere winter's morning Mandela woke at 4:30, as usual, got dressed, and made his bed . . . but then, behaving in a manner stunningly out of the ordinary for a creature as set in his ways as he was, he broke his routine; he did not go for his morning walk. He went downstairs instead, sat at his chair in the dining room, and ate his breakfast. He had thought through this change of plan the night before, giving him time to inform his startled bodyguards, the Presidential Protection Unit, that the next morning they could have one more hour at home in bed. Instead of arriving at five, they could come at six. They would need the extra rest, for the day would be almost as much of a test for them as it would be for Mandela himself.

Another sign that this was no ordinary day was that Mandela, not usually prone to nerves, had a knot in his stomach. "You don't know what I went through on that day," he confessed to me. "I was so tense!" It was a curious thing for a man with his past to say. This was not the day of his release in February 1990, nor his presidential inauguration in

May 1994, nor even the morning back in June 1964 when he woke up in a cell not knowing whether the judge would condemn him to death or, as it turned out, to a life sentence. This was the day on which his country, South Africa, would be playing the best team in the world, New Zealand, in the final of the Rugby World Cup. His compatriots were as tense as he was. But the remarkable thing, in a country that had lurched historically from crisis to disaster, was that the anxiety they all felt concerned the prospect of imminent national triumph.

Before today, when one story dominated the newspapers it almost always meant something bad had happened, or was about to happen; or that it concerned something that one part of the country would interpret as good, another part, as bad. This morning an unheard-of national consensus had formed around one idea. All 43 million South Africans, black and white and all shades in between, shared the same aspiration: victory for their team, the Springboks.

Or almost all. There was at least one malcontent in those final hours before the game, one who wanted South Africa to lose. Justice Bekebeke was his name and contrary, on this day, was his nature. He was sticking by what he regarded as his principled position even though he knew no one who shared his desire that the other team should win. Not his girlfriend, not the rest of his family nor his best friends in Paballelo, the black township where he lived. Everybody he knew was with Mandela and "the Boks", despite the fact that of the fifteen players who would be wearing the green-and-gold South African rugby jersey that afternoon, all would be white except one. And this in a country where almost 90 per cent of the population was black or brown. Bekebeke would have no part of it. He was holding out, refusing to enter into this almost drunken spirit of multiracial fellow-feeling that had so puzzlingly possessed even Mandela, his leader, his hero.

On the face of it, he was right and Mandela and all the others were not only wrong but mad. Rugby was not black South Africa's game.

Neither Bekebeke nor Mandela nor the vast majority of their black compatriots had grown up with it or had any particular feel for it. If Mandela, such a big fan suddenly, were to be honest, he would confess that he struggled to grasp a number of the rules. Like Bekebeke, Mandela had spent most of his life actively disliking rugby. It was a white sport, and especially the sport of the Afrikaners, South Africa's dominant white tribe – apartheid's master race. The Springboks had long been seen by black people as a symbol of apartheid oppression as repellent as the old white national anthem and the old white national flag. The revulsion ought to have been even sharper if, like Bekebeke and Mandela, you had spent time in jail for fighting apartheid – in Bekebeke's case, for six of his thirty-four years.

Another character who, for quite different reasons, might have been expected to follow Bekebeke's anti-Springbok line that day was General Constand Viljoen. Viljoen was retired now but he had been head of the South African military during five of the most violent years of confrontation between black activists and the state. He had caused a lot more bloodshed defending apartheid than Bekebeke had done fighting it, yet he never went to jail for what he did. He might have been grateful for that, but instead he had spent part of his retirement mobilizing an army to rise up against the new democratic order. This morning, though, he got out of bed down in Cape Town in the same state of thrilling tension as Mandela and the group of Afrikaner friends with whom he planned to watch the game on TV that afternoon.

Niël Barnard, an Afrikaner with the curious distinction of having fought against both Mandela and Viljoen at different times, was even more tautly wound up than either of his former enemies. Barnard, who was preparing to watch the game with his family at his home in Pretoria, more than nine hundred miles north of Cape Town, forty minutes up the highway from Johannesburg, had been head of South Africa's National Intelligence Service during apartheid's last decade. Closer than any man to the notoriously implacable President P. W. Botha, he was seen as a dark and demonic figure by right and left alike, and by people way beyond South Africa itself. By trade and temperament a defender of the state, whatever form that state might take, he had waged war on Mandela's ANC, had been the brains behind the peace talks with them, and then had defended the new political system against the attacks of the right wing, to which he had originally belonged. He had a reputation for being frighteningly cold and clinical. Yet when he let go, he let go. Rugby was his escape valve. When the Springboks were playing he shed all inhibitions and became, by his own admission, a screaming oaf. Today, when they were going to be playing the biggest game in South African rugby history, he awoke a bag of nerves.

Archbishop Desmond Tutu, on the details of whose private life Barnard used to keep dossiers, was in a state of similar nervous apprehension – or he would have have been had it not been for the fact that he was unconscious. Tutu, who had been Mandela's understudy on the global stage during the years of Mandela's imprisonment, was possibly the most excitable – and undoubtedly the most cheerful – of all Nobel Peace Prize winners. There were few things he would have enjoyed more than to have been at the stadium watching the game, but he was away in San Francisco at the time, giving speeches and receiving awards. After some anxious searching he had found a bar the night before where he would be able to watch the game on TV at the crack of dawn, Pacific time. He went to sleep troubled merely by his desperate desire for the Springboks to beat the odds next morning and win.

As for the players themselves, they would have been tense enough had this just been an ordinary World Cup final. But they bore an added burden now. One or two of the bluff sportsmen in the South African fifteen might have allowed a political thought to enter their heads at some point before the World Cup competition began, but not more. They were like other white South African men, who were like most males everywhere in that they thought little about politics, and much about sport. But when Mandela had come to see them a month earlier, the day before the World Cup competition began, the novel thought had gripped them that they had become, literally, political players now. On this morning of the final they understood with daunting clarity that victory against New Zealand might achieve the seemingly impossible: unite a country more polarized by racial division than any other in the world.

François Pienaar, the Springbok captain, woke up with the rest of his team at a luxury hotel in northern Johannesburg, near where Mandela lived, in a state of concentration so deep that he struggled to register where he was. When he went out for a limbering-up, mid-morning run his brain had no notion of where his legs were taking him; he focused exclusively on that afternoon's battle. Rugby is like a giant chess match played at speed, with great violence, and the Springboks would be meeting the grand masters of the sport, New Zealand's All Blacks (their name comes from their entirely black strip), the best team in the world and one of the finest ever seen. Pienaar knew that the All Blacks could beat the Boks nine times out of ten.

The only person with a graver responsibility than the Springbok players that day was Linga Moonsamy, a member of the Presidential Protection Unit. Assigned the job of "number one" PPU bodyguard, he would not be more than a step away from Mandela from the moment he left his home for the game until the moment he returned. Moonsamy, a former guerrilla in Mandela's African National Congress, the ANC, was intensely alive, in his professional capacity, to the physical perils his boss would face that day and, as a former freedom fighter, to the political risk he took.

Grateful for the extra hour of sleep his boss had granted him, Moonsamy drove to Mandela's Houghton home, past the police post at the gates, at six in the morning. Soon the PPU team that would be guarding Mandela that day had arrived, all sixteen of them, half of whom were white former policemen, the other half black ex–freedom fighters like himself. They all gathered in a circle in the front yard, as they did every morning, around a member of the team known as the planning officer who shared information received from the National Intelligence Service about possible threats they should look out for and the details of the route to the stadium, vulnerable points on the journey there. One of the four cars in the PPU detachment then went off to scout the route, Moonsamy staying behind with the others, who took turns checking their weapons, giving Mandela's grey armour-plated Mercedes-Benz a once-over and busying themselves with paperwork. Being formally employed by the police, they always had forms to complete and this was the ideal time to do it. Unless something unexpected happened, and it often did, they would have several hours to kill until the time of departure, ample opportunity for Moonsamy and his colleagues to engage in some serious pregame chitchat.

But Moonsamy, mindful of the special responsibility he had today, for the identity of the number one bodyguard changed from one assignment to the next, was as focused on the day's great task as François Pienaar. Moonsamy, a tall, lithe man, twenty-eight years old, faced his life's greatest challenge today. He had been at the PPU since the day Mandela had become president, and he had accumulated his share of adventures. Mandela insisted on making public appearances in unlikely places (bastions of right-wing rural Afrikanerdom, for instance), and he loved to plunge indiscriminately into crowds for some unfiltered contact with his people. He also liked making unscheduled stops, suddenly announcing to his driver to stop outside a bookshop, say, because he had just remembered a novel he wanted to buy. Without a care for the commotion he would cause, Mandela would saunter into the shop. Once in New York when his limo got stuck in traffic on the way to an important appointment, he got out and headed down Sixth Avenue on foot, to the astonishment and delight of the passers-by. "But, Mr. President, please . . . !" his bodyguards would beg. To which

Mandela would reply, "No, look. You take care of your job, and I'll take care of mine."

The PPU's job today was going to be of a different order from anything they had ever faced before, or would ever face again. That afternoon's game, or Mandela's part in it, was going to be, as Moonsamy saw it, Daniel entering the lion's den – save that there would be 62,000 lions at Ellis Park Stadium, a monument to white supremacy not far from gentle Houghton, and just the one Daniel. Ninety-five per cent of the crowd would be white, mostly Afrikaners. Surrounded by this unlikely host (never had Mandela appeared in front of a crowd like this one), he would emerge onto the field to shake hands with the players before the game, and again at the end to hand the cup to the winning captain.

The scene Moonsamy imagined – the massed ranks of the old enemy, beer-bellied Afrikaners in khaki shirts, encircling the man they had been taught most of their lives to view as South Africa's great terrorist-in-chief – had the quality of a surreal dream. Yet contained within it was Mandela's entirely serious, real-life purpose. His mission, in common with all politically active black South Africans of his generation, had been to replace apartheid with what the ANC called a "nonracial democracy". But he had yet to achieve a goal that was as important, and no less challenging. He was president now. One-person-one-vote elections had taken place for the first time in South African history a year earlier. But the job was not yet done. Mandela had to secure the foundations of the new democracy, he had to make it resistant to the dangerous forces that still lurked. History showed that a revolution as complete as the South African one, in which power switches overnight to a historically rival group, leads to a counterrevolution. There were still plenty of heavily armed, military-trained extremists running around; plenty of far-right Afrikaner "bitter-enders" – South Africa's more organized, more numerous, and more heavily armed variations on America's Ku Klux Klan. White right-wing terrorism was to be expected in such circumstances, as Moonsamy's political readings taught him, and white right-wing terrorism was what Mandela sought most of all as president to avoid.

The way to do that was to bend the white population to his will. Early on in his presidency he glimpsed the possibility that the Rugby World Cup might present him with an opportunity to win their hearts. That was why he had been working strenuously to persuade his own black supporters to abandon the entirely justified prejudice of a lifetime and support the Springboks. That was why he wanted to show the Afrikaners in the stadium today that their team was his team too; that he would share in their triumph or their defeat.

But the plan was fraught with peril. Mandela could be shot or blown up by extremists. Or today's pageant could simply backfire. A bad Springbok defeat would not be helpful. Even worse was the prospect of the Afrikaner fans jeering the new national anthem that black South Africans held so dear, or unfurling the hated old orange, blue, and white flag. The millions watching in the black townships would feel humiliated and outraged, switching their allegiances to the New Zealand team, shattering the consensus Mandela had striven to build around the Springboks, with potentially destabilizing consequences.

But Mandela was an optimist. He believed things would turn out right, just as he believed (here he was in a small minority) that the Springboks would win. That was why it was in a tense but cheerful mood that he sat down on this cold, bright winter's Saturday morning to his habitually big breakfast. He had, in this order: half a papaya, then corn porridge, served stiff, to which he added mixed nuts and raisins before pouring in hot milk; this was followed by a green salad, then – on a side plate – three slices of banana, three slices of kiwifruit, and three slices of mango. Finally he served himself a cup of coffee, which he sweetened with honey.

Mandela, longing for the game to start, ate this morning with special relish. He had not realized it until now, but his whole life had been a preparation for this moment. His decision to join the ANC as a young man in the forties; his defiant leadership in the campaign against apartheid in the fifties; the solitude and toughness and quiet routine of prison; the grinding exercise regimen to which he submitted himself behind bars, believing always that he would get out one day and play a leading role in his country's affairs: all that, and much more, had provided the platform for the final push of the last ten years, a period that had seen Mandela take on his toughest battles and his most unlikely victories. Today was the great test, and the one that offered the prospect of the most enduring reward.

If it worked it would bring to a triumphant conclusion the journey he undertook, classically epic in its ambition, in the final decade of his long walk to freedom. Like Homer's Odysseus, he progressed from challenge to challenge, overcoming each one not because he was stronger than his foes, but because he was cleverer and more beguiling. He had forged these qualities following his arrest and imprisonment in 1962, when he came to realize that the route of brute force he had attempted, as the founding commander of the ANC's military wing, could not work. In jail he judged that the way to kill apartheid was to persuade white people to kill it themselves, to join his team, submit to his leadership.

It was in jail too that he seized his first great chance to put the strategy into action. The adversary on that occasion was a man called Kobie Coetsee, whose state of mind on this morning of the rugby game was one of nerve-shredding excitement, like everybody else's; whose clarity of purpose was clouded only by the question whether he should watch the game at his home, just outside Cape Town, or soak in the atmosphere at a neighbourhood bar. Coetsee and Mandela were on the same side today to a degree that would have been unthinkable when they had first met a decade ago. Back then, they had every reason to feel hostile towards each other. Mandela was South Africa's most celebrated political prisoner; Coetsee was South Africa's minister of justice and of prisons. The task Mandela had set himself back then, twenty-three years into his life sentence, was to win over Coetsee, the man who held the keys to his cell.

CHAPTER II
THE MINISTER OF JUSTICE

November 1985

Nineteen eighty-five was a hopeful year for the world but not for South Africa. Mikhail Gorbachev came to power in the Soviet Union, Ronald Reagan was sworn in as president for a second term, and the two Cold War leaders held their first meeting, offering the strongest signal in forty years that the superpowers might prevail upon each other to shelve their stratagems for mutually assured destruction. South Africa was rushing in the opposite direction. Tensions between anti-apartheid militants and the police exploded into the most violent escalation of racial hostilities since Queen Victoria's redcoats and King Cetshwayo's battalions inflicted savage slaughter on each other in the Anglo-Zulu War of 1879. The exiled ANC leadership stirred their supporters inside South Africa to rise up against the government, but they pursued their offensive against the government across other fronts too. Through the powerful domestic trade unions, through international economic sanctions, through diplomatic isolation. And through rugby. For twenty years, the ANC had been waging a campaign to deprive white male South Africans, and especially the Afrikaners, of international rugby, their lives' great passion. Nineteen eighty-five was the year they secured their greatest triumphs, successfully thwarting a planned Springbok tour of New Zealand. That hurt. The fresh memory of that defeat injected an added vitality into the hammy forearms of the Afrikaner riot police as they thumped their truncheons down on the heads of their black victims.

The only prospect in sight that year, it seemed, was civil war. A national opinion poll conducted in mid-August found that 70 per cent of the black population and 30 per cent of the white believed that was the direction the country was heading in. But were it to come to that, the winner would not be Mandela's ANC; it would be their chief adversary, President P. W. Botha, better known in South Africa as "P.W." or, by the friends and foes who feared him, "die groot krokodil", the big crocodile. Botha, who ruled South Africa between 1978 and 1989, announced a state of emergency in the middle of 1985 and ordered 35,000 troops of the South African Defence Force, better known as the SADF, into the black townships, the first time the military had been called in to help the police quell what the government believed to be an increasingly orchestrated rebellion. Their suspicions were confirmed when the ANC's exiled leadership responded to Botha's move by calling for a "People's War" to make the country "ungovernable", prompting white people to flee the country – to Britain, to Australia, to America – in droves. Nineteen eighty-five was the year in which TV viewers around the world grew accustomed to seeing South Africa as a country of burning barricades where stone-throwing black youths faced up to white policemen with guns, where SADF armoured vehicles advanced like spidery alien craft on angry, frightened black mobs. Under the state of emergency regulations, the security forces were granted practically limitless powers of search, seizure, and arrest – as well as the comfort of knowing that they could assault suspects with impunity. In the fifteen months leading up to the first week of November that year 850 people had died in political violence and thousands had been jailed without charge.

In this climate, in this year, Mandela launched his peace offensive. Convinced that negotiations were the only way that apartheid could ultimately be brought down, he took on the challenge alone and, as it turned out, with one arm tied behind his back. Earlier in the year, doctors had discovered he had prostate problems and, fearing cancer, ruled that he needed urgent surgery. They had made the diagnosis at Pollsmoor Prison, where he'd been transferred from Robben Island three years earlier, in 1982. Pollsmoor, on the mainland near Cape Town, was where he shared the large cell with Walter Sisulu and three other prison veterans whom he would infuriate with his predawn indoor runs. The operation, carried out on November 4, 1985, was a success, but Mandela, now aged sixty-seven, had to remain under observation. Doctors' orders were for him to convalesce in the hospital for three more weeks.

During this interlude, Mandela's first spell outside bars in twenty-three years, he began his ten-year courtship of white South Africa. By a remarkable historical coincidence, this was the very month in which Reagan and Gorbachev met. Just as the American president set out to use his charm on the Soviet leader, Mandela prepared to use his on Kobie Coetsee, the man with the world's most contradictory job description, minister of justice of South Africa.

But while the superpower summit in Geneva was a media circus, this meeting was top secret. The press did not learn of it until five years later, but even if they had known about it at the time, even if the story had been leaked, they would have had trouble finding anyone to believe it. The ANC were the enemy, the purveyors of a Soviet-inspired "Total Onslaught", in P. W. Botha's term, against whom the state's security forces had launched what he called a "Total Strategy". Nothing was more unthinkable than the idea of the Botha regime negotiating with the "Communist terrorists", much less with their jailed leader.

But if anyone in government was to make that first contact with the enemy it was Coetsee, whose portfolio extended beyond justice to include correctional services, meaning the prison system. Botha chose Coetsee to be his secret emissary because he was blindly loyal – one of the few people in his cabinet whom Botha trusted to behave discreetly – and because, as minister of justice and of prisons, he was the appropriate member of his government to go and meet Mandela. Besides, it had been to Coetsee, as to his predecessors in the Justice Ministry, that Mandela had long been addressing letters requesting a meeting. In so doing Mandela had been following in a rather hapless ANC tradition, begun with the organization's founding in 1912, of seeking to persuade white governments to sit down and discuss the country's future together. But now at last it was going to happen: the very first talks between a black politician and a senior member of the white government. Botha's reasons for sanctioning the encounter were partly a matter of curiosity – the ANC had launched a Free Mandela campaign in 1980 and by now he was the most famous, least known prisoner in the world. But Botha was motivated more by the increasingly volatile situation in the townships and the intensifying pressure from the outside world. He felt that the time had come to dip a toe in the waters of reconciliation, to venture the first tentative test of whether one day an accommodation with black South Africa might be possible. As Coetsee would explain it later, "We had painted ourselves into a corner and we had to find a way out."

The curious thing was that while Mandela had been the supplicant, Coetsee was the one who felt uncomfortable. It was a mixture of guilt and fear – guilt because he would be seeing Mandela as the emissary of the government that was killing his people; fear because he had read the files on Mandela and he was uneasy at the prospect of coming face-to-face with an enemy so apparently ruthless. "The picture I had formed of him," he said during an interview in Cape Town some years after he had left government, "was of a leader determined to seize power, given the chance, at whatever cost in human lives." From Mandela's files, Coetsee would also have formed a mental image of an imposing former heavy-weight boxer who had had the temerity ten months earlier to humiliate his dour, scowling boss, P. W. Botha, before the entire nation. Botha had publicly offered to free Mandela, but he had issued preconditions. Mandela had to promise to abandon the very "armed struggle" that he himself had set in motion when he founded the ANC's military wing, Umkhonto we Sizwe (Spear of the Nation), back in 1961; he also had to conduct himself "in such a way that he will not have to be arrested" under the apartheid laws. Mandela replied through a statement read out by his daughter Zindzi at a rally in Soweto. Challenging Botha to renounce violence against black people, Mandela mocked the very idea that he might be set free when, so long as apartheid existed, every black person remained in bondage. "I cannot and will not give any undertaking at a time when I and you, the people, are not free," Mandela's statement said. "Your freedom and mine cannot be separated."

Coetsee had understandable misgivings about the meeting, but the balance was tilted heavily in his favour. Mandela was the prisoner, after all, and Coetsee the jailer; Mandela was thin and weak after his operation and wearing hospital clothes – bathrobe, pyjamas, and slippers – while Coetsee, in ministerial suit and tie, glowed with health. And far more depended on the outcome of the meeting for Mandela than it did for Coetsee. For Mandela it was a life-or-death opportunity that might not be repeated; for Coetsee it was an exploratory encounter, almost an act of curiosity. In Mandela's eyes this was the chance he had sought ever since he embarked in politics four decades earlier to begin a serious conversation about the future direction of the country between black and white South Africa. Of all the challenges to his powers of political seduction that he would subsequently face, none would hold greater risks. For had he failed, had he argued with Coetsee, or had the chemistry been wrong, that might have been the beginning and the end of everything.

Yet the moment Coetsee entered Mandela's hospital room the apprehensions on both sides evaporated. Mandela, a model host smiling grandly, put Coetsee at his ease, and almost immediately, to their quietly contained surprise, prisoner and jailer found themselves chatting amiably. Anybody watching unaware of who they were would have assumed that they knew each other well, in the way that a royal adviser knows his prince, or a lawyer his biggest client. It had partly to do with the fact that Mandela, at six foot one, towered over Coetsee, a small, chirpy fellow with big black-framed glasses and the air of a small-town real estate lawyer. But it had more to do with body language, with the impact Mandela's manner had on people he met. First there was his erect posture. Then there was the way he shook hands. He never stooped, he did not incline his head. All the movement was in the socket of the arm and shoulder. Add to that the massive size of his hand and its leathery texture, and the effect was both regal and intimidating. Or it would have been were it not for Mandela's warm gaze and his big, easy smile.

"He was a natural," Coetsee recalled, sparkling with animation, "and I realized that from the moment I set eyes on him. He was a born leader. And he was affable. He was obviously well liked by the hospital personnel and yet he was respected, even though they knew that he was a prisoner. And he was clearly in command of his surroundings."

Mandela mentioned people in the prison service they knew in common; Coetsee inquired after Mandela's health; they chatted about a chance encounter Coetsee had had with his wife, Winnie, on an airplane a few days earlier. Coetsee was surprised by Mandela's willingness to talk in Afrikaans, his knowledge of Afrikaans history. It was all terribly genteel. But both men knew very well that the significance of the meeting lay not in the words they exchanged, but in those that were left unsaid. The fact that there was no animosity in the encounter was in itself a signal, transmitted and received by both men, that the time had come to explore the possibility of fundamental change in how black and white South Africans related politically to one another. It was, as Coetsee would see it, the beginning of a new exercise, "to talk, rather than to fight".

. . .

The absence of cameras, the anodyne hospital setting, the pyjamas, the inconsequential affability of the chat all disguised the truth that Mandela had pulled off the seemingly impossible feat that the ANC had been striving towards for seventy-three years. How had he done it? Like everyone who is very good at what they do – be they athletes, painters, or violinists – he had worked long and hard to develop his natural talent. Walter Sisulu had spotted the leader in him the first day the two men met, in 1942. Sisulu, six years older than Mandela, was a veteran ANC organizer in Johannesburg; Mandela, twenty-five, had just arrived from the countryside. Mandela was a bumpkin to Sisulu's city slicker, but as he sized up the young man standing tall before him, the canny activist in Sisulu saw something that he could use. "He happened to strike me more than any person I had met," Sisulu said more than half a century after that first encounter. "His demeanour, his warmth . . . I was looking for people of calibre to fill positions of leadership and he was a godsend to me."

Mandela often joked that had he never met Sisulu, he would have spared himself a lot of complications in life. The truth was that Mandela, whose Xhosa name, Rolihlahla, means "troublemaker", went out of his way to court complication, deploying a gift for striking poses to valuable political effect during the peaceful resistance movement of the 1940s and '50s. Public acts had to be staged that would raise political consciousness and set an example of boldness to the black population at large. Mandela, as the so-called "Volunteer in Chief" of the "Defiance Campaign" of that period, was the first to burn his black man's identity document, known as "the pass book", a humiliating method the apartheid government imposed to ensure black people entered white areas only in order to work. Before burning the document, he chose the time and place with a view to maximum media impact. Photographs of the time show him smiling for the cameras as he broke that cornerstone apartheid law. Within days, thousands of ordinary black people were following suit.

As president of the ANC Youth League in the fifties, he stood out as a uniquely self-confident individual. During a meeting of the ANC's top leadership, a black-tie event at which he showed up in a dapper brown suit, he shocked everyone present by giving a speech in which he predicted that he would be the first black president of South Africa.

There was something of the brash young Muhammad Ali in him – quite apart from the fact that he boxed to stay in shape, a shape he also enjoyed displaying. A number of photographs show him posing for the cameras stripped to the waist in classic boxing stances. In photographs of him in suits, he looks the image of a Hollywood matinee idol. In the fifties, he was already the most visible face of black protest, and he dressed impeccably: the only black man who had his suits cut by the same tailor as South Africa's richest man, the gold and diamond magnate Harry Oppenheimer.

When the ANC took up the armed struggle in 1961, largely at his behest, and he became commander in chief of the ANC's Umkhonto we Sizwe, he shed the suits and took up liberation chic, modelling himself on one of his heroes, Che Guevara. At the very last public function he attended before his arrest in 1962, a party in Durban, he appeared in green camouflage guerrilla dress. He was the most wanted man in South Africa at the time, but such was the importance he gave to striking the right note of defiance, as well as the pleasure he derived from standing out in a crowd, that he refused his comrades' advice to shave off the imitation "Che" beard he sported in police Most Wanted photographs.

If his vanity was, in part at least, his downfall, he also put it to good use. In jail, facing charges of sabotage, he determined that at his first appearance in court he would again steal the show. He entered the courtroom with deliberately magisterial slowness, dressed, as befitted his status in the Xhosa clan where he was raised, in the elaborate garb of a high-ranking African chieftain – an animal skin across his chest, beads around his neck and arms. As he strode to his seat, a hush fell over the room; even the judge struggled briefly to find his voice. He sat down, then, on a nod from the judge, stood up, slowly surveying the room before beginning what would turn out to be an electrifying speech. It began, "I am a black man in a white man's court," and it achieved precisely the national purpose he sought, generating a mood of unbowed black defiance.

It was an important discovery. Prison could also serve as a political stage; even from behind bars he could make an impact. It transformed his outlook on the sentence that lay before him, and from then on, building on the skills he had acquired as a lawyer defending black clients in white courts during the fifties, he used prison as his practice ground, the place where he trained himself for the grand game that awaited him outside. He honed his natural ability for theatre towards the achievement of his political ends, rehearsing his role among his jailers and fellow prisoners for the triumphant destiny he had the temerity to believe awaited him outside.

The first challenge was to get to know his enemy, a task to which he applied himself with the same rigour he devoted to his physical exercises. He had two tools at hand: books – through which he learned about the history of the Afrikaners and taught himself their language – and the Afrikaner prison guards, simple men, occupants of the lowest rung in apartheid's great white labour preferment scheme. Fikile Bam, who spent time in prison with Mandela, remembered vividly the seriousness with which, right from the start of his sentence, Mandela set about understanding the Afrikaner mentality. "In his mind, and he actually preached this to us, the Afrikaner was an African. He belonged to the soil, and whatever solution there was going to be on the political issues was going to involve Afrikaans people."

At the time, the standard ANC position was that Afrikaner power was an updated version of European colonialism. For Mandela to challenge that view, to declare that the Afrikaners had as much right to be called Africans as the black Africans with whom he shared his cells, took some pluck. Nor did he disguise his newfound passion for finding out about the Afrikaners' past. "He had this very intense interest in historical Afrikaner figures, not least Afrikaner leaders during the Anglo-Boer War," Bam said. "He knew the names of the various Boer commanders."

In prison, Mandela took an Afrikaans language course for a couple of years, and he never missed an opportunity to work on improving his proficiency in the language. "He had absolutely no qualms about greeting people in Afrikaans, and about trying his Afrikaans out on the warders. Other prisoners had their doubts and inhibitions, but not Nelson. He wanted to really get to know Afrikaners. The warders served his purpose wonderfully well."

And not just for learning their language. Mandela looked at these men, the most visible and immediate face of the enemy, and he set himself a goal – to persuade them to treat him with dignity. If he succeeded, how much greater the chances, he figured, that he might do the same one day with the whites as a whole in the wider world.

Sisulu had observed him out of prison, observed him in prison, and – like the trainer who spots the young boxer who becomes heavyweight champ – congratulated himself on the astuteness of his choice. Sisulu was always, by preference, in Mandela's shadow, yet Mandela relied on him for advice on matters personal and political all his life. It was Sisulu, for example, who best understood how to thaw the white jailers' hearts. The key to it all, as he would explain much later, was "respect, ordinary respect". He did not want to crush his enemies. He did not want to humiliate them. He did not want to repay them in kind. He just wanted them to treat him with no-frills, run-of-the-mill respect.

That was precisely what the rough, undereducated white men who ruled over his prison wanted too, and that was what Mandela endeavoured to give them right from the start, however hellish they made life for him. His cell, his home for eighteen years, was smaller than the average white South African's bathroom. Eight feet by seven feet, or three Mandela paces long and two and a half across, it had one small barred window a square foot in size that looked onto a flat cement courtyard where the prisoners would sit for hours at a time breaking stones. Mandela slept on a straw mat, and three threadbare blankets provided the only protection against the windy cold of the Cape winters. Like the rest of the political prisoners, who enjoyed fewer privileges than the criminal occupants of the island's plusher wing, he was obliged to wear short trousers (long ones were provided only for the Indian or coloured prisoners, not for the black Africans), and the food was as scarce as it was grim: a corn gruel laced, on good days, with gristle. Mandela soon lost weight and his vitamin-deprived skin became sallow, yet he was forced to engage in hard labour, either working with a pick on the island's lime quarry or collecting seaweed that would be exported to Japan for use as fertilizer. To wash they were given buckets of cold Atlantic seawater.

Two months after Mandela's arrival on Robben Island, his lawyer George Bizos had his first chance to see the toll that prison had taken on him. Mandela was now much thinner and humiliatingly dressed in those short trousers and shoes without socks. Forming a box around him were eight smartly uniformed guards, two in front, two behind, and two on each side. But from the moment Bizos spotted his client, he could tell that Mandela carried himself differently from the typical prisoner. When he emerged from the prison van with his escort, he, not his guards, set the pace. Bizos threaded his way past the two guards in front and embraced his client, to the confusion of the guards, who had never conceived of the notion of a white man hugging a black one. The two men chatted briefly, Mandela asking after his old friend's family, but with a start he interrupted himself and said, "George, I'm sorry, I have not introduced you to my guard of honour." Mandela identified each of the officers to Bizos by name. The guards were so stunned, as Bizos would recall many years later, "that they actually behaved like a guard of honour, each respectfully shaking my hand".

It was not always thus. The guards and the commanding officers of the prison inevitably rotated, and some regimes were brutal, some relatively benign. Mandela, recognized by his fellow political prisoners as their leader from day one, refined the art of manipulating all of them, irrespective of their character. He strove to persuade the prisoners that deep down all the guards were vulnerable human beings; that it was the system that had made many of them brutish. But that did not mean that when the occasion required it Mandela failed to stand up aggressively for his rights. The one and only time on the island that a guard was clearly about to strike him a blow, Mandela, the lawyer-boxer, stood his ground and said, "If you so much as lay a hand on me, I will take you to the highest court in the land. And when I finish with you, you will be as poor as a church mouse." The guard huffed and puffed but held back from hitting him, before sheepishly walking away.

In the mini-South Africa that the island became, the black prisoners stood up to the white prison regime in much the way they had done to the government when they had been free. Civil disobedience was the general principle, and it expressed itself in hunger strikes, work go-slows, and a habit of salvaging every crumb of dignity they could. The prison guards whom Mandela met when he arrived on the island were accustomed to the prisoners addressing them as "baas". Mandela refused and, while subject to intimidation, never budged.

Prison conditions on the little island fiefdom, formerly a leper colony and a lunatic asylum, were very much the expression of the personality of the commanding officer at any particular time. A mild and affable one called Van Aarde was replaced in 1970 by Colonel Piet Badenhorst, the most fearsome character Mandela would encounter during his years behind bars. The new recruits Badenhorst brought with him to the island were very nasty too, and between them they set about a reign of terror that lasted a year. Badenhorst was incapable of opening his mouth without swearing, and he made a habit at first of singling out Mandela for his filthiest abuse. His guards followed their master's lead, jostling prisoners on their way to the quarry, submitting their cells to snap searches, and confiscating their cherished books, among which Shakespeare and the Greek classics were Mandela's and Sisulu's particular favorites. One day in May 1971 Badenhorst's guards entered the political wing, B section, early one morning, quite drunk. They ordered the prisoners to strip naked while they searched their cells. An hour later one of the prisoners collapsed, and when another one remonstrated, and then hit out, he was beaten so badly that his cell was spattered in blood.

Mandela kept his cool, and under his guidance the prisoners again took up the lessons they had learned in their political struggle outside. They turned for help beyond their microcosmic island world. They sent out messages via prison visitors and the International Red Cross. Help was also at hand from South Africa's most high-profile progressive politician in parliament, Helen Suzman, who visited the prisoners on the island, and was referred by them to Mandela, their unanimously elected spokesman.

The decisive moment came when three judges visited the prison toward the end of 1971. In the presence of Badenhorst, the three met with Mandela, who did not hold back from denouncing the harsh treatment the colonel had been meting out. He mentioned the sorry diet and the hard labour, but dwelled at length on the incident when the drunken guards had stripped the prisoners and beaten them. Badenhorst wagged his finger at Mandela and said, "Be careful, Mandela. If you talk about things you haven't seen, you will get yourself into trouble, you know what I mean?" Mandela seized on Badenhorst's mistake. Turning triumphantly to the judges, as if he were a lawyer in a courtroom again, he said, "Gentlemen, you see for yourselves the type of man we are dealing with as commanding officer. If he can threaten me here, in your presence, you can imagine what he does when you are not here." One judge turned to the others and said, "The prisoner is quite right."

Mandela had tamed his tormentor. After the judges left, prison conditions improved, and within three months word arrived that Badenhorst was to be transferred. But that was not the end of the story. The most interesting part was still to come, for it made an impact on Mandela that would help shape his attitude towards the Afrikaner "oppressors" for the rest of his life, and proved decisive when he was eventually allowed to join political battle with them.

A few days before Badenhorst was due to leave, the national commissioner of prisons, a General Steyn, visited Robben Island. He met with Mandela in Badenhorst's presence. When the meeting was over and Steyn had moved out of earshot, Badenhorst came up to Mandela and, strikingly polite in his demeanour, informed him of his impending departure. Then he said, "I just want to wish you people good luck." Mandela was momentarily struck dumb, but he collected himself sufficiently to thank him and wish him good luck too in his new posting.

Mandela dwelled on that incident, examining the lessons to be drawn from it, reflecting on how a man he had seen as callous and barbarous had in the end revealed himself in a gentler light. He tucked away those thoughts, but he also found ways to put them to immediate use. Applying the strategies he had developed during his seven years on Robben Island, he used all the help that he could from the likes of Helen Suzman and the judicial system towards making the prison a more livable place. By the late seventies not only was the quality of the food and clothing and bedding far better than in 1964, not only had the seaweed-picking and the forced labour on the quarry ceased, but all manner of unimagined luxuries had been added. The prisoners could watch films, listen to radio programmes on a prisonwide speaker system, and, best of all, play sports. Tennis, remarkably, was on the agenda. And so was football, black South Africa's favourite pastime. At the authorities' insistence, rugby was added to the list. The rule from above was that it would be one week football, the next week rugby, always alternating. The younger prisoners played rugby and listened to broadcasts of important matches on the radio. Even though, to a man, they noisily supported the rival teams when the Springboks played, the authorities persisted, as if hoping for a miraculous conversion.

That would happen much later. Before it, came Kobie Coetsee's conversion that November day in 1985.

When Mandela was discharged from the hospital on November 24, 1985, Botha agreed with Coetsee that he should not return to the large cell he had shared over the previous three years with his four old comrades. He would remain in Pollsmoor but would now be kept in a cell on his own, in an otherwise empty section of the prison. This was no punishment, but a first step towards freedom The idea was to keep further contacts between Mandela and the government as secret as possible, even from the other prisoners. Mandela was grateful too to have the space he needed to collect his thoughts and prepare his strategy. Besides, Coetsee saw to it that Mandela, alone in his cell, was pampered as no "baas" had ever pampered a black man in South Africa. His food was improved, and he received newspapers, a radio, and access to an invention unknown in South Africa when he went to prison, a TV.

He also had the company of a prison guard called Christo Brand, who had been transferred with him from Robben Island, and who doted on him. Brought up on a farm, Brand had had his first encounter with electricity at the age of ten and left school at fifteen. Half Mandela's age, he was a sweet-tempered man who came to regard his prisoner in a fatherly light. Mandela acted the part, among other things writing letters to Brand's wife complaining that her spouse wasn't doing enough to improve himself; that he had a fine mind and that if only he would be persuaded to study he could really get ahead in life. Brand's own son Riaan, who was born in 1985, became something of a surrogate grandson for Mandela. Brand smuggled Riaan into Pollsmoor when he was eight months old so that Mandela could hold him. Mandela did so with tears in his eyes; he hadn't been able to touch any of his six children in twenty-three years. As Riaan Brand grew up, Mandela never failed to inquire as to how he was getting on at school, and wrote letters to him punctually each birthday.

The more distant, senior officers at Pollsmoor were harder nuts to crack than Brand. Mandela had to keep his wits honed in order to win them over. The officer in charge at Pollsmoor's maximum-security C wing was a Major van Sittert, a man who, as Brand would relate, was more comfortable dealing with common criminals than political prisoners. "The major used to come and visit the cells once a month," Brand said. "He found the political prisoners annoying: they complained and asked for things a lot more than the regular criminal prisoners; also the major did not speak English very well and he felt uncomfortable with them for that reason too." Mandela, in addition, was world-famous by now, a celebrity in his own way. And that irritated Major van Sittert still more, made him more uneasy in his presence.

Mandela thought hard. He had subdued all his other commanding officers, but the prickly, insecure Van Sittert would put his powers of seduction seriously to the test. Mandela spoke to Brand, probing for weaknesses. And, through Brand, he found one. Sittert was a rugby nut. So Mandela, who had no special interest in rugby, set about zealously learning about the game in preparation for the major's monthly visit. He read the rugby pages in the newspapers for the first time in his life, watched the sports programmes on his TV, and generally boned up on all the latest news so that he could engage the major on his life's passion with seeming plausibility.

Mandela had an incentive beyond the political satisfaction of snaring more white prey. He had a particular need, a request he wished to make that would impinge significantly on his immediate well-being and that only the major could grant. He didn't want to wait another month for a chance to satisfy that need, so he had to seize the moment when it came. Mandela met Major van Sittert for the first time in the corridor outside his cell. And while he found himself at a sartorial disadvantage, as he had on the day he met Kobie Coetsee, wearing prison clothes while the major was decked out like an army officer, Mandela again was the master of the situation. He welcomed the major as if he were a guest at his home. Then, realizing how unhappy Van Sittert was speaking English, he addressed him in Afrikaans.

"Mandela was very polite, as usual," Brand recalled. "He greeted him with a big smile and then immediately started talking rugby. Well, I was very surprised! There he was saying that such and such a player was doing very well, but such and such was below his best, and had really disappointed in the last game, and maybe it was time to give such and such a young player a chance, because he seemed a very promising prospect, and so on, and on." Once the major got over his own amazement, he became quite animated, agreeing with Mandela on practically every point he made. "You could see all those doubts of the major's just melting away," Brand said.

Having laid the trap, Mandela lured the major into it. Gingerly, he steered him into his cell, casually mentioning that he had a little problem, one that he felt sure the major would not wish a rugby man like him to endure. He told him that he received more food for lunch than for dinner, and for this reason he had got into the habit of keeping some of his lunch until the evening came. The trouble was that by then the food was cold. But there was a solution, Mandela said. He had heard about a device called a hot plate. It seemed like just the thing to resolve his dilemma. "Major," he said, "would it be at all possible for you to help me obtain one?"

To Brand's surprise, Van Sittert capitulated without a struggle. "Brand," he ordered, "go and get Mandela a hot plate!"

He got all that and more, meeting again secretly with Kobie Coetsee, this time at his home. The minister, anxious to afford Mandela the dignity he saw he deserved, arranged for the prison authorities to dress him in a jacket for the first time in twenty-three years, and to drive him over not in a prison van but in a stately sedan. At this second encounter the content of the discussion was more explicitly political. Coetsee, pleased, reported to Botha that prison did indeed seem to have mellowed Mandela, that he was not the firebrand terrorist type anymore, that he seemed willing to explore an accommodation with the whites.

Mandela was rewarded with more privileges. Brand and Van Sittert were astounded to receive orders that Mandela be taken on drives around Cape Town. A small committee of Botha's confidants who were in on the secret talks (Coetsee; Niël Barnard, the head of intelligence; and one or two others) feared that if they let Botha's full cabinet know about the talks, someone might leak the story to the press. Even so, they considered it so important for Mandela to start getting acclimatized to life outside prison that they even authorized his prison minders to let him go for short strolls on his own, mingling with unsuspecting locals. Once Christo Brand took him to his home, to introduce Mandela to his wife and children. Another time, two other prison officers drove him all the way to a town called Paternoster, seventy-five miles north of Cape Town, on the Atlantic Ocean. As Mandela strolled alone on the town's pristine white beach, a bus-load of German tourists suddenly appeared. The two prison officials panicked, fearing he would be recognized. They need not have worried. The tourists, enraptured by the wild beauty of the setting, snapped photos, ignoring the grey-haired black man nearby. Mandela could have rushed into their midst and jumped on their bus, in search of political asylum, but he didn't want to get out of prison just yet, despite the clamour that had been building around the world for his release. He could do more good, he saw, by staying inside, talking.

CHAPTER III
SEPARATE AMENITIES

Justice Bekebeke was an angry young black man in November 1985, one of millions. Tall and stick-thin, like an African carving, he had a courteous manner and a soothing baritone voice that when he spoke carried a wisdom, hard won, beyond his twenty-four years.

Paballelo was where Bekebeke lived, a treeless township five hundred miles north of Mandela's Cape Town prison and five hundred west of Johannesburg, on the edge of the Kalahari Desert, in the back of beyond. A black township in South Africa was always paired with a white town. But while the townships invariably had a lot more people in them, only the white towns appeared on the maps. The townships were the black shadows of the towns. Paballelo was the black shadow of Upington.

Upington was a stark caricature of an apartheid town. An incurious visitor to a big city like Johannesburg might have missed the system's crasser racist edges. But in Upington those edges were sharp and blatant – "Slegs Blankes" ("Whites Only") signs at the public toilets, bars, drinking fountains, cinemas, public swimming pools, parks, bus stops, the railway station. Such nonsense, legally required by the Separate Amenities Act of 1953, sometimes generated dark comedy. Should a black woman carrying her "madam's" white baby travel in the "whites only" or "non-whites" section of a train? Or would a Japanese visitor who used a "whites only" public toilet be breaking the law? Or what was a bus conductor to do when he ordered a brown-skinned passenger to get off a whites-only bus and the passenger refused, insisting that he was a white man with a deep suntan?

Often, among the more liberal-minded white set in Cape Town or Johannesburg, these finer points of law were ignored. In places like Upington, deep in the Afrikaner heartland, they were obeyed with Calvinist rigour. Paballelo was poorer, dingier, and more cramped than Upington, but less stifling. There you could escape apartheid's pettier constraints. You could eat, shop, or sit wherever you pleased. To get to Paballelo from Upington you drove about a mile on the road west towards Namibia, until you reached the municipal slaughterhouse. There you turned left and before you stood a rusting sign that read "Welcome to Paballelo." The contrast between one place and the other, as always when you crossed over the white world to the black world in South Africa, was staggering, as if you had gone back a century, or stepped straight from suburban Buckinghamshire into Burkina Faso. One was bone-dry, a cramped labyrinth of matchbox houses on a flat expanse of scrub; the other was a man-made oasis of weeping willows, golf-green lawns, lovingly tended rose gardens, and large homes whose owners had not been shy about sucking up the resources of the nearby Orange River. Upington would have been almost gracious, had it been less unnatural, had the greenery not smacked of fake adornment amid the obliterating heat and desert drabness all around, had it not been a place where white people routinely called black people by that most hurtful, shaming of names, "kaffir" – South Africa's version of "nigger".

Three childhood memories had a lasting effect on the man Justice Bekebeke would become. The first dated from early in his childhood when he visited Cape Town with his family. Looking out over the Atlantic Ocean, he spotted a speck of land not far offshore. His father, who was barely literate but knew where he stood politically, told him that this was the place where "our leaders" were. The speck was Robben Island. Justice begged his father for a coin to put into a shore-line telescope so he could catch a glimpse of his leaders. He did not succeed, the island being seven miles away, but he saw the outlines of the buildings where the cells were – enough for him to construct a fan-tasy in his mind that he had actually been to the island. He went back home and recounted the fantasy as fact, impressing his school friends so much that before he knew it he had acquired the status in Paballelo as a leader himself, as someone from whom his young peers were pre-pared to take political direction.

Thanks to that episode, and thanks to the influence of his father, Justice allied himself from an early age with Mandela's African National Congress rather than with its rival, the more radical Pan Africanist Congress. The PAC was an openly, vengefully racist party that counted "one settler, one bullet" and "throw the whites into the sea" among its slogans, and almost became the dominant force in black politics dur-ing the 1960s. The PAC was South Africa's Hamas.

Imagine Yassir Arafat convincing Hamas to succumb to his leader-ship and unite the Palestinian people under the banner of his Fatah party and you have a sense of what Mandela achieved with his own much larger and more tribally disparate constituency. In black South Africa there were Zulus, there were Xhosas, there were Sothos and six other tribal groups, all of whom spoke different languages at home, most of whom had some history of animosity towards one another. Mandela, whom everybody knew to be a Xhosa of the royal house, ulti-mately won over 90 per cent of all black South Africans.

Bekebeke's second defining memory was sealed when he was ten. He heard about a black man who had been arguing with a white policeman. The dispute grew more and more heated until the policeman pulled out his gun and shot the black man, who, as he fell, thrust at the policeman with a knife and stabbed him to death. Justice didn't know the black man, but the story had the force of a parable on him. "I adored that man," he blazed, recapturing the mood of his youth, when he told the story much later. "I hero-worshiped him for standing up to the white policeman, for fighting back."

If that memory suggests the challenge Mandela would face in persuading his people to accept a negotiated end to apartheid, Justice's third great childhood memory illustrated how tough it would be to persuade them to support the Springboks. It concerned a rugby game in Upington in 1970, also in his tenth year.

Like most black children, he had little interest in the game. It was the brutish, alien pastime of a brutish, alien people. But this time curiosity, and the prospect of gloating over a rare defeat for his white neighbours, urged him on to the local rugby stadium. The New Zealand rugby team was on a tour of South Africa and had come to Upington to play against the big provincial team, North West Cape. The stadium was small, with a capacity of nine thousand, and space – where the sun beat hardest – for only a few hundred blacks. But Justice went along, trusting that the local team, the pride of Afrikaner Upington, would receive a good drubbing.

The Afrikaners, of Dutch descent mostly, speaking a language that most modern Dutch people could understand, made up 65 percent of South Africa's five million white people. The other 35 percent spoke English at home, were of mostly British descent (though there were a number of Portuguese, Greeks, and Lithuanian Jews), and were dominant in the business world, especially big business – which in South Africa meant the gold, diamond, and platinum mines. But in terms of

political power, the Afrikaners ruled supreme. They ran the state –
every cabinet minister, every army general, every police general, every
senior intelligence officer was an Afrikaner – and they owned and
farmed the land. So complete was the association between the Afrikaners and the land that the word "Boer," meaning "farmer" in Afrikaans,
was almost synonymous in practice with Afrikaner. This was hardly
surprising given that 50,000 white farmers owned twelve times as much
arable and grazing land as the country's 14 million rural blacks.

As keepers of the food and the guns, the Afrikaners were the protectors of the rest of white South Africa. Or, as P. W. Botha put it once,
"The security and happiness of all minority groups in South Africa
depend on the Afrikaner. Whether they are English, or German, or
Portuguese, or Italian-speaking, or even Jewish-speaking, makes no
difference."

Botha was heavy-handed but he was right. The Afrikaners were
apartheid's lords and protectors. That was why young Justice cheered
like mad that day for the New Zealanders, an all-white team known,
to the young Justice's confusion and delight, as the All Blacks. He had
plenty to cheer about.

Marshalled by a bald, stocky player named Sid Going, the visitors
thrashed North-West Cape 26–3. Justice, summoning up the childhood
memory, rubbed his hands with glee at the manner in which the New
Zealanders "murdered" the Upington Boers; those overfed giants who
humiliated him, his family, and his friends every day, who insisted always
on black people addressing them as "baas". From that day on, Justice
became a rugby fan, if only in the limited, strictly vindictive sort of way
that millions of black South Africans were. He enjoyed the game only
when the foreign rivals were good enough to beat the Boers.

Justice became a politically alert adolescent who understood
how important rugby was to the Afrikaners; how it was the closest they
got, outside church, to a spiritual life. They had their Old Testament

Christianity, otherwise known as the Dutch Reformed Church; and they had their secular religion, rugby, which was to Afrikaners as football was to Brazilians or cricket was to the residents of Kolkata or Mumbai. And the more right-wing the Afrikaners were, the more fundamentalist their faith in God, the more fanatical their attachment to the game. They feared God, but they loved rugby, especially when played in a Springbok jersey.

Successive South African national teams had built up a reputation during the twentieth century as the most bruisingly physical rugby players in the world. Mostly they were Afrikaners, though occasionally an unusually hefty, or tough, or fast "Englishman" (as the Afrikaners called them, when they were being polite) would sneak into the national side. And mostly, being Afrikaners, they were big-boned men of horny-handed famer stock, who as children learned the game playing barefoot on hard, dry pitches where if you fell, you bled.

As a metaphor for apartheid's crushing brutality, the Boks worked very well. That was why their distinctive green jersey had become as detestable to blacks as the riot police, the national flag, and the national anthem, "Die Stem" (The Call), whose words praised God and celebrated the white conquest of Africa's southern tip.

It was on such indignities that Justice dwelled in that fateful month of November 1985. Mandela, unimaginably, was meeting secretly with Kobie Coetsee, but Justice himself was in less mood for compromise than ever before. He seethed with the dark indignation of a man who knew that, because he was born black, he would never be able to exploit his natural gifts to the full. He had always been an unusually bright pupil, way ahead of his peers and of his parents (his mother never learned to read) by the age of fifteen. But the Upington authorities, who ran Paballelo, did not provide schooling for black children beyond that age. They stuck by the spirit and the letter of apartheid's chief architect, Hendrick Verwoerd, who in 1953, as head of the Department of Native Affairs, came up with a school curriculum designed, as he put it, for "the nature and requirements of black people". Verwoerd, who would go on to become prime minister, stated that the aim of his Bantu Education Act was to stop blacks from receiving an education that might make them aspire to positions above their station. The deeper purpose was to uphold the apartheid system's giant, covert job-protection scheme for whites. Justice's father, determined to do what he could to short-circuit the system, sent him far across the country to the Eastern Cape, to a Methodist school called Healdtown that Mandela himself had attended.

Justice spent the next ten years shuttling back and forth between Upington and the Eastern Cape, six hundred miles across country, in an often frustrating search for an education that would help him achieve his dream of becoming a doctor. He was beginning to get close, passing all the right exams to be admitted eventually to study medicine, when, at the end of 1985, disaster struck. He fell for a girl and made her pregnant. He was twenty-five years old but the Christian educational establishment he now attended found such behaviour intolerable. He was expelled, returning home to Paballelo in the first week of November, burning with frustration.

Justice's return coincided with the township's first serious episode of what the apartheid authorities called "black unrest." It was happening all over the country but was a novel phenomenon for a backwater like Paballelo, where until now political resistance had dwelled underground. During Justice's first weekend back, on Sunday, November 10, his township erupted. The "unrest" followed the grim choreography that was by now familiar to viewers of television news everywhere in the world, except for South Africa, where such images were censored. A group of black people gathered in an open space in Paballelo to denounce the latest litany of social injustices. The local police had been fearing for some time that their hitherto tame blacks ("our blacks" was the phrase they would use, ignorant of the rebellious thoughts that swirled inside their heads) were in danger of following the violent lead of their uppity cousins in Johannesburg and Cape Town. Certain now that the dread day had finally come, they followed the script of their unrest-hardened metropolitan peers and fired tear gas into the small crowd of protestors. Justice was not actually present that day, but there was no shortage of other angry young blacks around to respond by hurling stones at the police, who replied by hurling themselves into the crowd, setting their dogs on the stone-throwers, chasing them, and beating those they caught with their truncheons.

The police were unprepared to cope with the ensuing mayhem, in which rioters burned houses and vehicles owned by those perceived as black collaborators, people such as the black town councillors paid by the regime to give it a veneer of democratic respectability. The police opened fire, killing a pregnant black woman. They said later she had been throwing stones at them. But the truth, as far as Paballelo was concerned, was that she had simply stepped out of her house to buy some bread.

The revolution had finally come to Upington. Over the next two days, Monday and Tuesday, Paballelo residents engaged in running battles with the police, this time with Justice at the forefront.

On Tuesday afternoon, police reinforcements arrived from Kimberley, the nearest city, 180 miles away. At the head of them was a certain Captain van Dyk, who proposed peace talks. That evening Justice and other local leaders met with him in the township. No resolution was reached, but they agreed to meet again the next morning, this time with the whole community present, at the dusty local football pitch. The idea, to which Captain van Dyk assented, was that the residents of Paballelo should air the grievances that had occasioned all the trouble in the first place. If the police captain were able to provide some sort of satisfaction, some sense that the matters raised would be addressed at a political level, then tempers might cool and they would avoid the violent confrontation that loomed. Justice and his fellow leaders were encouraged by Van Dyk's reasonable manner. He was a different breed from the uncouth variety of policeman they had grown accustomed to in Upington.

The next morning, November 13, thousands turned up at the football pitch. Again, the choreography followed a familiar pattern, replicating the sequence of events at thousands of other such protest meetings nationwide. Observed by a phalanx of riot police in grey-blue uniforms and a column of clunky yellow armoured vehicles with huge wheels called Casspirs, an orderly crowd of black people gathered at the centre of the pitch. The proceedings began, as always, with the official anthem of black liberation, "Nkosi Sikelele iAfrika". The words, in Mandela's language, Xhosa, meant :

> God Bless Africa
> May her glory rise high
> Hear our pleas
> God bless us
> Us your children
> Come Spirit
> Come Holy Spirit
> God we ask you to protect our nation
> Intervene and end all conflicts
> Protect us
> Protect our nation
> Let it be so
> For ever and ever

It was generous, mournful, defiant, and had the iterative power of an ocean wave. To black South Africans and those who sympathized with their cause, it was a call to courage. To the apartheid authorities, and in particular to the young white policemen whom the anthem had in its immediate sights, it was a menacing expression of the vast black sea that might rise and engulf them.

After "Nkosi Sikelele" came a Christian prayer. While the thousands addressed themselves to their God, heads bowed, and before anyone had even begun to broach the political matters at hand, a local police officer, Captain Botha, wrested command away from Captain van Dyk. Botha was from Upington.

To Van Dyk's dismay, Botha lifted a bullhorn to his lips and announced, in a cry familiar to all veterans of black protest in South Africa, that the crowd had "ten minutes to disperse". The only thing that was unusual about the warning was that it should have come quite so early on, before the prayers had even finished. Captain van Dyk might well have reached the same point himself, but he would have observed the religious decencies a little more, and might have at least gone through the motions of seeking a negotiated outcome.

Captain Botha didn't wait for the full ten minutes to tick by. Before two minutes had passed he ordered his troops to open fire with tear gas and rubber bullets, to let loose their snarling dogs. Some of the younger blacks hurled stones, but most of the crowd ran off, the screams of the women drowned out by the fearsome revving of the pursuing Casspirs. Most routes had been blocked off by policemen carrying guns, stroking truncheons, or cracking sjamboks, thick leather whips, on the stony ground. Seeing a gap, Justice led a group of about 150 people – men and women, young and old – down Pilane Street, leaving the white policemen behind them.

Suddenly, from one of the small grey-brick houses on the street, shots rang out. A child fell, seriously wounded. Then a man charged out of a house with a gun above his head. Straight into the anger, the fear, the chaos ran the man who had fired the shots. His name was Lucas

Sethwala. He was that peculiarity in apartheid South Africa, a black policeman; he and other "collaborators", the butt of the rioting on Sunday night. Somewhere at the back of Justice's mind, driving him on, were the images that had shaped him, Robben Island and the suffering of "our leaders", the transient joy of watching the All Blacks murder the Upington rugby team, the Separate Amenities Act, the Group Areas, the schooling that ended at the age of fifteen, the thrilling example of the hero who stabbed the white policeman to death . . . all those memories and more ate away at him. But at that moment, as he broke away on his own and chased after police constable Lucas Sethwala, the foremost sensation was frenzy; the sole purpose was revenge.

"There was no time to stop and think. There was no rational choice made. It was pure emotion," Justice remembered.

The fact that Sethwala still had the gun in his hand and Justice carried no weapon, that Sethwala turned around as he ran down the road and fired at Justice, showed just how irrational Justice's response was. But the shots missed and Justice caught him, forced the gun out of Sethwala's hand, and beat Sethwala over the head with it. He only hit him twice, but twice was enough. He lay still, dead. Justice got up and kept running, but the group behind him, who had celebrated Sethwala's capture and pummelling with a cry, did as black South African crowds ritually did too often in such circumstances. They kicked Sethwala's inert body and then someone ran off to get a can of petrol. Justice did not see this; he was told about it later. About a hundred people gathered round the body, whooping with delight. It was a victory at last, or something that in the madness of the moment felt very much like it for Paballelo. They doused the body with petrol, scratched a match, and set it alight.

Justice fled across the border to Windhoek, the capital of Namibia. But then it was not yet an independent country; it still belonged to South Africa. Six days later, on November 19, he was arrested and brought back to Upington, where he and twenty-five others were jailed and charged with murder. The law of Common Purpose, as it was called, allowed for the prosecution not only of the person or persons directly responsible for a crime, but also of all those who might have shared in the desire to commit it, who had lent their moral support. Given such a loose definition, the police could have rounded up two people, or five, ten, twenty, or sixty-two. They opted for twenty-six, charging them all with the murder of the one man. Among the defendants was a married couple in their sixties who had eleven children between them and no criminal – or even mildly political – record. The police investigators made no effort to distinguish between the old couple's degree of guilt and Bekebeke's. They didn't know that Bekebeke had been the one who had administered the decisive blows. Nor would they find out in the course of the long trial that followed. If found guilty, the "Upington 26" would face the same sentence Mandela had prepared for when he had stood at the dock in Pretoria twenty-one years earlier: death by hanging.

CHAPTER IV

BAGGING THE CROC

1986–89

Kobie Coetsee had succumbed more quickly than either he or Mandela would have expected. But Mandela doubted his next target would roll over quite so easily. His ultimate goal – a meeting with Botha himself – could only be attained after, or if, he won over the man guarding the presidential door, the head of the National Intelligence Service, Niël Barnard. Barnard, who had studied international politics at Georgetown University in Washington, D.C., acquired a reputation in his twenties as a boy genius. Botha first heard about him when Barnard was a lecturer in political science at the University of the Orange Free State. Impetuously, Botha hired him out of the university, aged thirty, to head up the NIS. That was on June 1, 1980. Barnard was to remain in the job until January 31, 1992, serving Botha for nearly ten years and his successor, F. W. de Klerk, for two.

No one in the apartheid state apparatus knew more about what was going on in South African politics than Barnard, who had informers everywhere, some of them deep in the ANC. He was shrewd and discreet, a civil servant to the marrow, with a powerful sense of duty. During the twelve years he remained as head of the NIS, an organization that the likes of the CIA and MI6 came to respect, if not love, his face was as unknown to the general public as Mandela's had been in prison. There was no man Botha trusted more.

Barnard was a tall, sleek, dark-haired, humourless fellow. An Afrikaner Mr. Spock, he spoke in a monotone and his features were so blankly set that if you were to run across him a day after meeting him you would probably fail to recognize him. But the workings of his mind were crystal clear, and while he had a stilted way of talking, years later his memory remained sharp regarding the political mood and the fights within government in the 1980s.

"Some people, specifically in the military, but in the police as well, deep down believed that we had to fight it out in some way or another," he recalled. "We at the NIS believed this to be the wrong way to go about things. We took the view that a political settlement was the only answer to the problems of this country." That was a very hard message indeed to sell to the South African government apparatus. Barnard had no illusions about that. "But the important thing was that P. W. Botha, who was more or less born and bred within the security establishment, firmly believed that in some way or another we had to . . . how should I say . . . stabilize the South African situation, and then from there try to find some kind of political solution."

Botha summoned Barnard to his office one day in May 1988, and told him, "Dr. Barnard, we want you to meet Mr. Mandela now. Try to find out what you have been advocating for some time. Is it possible to find a peaceful settlement with the ANC, with this man Mandela? Try to find out his views on communism . . . and then try to find out, are Mr. Mandela and the ANC interested in a peaceful settlement? For we also have deep suspicions about what they would be interested in."

Barnard's first meeting with Mandela was held in the office of Pollsmoor's commanding officer. As Barnard remembered it, recalling Kobie Coetsee's first impressions, "Mr. Mandela came in and I saw immediately that, even in an overall and boots, he had a commanding kind of presence and personality." The two men sat down, both understanding that the real purpose of this meeting was to become acquainted, to develop a relationship that could sustain the political negotiations that might follow. They made some small talk – Mandela asking him what part of South Africa he was from and Barnard inquiring after his health – and agreed to meet again.

Before they did, however, Barnard ruled, just as Coetsee had done, that Mandela should be kitted out in clothes more befitting a man of his stature. As Barnard explained, "Talking about the future of the country in overall and boots: this was obviously not acceptable. We arranged with Willie Willemse, the commissioner of prisons, that at any future meeting he would be clothed in such a way that it serves his dignity and his pride as a human being." It was not only on the matter of clothes that Mandela should be accommodated, Barnard decided. A more fitting meeting venue was required. "Mr. Mandela had to be on a par, as an equal, at any future meeting, this much was clear to me. I remember saying with Willie Willemse that we could never again hold such a meeting within the prison building. That would not create an equal situation." From now on, Barnard and Mandela would meet in Willemse's home on the Pollsmoor grounds rather than in his nondescript office.

This began with the second meeting, at which Mandela turned up for dinner at the Willemses' dressed in a jacket. "He was a wonderful guest," Barnard recalled, his natural reserve thawing at the recollection. At these meetings, Willemse's wife cooked delicious meals, wine flowed, and the two men talked for hours about how to end apartheid peacefully.

For his part, Kobie Coetsee came to the conclusion that keeping this prisoner in prison was as improper, and as unhelpful to the talks' broader goal, as dressing him in prison clothes. Not that he was being treated badly at Pollsmoor. Compared to the claustrophobia he had learned to endure on Robben Island, his cell in Pollsmoor felt like the open sea. But where he went next was a luxury cruise liner.

The worse the Botha regime treated the blacks out on the street, the better it treated Mandela. He could have protested. He could have raged at Barnard, made demands, threatened to call off the secret talks. But he did not. He played the game, because he knew that while his power to intervene in contemporary events was practically nil, his potential to influence the future shape of South Africa might be immense. And so when in December 1988 General Willie Willemse, the top man in the South African prison service, informed him that he would be moved from his big lonely cell in Pollsmoor to a house inside the grounds of a prison called Victor Verster in a pretty town called Paarl, an hour north by road in the heart of the Cape wine country, Mandela raised no objections.

He traded his cell for a spacious home under the supervision of – or rather, looked after by – another Christo Brand, another Afrikaner prison guard who had been with him both in Pollsmoor and on Robben Island. His name was Jack Swart and his job was to cook for Mandela and to play the butler, opening the door to his guests, helping him organize his diary, keeping the house tidy and clean. The kitchen was ample and fully equipped, including devices technologically unimaginable when Mandela went to prison. He was allowed to receive visits from other, still incarcerated political prisoners. One of them was Tokyo Sexwale, an Umkhonto we Sizwe firebrand who spent thirteen years on Robben Island on terrorism charges. Sexwale was one of a small group of young ANC Turks who had got close to Mandela on the island, who not only listened to him talking politics but relaxed with him, engaging him in games of Snakes and Ladders and Monopoly before

Mandela was transferred to Pollsmoor. Recalling that visit to Mandela at Victor Verster, Sexwale laughed. "We saw one television set in the house. That was bad enough. But then we saw another. Two television sets! This, surely, was definitive proof, we thought, that he had sold out to the enemy!"

Smiling broadly, Mandela assured them that this was not a television set. He explained to his openmouthed guests that this machine could boil water. He took a cup of water, and gave them a triumphant demonstration, placing the cup inside and pressing a couple of buttons. A few moments later, Mandela removed the cup of steaming water from the microwave – a device his guests had never seen before.

With Jack Swart ever in attendance, Mandela would entertain dinner guests as varied as Barnard, Sexwale, and his lawyer George Bizos at his new "home". Before the guests arrived, Swart and Mandela would discuss such matters of etiquette as which might be the correct wine to serve first. As for the vegetables, some came from Mandela's own garden, which had a swimming pool and a view of the magnificently craggy mountains surrounding the lush valleys of the Cape winelands. Paradise for Mandela wouldn't have been complete without a gym, furnished with exercise bike and weights, where he toiled diligently every day before dawn.

The idea, as Barnard explained it, was to ease his transition, after what was now twenty-six years of hibernation, into a brave new world of microwaves and personal computers. "We were busy creating a kind of atmosphere where Mr. Mandela could stay and live in at least as normal a surrounding as possible," Barnard said. The deeper purpose, or so Barnard claimed, was to help him prepare for government and a role on the world stage. "Many times I told him, 'Mr. Mandela, governing a country is a tough job. It's not like, with a lot of respect, sitting in London in a hotel and drinking Castle beer from South Africa and talking about government. [Barnard was aiming a barb at the ANC's exiled leaders.]

I told him, 'Government is a tough job, you must understand that it is difficult.'"

Barnard also bore the more difficult task of preparing President Botha, the "krokodil", to meet with Mandela. The initial pressure for such a meeting came from Mandela himself, who began to express some impatience with the pace of progress. He wanted these talks to pave the way for a negotiations process involving the ANC, the government, and all other parties that wished to take part, aimed at ending apartheid by peaceful means. When 1989 came around, after more than six months of meetings between prisoner and spy, Mandela had had enough. "It is good to have preliminary discussions with you on the fundamental issues," Mandela said to Barnard, "but you will understand that you are not a politician. You don't have the authority and the power. I must have a discussion with Mr. Botha himself, as quickly as possible."

In March 1989, Barnard delivered a letter from Mandela to his boss. In it Mandela argued that the only way a lasting peace could be reached in South Africa would be via a negotiated settlement. He said that the black majority had no intention, however, of accepting the terms of a surrender. "Majority rule and internal peace," he wrote, "are like the two sides of a single coin, and White South Africa simply has to accept that there will never be peace and stability in this country until the principle is fully applied."

Perhaps more significant than this letter was the fact that Mandela had already convinced Barnard of the argument it contained. Barnard would convince his boss, even if the letter could not.

"Yes . . . ," Barnard said, a fondness creeping into the steely flatness of his voice, "the old man" – he meant Mandela – "he is one of those strange individuals who captivates you. He has this strange charisma. You find yourself wanting to listen to him . . . So, yes," continued Barnard, "there was, in our minds, looking from an intelligence perspective, never the slightest doubt. This is the man – if you cannot find a settlement with him, any settlement will be out."

That was the point he argued before Botha. But there were other arguments he recommended the president consider too. The world was changing fast. The anti-communist Solidarity movement had come to power in Poland; demonstrations in Tiananmen Square were calling for Chinese reform; the Soviet army ended its nine-year occupation of Afghanistan; the Berlin Wall was tottering. Apartheid belonged, like communism, to another age.

Barnard's arguments influenced Botha, yet the president might have continued to dither, bristle, and pace inside his mental fortress had biological destiny not intervened. A stroke he suffered in January 1989 injected a new urgency into his dealings. He was more respected than loved by his cabinet peers, and some of them feared him. His enemies within his own National Party, sensing weakness at last, were circling for the kill. Barnard, one of the few people who actually felt affection for Botha, sensed that his boss's days in office were numbered and that he had to act quickly. "I remember telling him that the time was absolutely right to meet Mr. Mandela, as quickly as possible. If not, we are going to slip, perhaps, one of the most important opportunities in our history. My views with Mr. Botha were the following: 'Mr. President, if you meet Mandela and it becomes the basis, the foundation for future development in our country, history will always acknowledge you as the man who started this due process. In my considered opinion, there is only a win-win situation.'"

It was a polite way of saying that here maybe was the last opportunity Botha would have to be remembered not entirely as a large, terrifying reptile. Botha got the message and Barnard reported back to Mandela with the happy news that the president had agreed to meet him. "But I warned him, 'Listen, this is an ice-breaker meeting. It is not about fundamental issues. Come to learn about the man. Talk about all those easy things in life. And don't mention the issue of Walter Sisulu. . . . If you mention the release again of Walter Sisulu, Mr. Botha will say no. I know him. And if he says no, it's no . . . Leave that aside. There's another way to tackle the issue. Furthermore, don't tackle difficult issues, that's not the reason for the first meeting."

Mandela listened politely, but he had no intention of following the instructions of this bright, impudent, slightly odd young man more than thirty years his junior. The two had talked a great deal about the possible release of Sisulu, who had been in prison for twenty-five years now, and if Mandela considered it fit, he would raise the matter with Botha. He did not, however, turn down Barnard's offer of a special outfit for the occasion. Courtesy of the NIS, a tailor measured him for a suit. When the suit was delivered Mandela studied himself in the mirror and was pleased with the effect. This was the most important meeting of his life and he was eager to get the atmosphere right. Like an actor about to go onstage, he read over the notes he had been preparing for several days, rehearsed his lines, played himself into the role. He would be meeting his jailer-in-chief in the guise of an equal. Two chieftains representing two proud peoples.

On the morning of July 5, 1989, General Willemse picked up Mandela at Victor Verster to accompany him on the forty-five-minute drive from Paarl to the stately presidential residence in Cape Town known as Tuynhuys, an eighteenth-century monument to white colonial rule. Just before they got in the car, Willemse, momentarily taking over the part of Jeeves from Jack Swart, leaned over to Mandela and helped him adjust his tie. Mandela, a dandy before he went to prison, had lost the knack.

About an hour later, after Mandela had stepped out of the car and was preparing to step into Botha's office, the waiting Barnard did a remarkable thing. Eager for his charge to make a good impression, he kneeled before Mandela and tightened the old man's shoelaces.

. . .

Mandela stood smiling on the threshold of the crocodile's lair, sensing that if he struck the right tone and chose his words wisely the triumph he had been building up to for a quarter of a century might finally be in his grasp. He knew that Botha's decision to meet was an acknowledgment that things could not go on as they had. That was why he had not agonized about the appropriateness of sitting down and talking to the most violent bunch of rulers South Africa had known since the establishment of apartheid in 1948.

Mandela understood, first of all, and in a way that the Justice Bekebekes out there on the firing line could not, that the violence Botha had unleashed on the black population over the previous four years signified a growing weakness and despair. With the illusion of legitimacy gone, the only instrument left to keep apartheid going was the barrel of a gun. If Mandela had learned one thing in prison it was to take the long view. And that meant not being sidetracked by present horrors and keeping his eye firmly fixed on the distant goal.

And there was something else. In all his years studying the Afrikaners, their language and culture, he had come to learn that what they were, above all else, was survivors. They had arrived from Europe and settled in Africa and made it their home. In order to have succeeded in that, they had had to be tough, but also pragmatic. There were two P. W. Bothas. There was the pitiless bully, and there was the man who once warned Afrikaners in a celebrated speech that they had to "adapt or die".

Barnard knocked on the president's door, opened it, and entered the plush salon, decorated in Versailles upholstery. Mandela recalls the moment in his autobiography, *Long Walk to Freedom*: "From the opposite side of his grand office PW Botha walked towards me. He had his hand out and was smiling broadly, and in fact from that very first moment he completely disarmed me." Kobie Coetsee, who stood in

the wings of the meeting alongside Barnard, and watched in astonishment as Botha poured Mandela a cup of tea, judged that the disarming
was mutual. Mandela put the gruff old crocodile at his ease, soothed
him with his frank smile and stately manner, and by speaking to him in
Afrikaans. "I would say there was almost relief as they approached each
other for the first time," Coetsee said.

Botha showed Mandela unqualified respect. Mandela too was
politeness itself, but where he had the edge over the president was in
the guile of his seductive arts. He reached out by drawing analogies
between black people's present struggle for liberation and the Afrikaners' similar endeavour in the Anglo-Boer War, nearly a hundred years
earlier, to shake off the British imperial yoke. Botha, whose father and
grandfather had fought the British in that war, was impressed by Mandela's knowledge of his people's history.

Having judged that he had softened up the president, Mandela went
ahead and disobeyed Barnard's instructions, raising the subject of his
friend Sisulu's release. It was of deep importance, both for political and
personal reasons, that Sisulu, whose health was not perfect, should be
set free, he argued. "Strangely enough," Barnard recalled a decade later,
"Mr. Botha listened, and he said, 'Dr. Barnard, you know the problems
we have. I take it that you've explained to Mr. Mandela, but I think we
must help him. I think it must be done. You will give some attention to
that.' I said, 'All right, Mr. President.'"

It was not all easy going between the two men. "There were
moments of great sincerity," Coetsee recalled, "and both parties were
very serious in their position." Mandela may have had to bite his lip
when Botha, as Coetsee remembered it, began banging on about "standards and norms, civilization and the scriptures", which was National
Party politicians' coded way of contrasting the merits of their culture
with the benighted barbarism of the world inhabited by the blacks.
Botha would not have been thrilled, for his part, to hear Mandela

restate his view that the Communist Party was a longtime ally and he was "not now going to shed partners who had been with the ANC throughout the struggle".

Yet the two men parted as affably as they had met. The chemistry Coetsee identified had worked because Botha confirmed immediately one of the impressions Barnard had reached: Mandela was a man of strong convictions and was unafraid to state them. "Mandela was very sincere, even rudely straightforward at times," Barnard said. "Afrikaner people like that." Botha looked at the leader of black South Africa and he chose to see an idealized version of his own blunt self. Appealing to his vanity and to his Afrikaner pride, Mandela had conquered the "krokodil". "Mandela," Barnard said, "knew how to use his power subtly. It is like comparing old money and new money. He knew how to handle power without humiliating his enemies."

An official statement after the meeting rendered Mandela's victory in bland language: the two men had "confirmed their support for peaceful developments" in South Africa. Botha had committed himself, in other words, to the plan Mandela had been hatching for twenty-seven years in prison: peace through dialogue. Preparations towards full negotiations between the ANC and the government, blessed now by the Afrikaner-in-chief, would continue apace. Also, there had been the pleasing bonus of apparent movement on the release of Walter Sisulu and half a dozen other veteran prisoners, which happened three months later, even though Botha himself would be out of office by then, replaced by F. W. de Klerk.

Both men left that meeting in Tuynhuys feeling better about themselves and the world than when they had gone in. Mandela, in particular, left in a mood of quiet triumph. As he would write in his autobiography, "Mr. Botha had long talked about the need to cross the Rubicon, but he never did it himself until that morning in Tuynhuys. Now, I felt, there was no turning back."

That was the end of Mandela's political work behind bars. He had won over his immediate jailers, like Christo Brand and Jack Swart; then the prison bosses – the Colonel Aucamps and the Major van Sitterts; then Kobie Coetsee, Niël Barnard, and, against all odds, the big crocodile himself. The next step was to leave jail and start practising his magic on the population at large, broadening his charm offensive until it embraced all of white South Africa.

CHAPTER V

DIFFERENT PLANETS

The world Mandela found himself inhabiting in 1989 was far removed in time and moral space from the harshness of life in South Africa, especially black South Africa. As he dressed up for a night out at the home of that nice Willemse couple, as he messed around with his microwave oven, discussed wine with his butler, splashed in his pool, and admired the view from his garden, the most powerful men in the country – the very ones with whom he would sit and sip those genteel cups of tea – would sneak out of the back door and put on their vampire suits, venting the furies on the people Mandela had dedicated his life to setting free.

Apart from the usual riot police mayhem in the townships, the police and army death squads whose creation Botha had approved were bumping off activists they considered a particular danger to the state. And Kobie Coetsee still presided over a judicial system that was sentencing more people to death than Saudi Arabia and the United States (though fewer than China, Iraq, and Iran) and was passing one unjust judgment after another. In April 1989, two white farmers found guilty of beating a black farm employee to death had been sentenced to a fine of 1,200 rand (then about $500), plus a six-month jail sentence suspended for five years. On the very same day another court had found three policemen guilty of beating a black man to death, but jailed just one of the policemen, the one who happened to be black, for twelve years.

Nothing quite compared, though, with what Coetsee's people were getting up to in a courtroom in downtown Upington. Of the twenty-six individuals accused of the murder of Lucas Sethwala, the black policeman who had fired into the crowd, they had contrived to find twenty-five guilty. What still remained to be decided in the middle of 1989 was whether the twenty-five, who had all been in jail since the end of 1985, would receive the mandatory death sentence.

Paballelo was consumed by every detail of the trial. But for the white population of Upington it might have been unfolding in Borneo, for all the interest it held. Save for the policemen on duty, not one white Upingtonian turned up during the whole three and a half years that the trial lasted. Drama works on the premise of a shared humanity with the protagonists. For Upington, Paballelo was a dimly lit parallel world inhabited by an alien species; best left well alone.

It would be unfair to suggest that Upington had cornered the market on white racism. The trial under way there, and the circumstances around it, could have happened in any of a hundred other towns in South Africa. Upington, sitting out there in the desert, did provide a sharply focused vision of apartheid, of the neatly drawn lines that kept the races apart. But the local white burghers were by no means alone, or substantially different from most of their pale-skinned compatriots. And while they were satirized and pilloried the world over, you would have to wonder whether the average citizen of the United States, Canada, or Australia, had he or she been born in apartheid South Africa, would have behaved much differently. They inhabited the same general orbit as the most privileged people in the Western world. Their lives centred on home and work, on leading an enjoyable and comfortable life. Politics rarely came into it. The difference lay in that they happened to live side by side with some of the poorest, most badly treated people in the world, and that their good fortune, the reason why white South Africans enjoyed quite possibly the world's highest average standard of living, and most definitely the most comfortable quality of life, depended on the misfortune of their black neighbours.

Choose a family from among the lower economic rungs of white South Africa. Choose, say, the family of François Pienaar, who would end up as Springbok captain in the 1995 Rugby World Cup final. Pienaar's father was a blue-collar worker in the steel industry. His family was not well-off by the standards of white South Africa. Life for them was a financial struggle. Pienaar was embarrassed by the battered old family car, by the presents he received at Christmas, less extravagant than other boys'. Yet the Pienaar family had a home large enough to accommodate two live-in black maids, who would address François and his three younger brothers as "klein baas", "little boss". This kind of relationship between six-year-old white boys and maids old enough to be their mothers or grandmothers was normal in white homes – as it had been for a long time. P. W. Botha once described in an interview with the *New York Times* his relationship with black people as he grew up. "I was taught by my father to be strict with them," he said "but to be just."

Pienaar grew up in an industrial town south of Johannesburg, five hundred miles east of Upington, called Vereeniging. White Vereeniging had the same relationship with its nearest black township, Sharpeville, as white Upington did with Paballelo. Sharpeville occupied a place in the minds of the Pienaar family barely more meaningful to them than Selma, Alabama. Yet Vereeniging weighed heavily on the minds of Sharpeville's residents. It was the place from which death had been famously visited on them. Sharpeville endured the single worst atrocity of the apartheid era; in 1960 police opened fire on unarmed, fleeing black demonstrators, killing sixty-nine.

There was probably more hatred concentrated toward whites in Vereeniging than anywhere else in South Africa. Sharpeville was the township where the PAC – the "one settler, one bullet" people – had their strongest base of support. Yet Pienaar had little notion that the blacks viewed him as a mortal enemy, and no sense of Sharpeville's existence, let alone its history, as he grew up. Black people drifted around the fuzzier outside edges of his youthful consciousness. As he would admit, "We were a typical, not very politically aware working-class Afrikaner family who never spoke about politics and believed a hundred per cent in the propaganda of the day."

That was the way it was for practically everybody who grew up in Pienaar's world. It didn't cross their minds to question the justness of whites having bigger homes, better cars, better schools, better sports facilities, or the ancestral right to jump the line ahead of black people at the post office. Even more remote for Pienaar, as for the vast majority of Afrikaners of his social class, was the notion that this privileged life whites led had been dubiously acquired, and could be roughly taken away one day. In his adolescence, the notion that black people might organize themselves into a force meriting the title of "enemy" would have seemed far-fetched. The enemy, as far as the rugby-playing François was concerned, were "the Englishmen". They also played rugby, though never as well as the Afrikaners, whom the English-speaking whites called "Dutchmen". The young Pienaar took great pride in the fact that during his entire school career, his team never lost once to a school whose predominant language was English.

The gap between the Pienaar family's passion for rugby and their lack of interest in politics was revealed during the Springboks' 1981 tour of New Zealand. Ordinarily one of the most politically placid countries in the world, New Zealand was split dangerously down the middle by the tour, such was the strength of feeling between the half of the country that shared the Afrikaners' blind devotion to the game and the half that abhorred South Africa's great "crime against humanity". Never before had the population of the island nation been more polarized. The tour lasted eight tumultuous weeks, and everywhere the Springboks went they were met by frenzied demonstrators, helmeted riot police, soldiers, and barbed wire. The stadiums were always full, but the streets outside were packed with just as many demonstrators laying siege. The tour's final game in Auckland was disrupted by a low-flying light plane that dropped flour bombs on the field. Combined with images of policemen clubbing demonstrators dressed in clown costumes, it all made for great TV. The Pienaar family was watching. But they were frankly puzzled by what they saw.

Arnold Stofile called rugby "the opium of the Boer". A black man who, like Bekebeke, had not allowed the indignities of apartheid to thwart his powerful personality, he was raised on a farm, joined an ANC front organization in the early sixties, became a theology lecturer at the University of Fort Hare (where Mandela had studied), was ordained a Presbyterian minister, and played rugby, a phenomenon less uncommon among black men from his native Eastern Cape than elsewhere in South Africa. But he did not let his personal passion for the game cloud his view of the bigger political picture. He became one of the most militant organizers of the international sports boycotts. "We always defined sport as apartheid in tracksuits," Stofile said. "It was a very important element in the foreign affairs of this country, sports icons being de facto ambassadors for South Africa, a key part of the effort to make apartheid less unacceptable. And as far as internal policy was concerned, it was the barrier that kept white youngsters secluded from blacks and so had big support from government, and big business got big tax rebates from supporting sport. So it was the opium that kept whites in happy ignorance; the opium that numbed white South Africa."

Denying white South Africa the happy drug, and the government its "ambassadors", was the mission to which Stofile dedicated nearly twenty years of his life. "A workers' strike, even a bomb, would affect a small group," he explained. "This affected all of them, every white male, every household in a sports-mad country whose main source of pride regarding the rest of the world was its sports prowess."

Niël Barnard, on the receiving end of Stofile's offensive, did not disagree. "The ANC's policy of international sports isolation, especially rugby isolation, was very painful to us Afrikaners. Psychologically it was a cruel blow, because rugby was one terrain where we felt as a small nation that we could hold our heads high. Preventing us from playing rugby with the rest of the world turned out to be a hugely successful lever of political influence."

Stofile's most spectacular success came in 1985, the watershed year in which practically everything seemed to happen in South Africa. He sneaked illegally out of the country and made it, with the help of a former All Black who was his country's high commissioner in Zimbabwe, into New Zealand. There he lent his weight in a decisive manner to a campaign to stop the All Blacks from mounting a planned tour of South Africa.

New Zealand was so divided and angry that the whole culture of rugby, the country's pride and passion, was under threat. Parents were refusing to allow their children to play the game at school, and threatening to stop them from ever playing it again, such was the strength of feeling of the anti-tour camp. Stofile recalled with relish how he went on a propaganda offensive, addressing large crowds, appearing on radio and TV, elevating the national argument beyond abstract notions of black and white, giving the cause a face and a name. When he arrived in New Zealand, support for the sports boycott stood at 40 per cent. Three weeks later the figure had climbed to 75 per cent. Still, the New Zealand rugby board decided to go ahead with the tour, but then players themselves stepped in, a group of them taking the issue to court. Stofile's appearance as a witness in the case proved decisive. A chunky fellow who loved rugby as much as the average New Zealander, he argued that there was a higher cause at stake here, and then proceeded to give an eloquent firsthand account of the crasser injustices black people endured, making special emphasis on the Separate Amenities Act and what it meant to black people's daily lives. He concluded by reminding the court that a country with the admirable democratic tradition of New Zealand should be ashamed to collude with a regime that had the cheek to portray a Springbok team drawn from only 15 per cent of the population as the authentic representatives of the whole of South Africa. "I was witness number two," said Stofile, grinning at the memory, "and when I finished the case was won. The tour was called off. It was a great victory."

Stofile was arrested on his return home and given a twelve-year jail sentence. Black South Africa celebrated his accomplishment as they had celebrated the scenes of Antipodean "white unrest" four years earlier that had so baffled the Pienaar family.

For Pienaar, rugby was just a game, his chief entertainment as a child along with fighting. His life, from a very early age, was violent, but it was never political or criminal in intent, as it was in the ungentle townships; it was violence for violence's sake. When Pienaar was seven, members of a rival gang hanged him from a tree. Had an adult not passed by he would have died. As it was, the rope left deep welts on his neck. Later, while at university, at around the same time as Bekebeke was killing Sethwala, Pienaar nearly did the same – or feared he had – to a stranger he came across outside a bar on a Johannesburg street late at night. During a drunken brawl he floored the man, who landed with his head on the pavement with a terrible crack. In between those two incidents, he cracked more ribs and broke more teeth, on and off the rugby field, than he could remember.

Viewed from the perspective of Justice Bekebeke's world, where soccer and dancing were what people did for fun, rugby was a puzzlingly savage sport, one in which players were stretchered off the field like soldiers from battle; in which the inevitably large, inevitably drink-sodden spectators, in their game-ranger Boer uniform of khaki shorts and shirts, heavy socks and boots, chewed with ferocious gusto on their traditional *boerewors* beef sausages and drank their favourite drink, brandy and Coke. As for the boys, they seemed to take their lead in black South African eyes from their dads. Their lives seemed to consist of one bruising, bloody fight after another, in which children were permanently smashing each other over the head with chairs, when they were not hanging their little friends from trees.

Hanging was very much in the mind of an Afrikaner called J. J. Basson on the morning of May 24, 1989. Basson, the judge who had reached the record-breaking verdict in the Upington case, had been listening for almost six months to arguments from the defence lawyers, chiefly Anton Lubowski, in favour of finding extenuating circumstances that might mitigate the death sentences of Justice Bekebeke and the other twenty-four convicted murderers.

Lubowski was a tall, handsome, thirty-seven-year-old Afrikaner raised in Cape Town whose looks suggested, as his name did, a dashing Polish count. An activist deeply immersed in the political struggle against apartheid, he belonged to that less than 1 per cent of the white population who not only saw South Africa the way the rest of the world did, but who acted on that understanding – who took risks, who made

the conscious decision to swim against the fierce currents of conventional *volk* wisdom. He was that rare white person who really knew his
country, all of it; who spent time in the black townships, socializing as
well as plotting; who made an effort to learn a smattering of a black
language.

Lubowski was a character with whom the journalists covering the
trial became friendly during those first months of 1989. Justice Bekebeke was only a face then across a crowded courtroom. But years later it
was Bekebeke who talked about that time. "Anton was one of us," he
said, with pained solemnity. "He and we were one. We called him
'Number 26,' as if he were the twenty-sixth accused. He was so much
more than just our lawyer." Inside the Upington court building there
was a special consulting room where lawyers met with their clients.
"But he did not want to meet with us there. He wanted to meet with us
in our environment, so he came down to our cells to talk to us. He said
he was more comfortable there. He was our comrade. We didn't see his
whiteness, that he was an Afrikaner."

Lubowski would go down to the cells below the court and sing
protest songs with them, join them in their dances of defiance. And
then he would stand up for them, imposingly tall in his flowing black
advocate's gown in the desert heat of the courtroom, where the win-
dows stood wide open in the hope of snatching a passing breeze. He
would face down Basson, arguing in subdued legal tones or, when all
else failed, raging at him. Mandela would have been more ready than
Lubowski to forgive Basson, would have been more disposed to see his
callousness as the consequence of the world in which he was raised.
But Mandela would also have known that Lubowski offered a vision of
that better world he wished to create in South Africa, and that it was in
large measure thanks to South Africa's Lubowskis that he could argue
convincingly to his black compatriots that because a person was white,
it did not mean that he was bad.

Early in the morning of May 24, the day Basson would give his verdict, Lubowski confessed over breakfast that the best one could seriously hope for was a ray of benevolent paternalism to penetrate
Basson's icy heart. Lubowski harboured most hope for the married
couple in their sixties, Evelina de Bruin and her husband, Gideon Madlongolwana. "I don't think even Basson could be so mad as to hang
them," he said. They had ten children, two still of school age. Evelina
was a plump domestic servant who walked with a limp. Gideon had
worked loyally for South African Railways for thirty-six years. Neither
had a criminal record. They would be okay, Lubowski figured. The
accused for whom he held out no hope at all was Justice Bekebeke,
who was twenty-eight years old at the time, and the most articulate, and
militant, member of the group.

If he had been singled out and the rest spared there would have been
some harsh logic in that. "The real guilty party was me," Justice said.
"Towards the end of that mitigation phase of the trial Anton came
down to the cells and told us our chances. My response was to say to the
guys that I felt I should come clean for the sake of the group. They
hardly let me finish. They all jumped on me. They were enraged. They
said, 'We would rather kill you ourselves than let them kill you.' They did
not want me to own up to this white judge. It was a question of dignity
and solidarity and it was immediately clear to me that there was no possibility of further discussion. Anton was present and he said, 'Okay,
guys, I did not hear this. This conversation never took place.'"

As it turned out, Bekebeke's fellow accused made an immense
sacrifice, for Judge Basson surpassed Lubowski's worst expectations.
He ruled that extenuation would apply to only eleven of the accused;
that along with Justice Bekebeke, Evelina de Bruin, and Gideon Madlongolwana should be counted among the fourteen in whose behavior
he saw no excuse, whose purpose on November 13, 1985, he judged to
be murder.

Cries of pain, amazement, and anger filled the courtroom as the accused and their relatives clutched their faces in despair and disbelief, for this was not what their lawyers had told them to expect. Evelina de Bruin leaned against her husband and wept. Basson, impassive, postponed final sentence until the following day. But the emotions he had unleashed in the courtroom spilled onto the streets. Forty or fifty women, youths, and old men gathered, watched by an equal number of heavily armed policemen. They wept, then burst into song, protest songs of the type heard throughout South Africa at funerals, demonstrations, or political trials.

One teenage boy broke from the crowd and exploded into a Toyi Toyi, a war dance symbolic of angry resistance to apartheid. Hissing, "Zaaa!! Za-Zaaa! Zaaa! Za-Zaaa! Zaaa! Za-Zaaa!" and stamping so hard that his knees jerked up to his chin, he spun around and around as if in a trance, arms flailing, fists so clenched they turned white. But he was not carrying a spear and the policemen had guns and dogs baring their fangs, and a video camera pointed right at him.

The women looked at him and shook their heads. They trembled for him. They were right to. That night the police went berserk. Quite why, it was hard to tell. Perhaps it was because the mothers of the condemned had upset the prim, pristine equilibrium of white Upington's town centre by gathering there, to shed their tears and sing their sad songs. Perhaps it was because, in the one moment of light relief on a day of woe, the black women outside the court had burst into hoots of laughter and ribald applause when a police car slammed accidentally into the side of a passing Toyota. Perhaps it was just that Upington had not yet fully sated its revenge, was still outraged by the intrusion of black unrest into the comfortable certainties of their apartheid lives.

For whatever reason, at nightfall that Thursday a police riot squad stormed past the slaughterhouse on the edge of town, turned left into Paballelo, and assaulted everyone who came into view. At least twenty people were severely beaten. Some were clubbed unconscious. Some were stamped on. Some were kicked in the abdomen till they bled. Of the twenty who had to be hospitalized, five were thirteen years old, and four fifteen.

Next day, the final one of the Upington trial, the courtroom was again furnace hot. Yet Justice J. J. Basson, wrapped in his ceremonial red robes, did not break a sweat. He was going to pass death sentences that morning, but it was with an absent voice – like a bureaucrat impatient to head home at the end of a long day – that he invited each of the accused to make a brief address to the court, as the law allowed.

Justice Bekebeke had been asked by the fourteen to speak on their behalf. He had planned to write something but in the end he could not. He just spoke from the heart.

"In a country like South Africa," he began, addressing himself to Basson, "I wonder how justice can really be applied. I certainly haven't found it. But, my lord, I would like to ask, Let's forget our racial hatred. Let us see justice for all humanity. We are striving for each and every racial group to live in harmony. But is it possible, in the name of the Lord? Is it possible in such a country? . . . I would like the Lord to give you many years so that one day you can see me, a black man, walking on the streets of a free South Africa. . . . And, my lord, may the Lord bless you, my lord."

At those words a small old man standing at the back of the courtroom muttered, "Amen!" He stood erect, propped up with the aid of a wooden ivory-headed cane, impeccably dressed in three-piece suit and tie. He was the father of one of the accused, and – about Mandela's age – a picture of elderly distinction. But when Judge Basson announced his verdicts, he sat down very slowly and his whole body crumpled, his head in his hands. It was death by hanging for Justice Bekebeke and the thirteen others. Basson made the announcement in a deadpan voice before dismissing the court for the last time. The prisoners went down to the holding cells under the courtroom, where Lubowski joined them. He was devastated. "We were the ones consoling him," recalled Bekebeke.

The Upington 14, as they soon became known, were bundled into a big yellow police truck and driven off to Pretoria Central, the maximum-security prison more commonly known then in South Africa as Death Row. Brown fingers clung to the vehicle's metal grille. Led by Bekebeke, the condemned sang "Nkosi Sikelele", the one gesture of defiance they had left.

They arrived at Death Row on the following afternoon, a Saturday, and at dawn on Monday a woman prisoner was hanged. More prisoners were killed on a weekly basis during the rest of 1989. Since 1985, South Africa had carried out six hundred legal executions. A prisoner would be given a week's notice of his death, and then placed in a cell known as "the pot", two cells away from where Justice Bekebeke had his permanent lodging. Before the morning of an execution he would hear the condemned prisoners crying all night long. He would hear the jailers opening the cell at dawn, he would hear prayers being said, he would hear the weeping prisoner led up some stairs to the gallows. When the crying stopped he knew the prisoner was dead. "The horror of it all," Justice said, "was compounded by the knowledge that next week it could be you."

It wasn't him. It was Anton Lubowski. The Upington 14 endured many sorrows on Death Row, but none worse than when they heard on the radio on September 13, 1989, two months after Mandela's tea at Tuynhuys with Botha, that the previous night Lubowski had been gunned down at the entrance to his home in Windhoek, Namibia. Justice never forgot that moment. "There were six of us from Upington together in my cell that morning. We reacted first with disbelief. It could not be true. Then, as time went by, the truth sank in and we were destroyed, devastated – inconsolable. We knew who had done it. Of course we knew. It was the state."

CHAPTER VI

AYATOLLAH MANDELA

1990

After years in the wilderness, the myth became man; the aging patriarch made himself visible to his people again, vowing to set them free. The embodiment of revolutionary virtue, he was met everywhere by vast, enraptured crowds. "I will strike with my fists at the mouths of the government," he cried on the day he returned from his long exile, and within ten days, on February 11, 1979, the state had collapsed and his militias controlled the streets. To rapturous acclaim, the Ayatollah Khomeini proclaimed himself head of a new revolutionary government.

Exactly eleven years later, on February 11, 1990, Nelson Mandela put an end to his own exile, walking out of jail. The coincidence in dates was not lost on the South African government. They feared that in releasing him, and in allowing the ANC to operate legally again after a thirty-year ban, they would unleash what they described to each other, in moments of panic, as "the Ayatollah factor". Niël Barnard was less worried than most. But even he was concerned, in some corner of his sceptical spy's heart, that maybe Mandela had taken him for a ride, had conned him. State officials' nightmare was that after being released in Cape Town, Mandela would set off on a long march north to the political heartland of Johannesburg and Soweto. "There would be a momentum building up and he would be moving through the country," was how Barnard put it, "and he would get to Johannesburg and it would be almost like the Ayatollah – a rolling momentum . . . hundreds of thousands of people on the rampage, shooting and killing. The anxiety was whether it would be possible for us to go through the first twenty-four, forty-eight, seventy-two hours without a major people's uprising, without a revolution."

If the Iranian precedent had given the government pause, it was a more recent foreign episode that impelled the new president, F. W. de Klerk, to push ahead urgently with the work P. W. Botha had initiated. The fall of the Berlin Wall, which had happened barely two months earlier, offered grounds to believe that, whatever happened in South Africa, communism would never again be viable, whether in Eastern Europe or South Africa. Besides, if apartheid had been an embarrassment before, now it was internationally unsustainable. It was fortunate for De Klerk that his predecessor had had the wisdom to pave the way for Mandela's release and for the start of negotiations.

But on that day, February 11, 1990, De Klerk dwelled less on his good fortune than on the perils that might lurk around Mandela's release. It didn't help his or anybody else's state of mind in the government that Mandela's release, for reasons that De Klerk watching on television did not at first understand, went wildly beyond schedule. A battery of television cameras was perched at the entrance to Victor Verster prison and millions of people were watching worldwide, but two hours had passed after the advertised time of his appearance, and still nothing.

When Mandela eventually emerged, striding purposefully out of the main gate of the prison in bright mid-afternoon sunlight, the triumphant smile he wore, happy as a soldier back from war, masked the fact that a little while earlier he had been fuming. His wife, Winnie, looking not quite so cheerful next to him, was the reason. The delay had been on her account, for she had arrived late that morning from Johannesburg, having been detained by a hairdresser's appointment. One consequence was that Mandela gave her a stern reprimand; another was that tensions were rising dangerously at the Parade, the great open square in Cape Town where Mandela was due to deliver his first address as a free man. A huge crowd had gathered under the hot sun, many among them black youths who had little reason to be well inclined toward the host of white policemen on Ayatollah watch. Scuffling broke out, tear gas was fired, stones thrown. It was not a bloodbath, or anything close to it, but enough to send people running in all directions.

Word reached Mandela's retinue, by now in a convoy of cars, that they had better wait for things to calm down. It was not the most auspicious start, but prison had taught Mandela patience. His security people told him the wisest course would be to stop the convoy and wait, and he agreed. They chose to park on the city's outer periphery, in a genteel, politically liberal white suburb called Rondebosch, where lived a young doctor called Desmond Woolf with his wife, Vanessa, and their twin baby boys Daniel and Simon.

The Woolfs were watching the day's events on television, with Dr. Woolf's mother. Dr. Woolf and his wife belonged to a small, politically sensitive sector of white society that was warmly in favour of Mandela's release. They had even debated among themselves whether they should go and join the crowds down at the Parade. The question right now, though, was whether Mandela himself would make it. From what they were saying on the television, no one seemed to quite know where he was.

Suddenly there was a knock at the door. A friend of Vanessa Woolf's told them that Mandela was sitting in a car outside their house. "Come on, don't be ridiculous!" Dr. Woolf said. "No," said the friend. "He is right here. Come outside, quick!."

The couple went out with their two children and Dr. Woolf's mother, and before them they saw a line of five parked cars. "And there he was," as Dr. Woolf would tell it, "sitting in the middle car. We stood . . . and gazed at him in astonishment. The whole world's attention was focused on him and there he was outside our house, when he was supposed to be somewhere else. And we just stood and watched and he rolled down the window, beckoned us towards him, and said, 'Please, come over.'"

Dr. Woolf introduced himself and Mandela introduced himself and they shook hands. Dr. Woolf was carrying Simon, who was barely one, and Mandela reached out to touch the child's hand before asking his father's permission to pick him up and take him through the open window into the car. "He bounced him on his knee for a while and he asked what his name was. Then he wanted to know why we had called him Simon, whether there was any particular significance in the name. He seemed very pleased to be able to hold a child." Vanessa Woolf introduced herself and Mandela exchanged Simon for Daniel. Then Dr. Woolf's mother came up to say hello, completing the cheerful Sunday afternoon scene.

Another Rondebosch resident, Morné du Plessis, had also been debating earlier in the day whether to go to the Parade, deciding eventually that yes, he would. One of the most famous people in the crowd – and certainly the most famous white one – to Afrikaners he was something of a god.

Du Plessis had been captain of the Springboks in the bad old days, as had his father before him. Felix du Plessis led the South African rugby team to four famous victories over New Zealand in 1949, the year after the National Party's first electoral victory, the one that entrenched apartheid in South African life for the next forty years. Morné, who was also born in 1949, would end up improving on his father's record, not only inflicting similar punishment on the All Blacks but retiring in 1980 with an international record of eighteen victories in twenty-two games. Under his captaincy South Africa won thirteen matches and lost only twice. He was an Afrikaner national hero during the nine years he played for his country and, as such, the most visible expression of the racial oppression that the green Springbok jersey symbolized for black South Africans. Unlike some of his teammates, he was not blind to it. He never forgot how in really big games in 1974 against the British Lions and in 1976 against the New Zealand All Blacks the few black people in the stadium were, as he put it, "fanatical in their support of the other side".

It was thus only partly surprising – Du Plessis was quite possibly the tallest of the tens of thousands of people gathered at the Parade – that a black man, apparently drunk, came up to him that afternoon and told him in abusive language to go away, that this was a ceremony at which he did not belong. "But it wasn't the guy's threatening behaviour that stayed with me," Du Plessis said. "It was the fact that immediately another black man admonished him. Then others joined in, angry that he should have treated me that way, and escorted the man away." They were poor people who spoke in Xhosa, Mandela's language, but Du Plessis understood that they had the political sophistication to see that the more whites who could be persuaded to join the Mandela release celebrations, the better for everybody.

Du Plessis was here today because he had a keen sense of the historical significance of this moment and he wanted to be part of it. But the deeper explanation went all the way back to the man who first steered the political course he would take, his father. Felix du Plessis was Springbok captain during the first flush of National Party power, but he was always a supporter of the gentler, more liberal – or, at any rate, less illiberal – United Party, which the National Party had defeated in 1948. He had also fought in the Second World War with the Allies, another factor that set him in opposition to the anti-British, in some cases ambiguously pro-Nazi, Nats. Morné's mother was an English-speaking white South African, and if anything more decidedly anti-Nat than her husband. This did not mean they favoured majority rule. The United Party were against apartheid because they found it to be too crudely racist, but the Du Plessis parents never questioned the fundamental desirability of white power.

Neither did their son, who was born in the same town as François Pienaar, Vereeniging, a surprising coincidence given that not only did they both end up as Springbok captains but also that exactly five years after Mandela's release Du Plessis would go on to become manager of Pienaar's World Cup team. Where the coincidence ended was in the relative political enlightenment of the better-off Du Plessis family, though in truth, politics counted for little more in the young Morné's life than it did in the young Pienaar's.

In 1970, however, Du Plessis came across a man who nudged those faint embers of rebellion his parents had sparked in him. His name was Frederik van Zyl Slabbert. A sociology lecturer at Stellenbosch University, where Du Plessis was studying, Slabbert was a progressive thinker, brilliant academically but notorious in the eyes of the Afrikaner establishment, who also happened to be a good provincial-level rugby player. The combination of the two – a rugby man who was in favour of one-man-one-vote – was startling. Du Plessis made the eye-opening discovery that it was actually possible to admire someone who thought apartheid was wicked.

If Slabbert gave Du Plessis a gentle nudge, his Springbok debut on a

1971 tour to Australia proved a blunt eye-opener. In sporting terms it was a great success. South Africa beat Australia three times out of three and Du Plessis became an instant hero back home, heralded as rugby's new bright star. But Morné's debutant joy was dampened by the hostility of the reception the team received from a broad chunk of the Australian public. "It was staggering to see such ferocity of feeling in people so far away," he recalled. "The images of those enraged Australian faces, the way they seemed actually to hate us, never left me."

A notion was born inside Du Plessis that something was "seriously amiss" in his country. But it was one thing to feel uneasy, quite another to let politics distract him from his rugby career. He never made a stand – as he might have done, to sensational effect – during his nine years as a Springbok star. He never spoke up about his misgivings, or even about his support for the Progressive Federal Party, to which Helen Suzman, Mandela's old prison visitor belonged and which Slabbert joined, becoming a member of parliament for Rondebosch in the mid-seventies and soon thereafter party leader. Viewed as oddball free-thinkers within the insular little world of white South Africa, the "Progs" were conservative by global standards. Representing what was largely a well-heeled English-speaking constituency, ready to tut-tut the Boers' rough treatment of the poor blacks but unlikely ever to go into a township to meet them, the PFP nevertheless had the merit of offering a legal public voice opposed to apartheid inside South Africa, as well as a bridge to ease the transition towards the changes that would come later. Slabbert himself would become a critical intermediary in early secret contacts between the government and the ANC in 1987, soon after Mandela's first prison encounters with Kobie Coetsee.

Morné du Plessis, brave as he was on the rugby field, did not take any political risks off it. Not till that afternoon of February 11, 1990, at Cape Town's Parade. He went because he hoped, as Joel Stransky did, that Mandela's release would heal a country that he had long known to be sick. Stransky watched Mandela's release on television in a café in France. It was not quite as impressive as turning up at the Parade, but it showed more interest than most of his future Springbok comrades, whose attitude was summed up by one of the team's giant forwards, Kobus Wiese. Asked much later about his reaction to Mandela's release, his straightforward reply was, "I wasn't paying much attention, to be honest." Yet Stransky felt, as he would recall, "absolutely excited".

Stransky's life was consumed by sports, but not so completely as to prevent him from experiencing two fleeting moments of political awakening. The first clue came following an event of which he would hardly have been aware: the Soweto uprising of 1976 by schoolchildren no older than he. One consequence was that his parents began to suspect that their child's school might be burned down. "I remember my dad having to go and stand guard at our school at night during the riots and the unrest. I'm not sure whether I knew exactly what was wrong because the grown-ups didn't really talk about it, but it was very clear to me from that moment on that things were messed up in this country."

Stransky's second clue came during the Springboks' riot-strewn 1981 tour of New Zealand, when he was fourteen. He realized that there had to be a good reason why half of New Zealand was outraged by his countrymen. Stransky offered the very image of the effect that Arnold Stofile and his fellow ANC anti-rugby campaigners were hoping to have on the white population. By denying them their happy drug, they were rousing them out of their torpor. They were creating the conditions for political change. In some they found a more receptive audience than others. In Stransky they found the perfect response, for he was thrilled when Mandela got out.

Stransky also suspected that Mandela's release might be good for his rugby career. He was already recognized as one of the best players in the country. He had become a key player by the age of twenty for Natal Province, one of the four biggest teams in South Africa. Not being the big, powerful, bone-crushing type, he had to be brave and resilient enough to take a pounding from Pienaar-sized rivals a dozen times a game. But Stransky occupied the one position in a rugby team where neither unnatural speed nor unnatural bulk were required – fly half, the player who dictates play, in whom brains and ball skill are paramount. He also kicked like a dream.

And he was ambitious. That was why when the South African rugby season ended in October 1989, at the start of spring, he played club rugby in France. The game there was not quite as manically intense as it was in South Africa, but it allowed him to keep in shape over the South African summer so that when the season resumed in April 1990 he could hit the ground running, physically fit and match fit. It worked. After Stransky's return from France, Natal Province ended up national champions. Mandela's release would work for him too, in the way he had hoped. For Stransky, a free Mandela meant liberation for the Springboks from the international boycott. Sitting in that French café, he imagined that one day he might play rugby in the colours of his country.

Mandela had been expected at the Parade at around three in the afternoon, but such was the pandemonium that he eventually made it nearly five hours later, arriving as dusk fell. And, adding to an odd sense of anticlimax that dulled the day's historic proceedings, he gave a speech that fell short of expectations, failed to stir.

The next morning, the first on which he had awoken a free man in twenty-seven years and six months, held what would have seemed a stiffer test: a news conference before the world's press. There were two hundred journalists there, many of them TV news personalities who were household names in their own countries: Jeremy Paxman, David Dimbleby, America's Dan Rather, and their equivalents worldwide. South Africa did not have television when Mandela went to jail. He himself had appeared before a TV camera only once – a one-on-one interview with a British reporter a year before his arrest, in 1961. By 1990, every politician alive had undergone a course on how to handle himself before the cameras. And here was Mandela, who was as famous as he was bereft of experience in the mass media age, about to face the exercise politicians everywhere dreaded, a no-holds-barred news conference. He had no way of knowing what the journalists might ask. And his less than charismatic speech the night before had created doubts as to the quality of his performance this morning. After all, he was seventy-one years old, and had spent almost three decades in prison. How well could he be? How sharp?

The news conference was held early in the morning at the garden of the official Cape Town residence of the head of South Africa's Anglican Church, Archbishop Desmond Tutu, who until that moment, as the winner of the 1984 Nobel Peace Prize, had been the most visible face of resistance to apartheid around the world. The mansion, in the gabled Cape Dutch style, sat on the steep, thickly wooded foothills of Table Mountain, the monolith whose rectangular outline Mandela would gaze upon across the water from Robben Island. With Mandela the 4.30 a.m. riser it was always an early start: reporters had to be there by 6:30. When he emerged from the house, his wife, Winnie, by his side, the dew still lay on the leaves. Mandela and wife smiled and waved their way down a set of stone steps to the lawn where the press awaited. Tutu, jigging with delight, happy no longer to have to play the part of the world's most prominent anti-apartheid celebrity, led the way. There was just the one jolt, when Mandela stopped at his table and glanced at an artillery of furry cylinders that would be arrayed before him when he sat down. One of his aides whispered something in his ear, to which Mandela responded with a nod and an "Oh, I see . . ." The furry objects were microphones.

From that moment on it was smooth sailing. He placated his own supporters and fellow leaders in the ANC by restating his symbolic commitment to the armed struggle and to the hoary old ANC policy (soon to be ditched) of nationalizing the country's mineral wealth. At the same time he signalled his resolve to show strong leadership by taking the bold step of describing President F. W. de Klerk – a twenty-year veteran of apartheid government who had just come to power in yet another whites-only "general" election – as "a man of integrity"; and he reached out reassuringly to white South Africa at every possible opportunity.

There was an acknowledgment of his kinder jailers – the Christo Brands and the Jack Swarts and the Willem Willemses – when he was asked the big obvious question that had to be asked, whether he felt any bitterness after his twenty-seven and a half years in captivity. He also offered a fleeting but potent recognition of the value prison had played in shaping his political strategy. "Despite the hard times in prison, we had also the opportunity to think about programmes . . . and in prison there have been men who are very good, in the sense that they understood our point of view, and they did everything to try and make you as happy as possible. That," Mandela said, emphatically, as if underlining the sentence as he spoke it, "has wiped out any bitterness that a man could have."

Asked what had most surprised him upon re-entering the world, he declared that he was "absolutely surprised" by the number of white people who had been on the streets to greet him the day before. Most important of all, Mandela stated that the way to a negotiated solution lay in a simple-sounding formula: reconciling white fears with black aspirations. "The ANC is very much concerned to address the question of the concern Whites have over the demand of one person, one vote," he said. "They insist on . . . guarantees . . . to ensure that the realization of this demand does not result in the domination of whites by blacks.

We understand those feelings and the ANC is concerned to address that problem and to find a solution which will suit both the blacks and whites of this country."

Hearing in public those words that he had heard so often in private, Niël Barnard heaved a sigh of relief. This was not the language of insurrection. This was not an Ayatollah smashing fists into people's mouths. When the press conference ended, forty-five minutes after it had begun, all the earlier anxieties seemed absurdly misplaced. Mandela had transformed what had been advertised as his first public grilling into the balmy outdoor equivalent of a cozy fireside chat. He had planted the seed of a notion among some white South Africans that a black man might be capable of touching their hearts. François Pienaar, still far from a political animal, found himself surprisingly moved by the sight of Mandela on TV. "I cannot recall any emotion other than sadness," he told me. "I felt sad that he had been in jail for so long and, although his face brimmed with pride, I felt that he had lost so much time."

Other white television viewers would have been less sympathetic, and many would have snarled. A significant chunk of right-wing opinion held that the white establishment had made a mistake not to hang Mandela, whose influence as a source of inspiration to black revolutionaries had endured throughout his captivity. Such people watched Mandela's release on television and felt only bitterness and contempt towards De Klerk and what they perceived as his traitorous government for selling out white South Africa, for releasing the terrorist in chief onto the streets.

He had a very different effect on those journalists standing before him on Archbishop Tutu's lawn on the morning of February 12, 1990. All it took was those forty-five minutes for Mandela to wrap the world's media in his astute embrace. The journalists did not quite realize it then, for they were too benumbed, but in due course they would understand that Mandela was a canny strategist, a talented manipulator of mass sentiment. His gift for political theatre was as sophisticated as Bill Clinton's or Ronald Reagan's. At that news conference, Mandela pulled off a coup that both Clinton and Reagan would have envied. The session ended with all two hundred assembled journalists doing something that they had never done before. The human being within all of them got the better of the journalist and they found themselves, to their confusion and surprise, breaking into spontaneous applause.

Getting the Afrikaans press on his side was not quite so simple. Because whites generally and Afrikaners in particular were uncertain and afraid of the consequences of his release, they seized on the more alarming things he said – the policy on nationalization; the "armed struggle"; the ANC's loyalty to its Communist Party allies – while failing to register the esteem he expressed for his prison guards or his desire to reach an accommodation acceptable to all. He faced a comparable challenge in keeping his own people on board, both at leadership level, where there had been some complaints about his unilateral decision to engage in secret talks with the government, and among the great mass of the population, for whom Mandela was a powerful myth but, as flesh-and-blood leader, an unknown quantity.

To address both these challenges, Mandela flew up to Johannesburg, two hours away, on the morning of the news conference, and from there drove to Soweto, where that afternoon Arrie Rossouw went to see him at the small family home he had left when he had gone to prison. It was one of those drab little matchbox houses, identical rows and rows of which lined every township in South Africa, almost identical to the place where Justice Bekebeke had lived before he went to prison. Rossouw was the chief political reporter of *Beeld*, the newspaper of the Afrikaans establishment. He was one of five Afrikaner journalists invited to a joint interview inside that little faded red-brick house with the man that their papers had taught readers for decades to see as the incarnation of "swart gevaar," the "black danger". Rossouw himself was rather more sophisticated than the average member of the *volk*. Having had contact with the ANC in exile, aware of the need for white South Africa to strike a deal with black South Africa, sufficiently alive to the way apartheid was viewed around the world to feel awkward and ashamed when he travelled abroad, he was ahead of most of his readers – much as Niël Barnard was ahead of the people who voted for the National party. Rossouw, nevertheless, had reason to be nervous. It was still too early to declare the Ayatollah alert conclusively over (a mass rally, as the ANC called it, had been prepared in Soweto the following day).

Instead, Mandela put the same spell on Arrie Rossouw as he had done hours earlier on his foreign colleagues at the news conference in Cape Town. "There he was in the tiny front room of his little brick home and he greeted us like a king, the most charming king imaginable," Rossouw said. "He actually introduced himself to me. 'Hello, I am Nelson Mandela, how are you?' And then I introduced myself and he knew all about me. He knew exactly who I was. He said he had been reading me with great interest for some time and he actually remembered pieces I had written months earlier!"

The Afrikaners were the first group of journalists Mandela saw in such small numbers – before the black press or the white liberal press or the international press. "He deliberately chose us to convey a message that all South Africans had a place in the nation of the future; above all that he was not emerging from prison with revenge in his heart. He saw, of course, that the Afrikaners were the key to a lasting peace, and he sought through us to address their fears literally from day one."

Rossouw was shrewd enough to understand that Mandela was

doing a number on him. But he fell for it anyway. "You could see he had a feel for what made Afrikaners tick. Basically what he told us was, 'Look, I know you and your people and I know Afrikaners have done much for this country and I know your fears, but let's discuss them and be friends.' And as he talked he would make self-deprecating jokes so that you would not feel overawed by him, but at ease. Suddenly I felt a tremendous sense of privilege to be in his presence. I just sat there, looking at this guy, and I remembered there were rumours flying about that he was ill, seriously ill, and I thought, 'Please God let it not be true!' Because I understood the vast importance this man would have for the welfare of our country."

One difference between politically astute white South Africans like Rossouw and the average black South African was that the latter didn't have to process Mandela's release through the logical part of the brain to understand the happy momentousness of the day. Save for a danger-ous redoubt of conservative, time-warped Zulus in the east of the country, no one disputed Mandela's automatic right to leadership. Not even Justice Bekebeke, who might have felt forgotten or bitterly out of sync with the times. Despite nine months and forty hangings in Death Row, he too suspended all reason, forgot about his own plight, and cel-ebrated as if Mandela's release had been his own. "We used to have one hour of exercise every day but on that day we all stayed in our cells to listen to the radio. They played a song as we waited and waited. 'Release Mandela', by Hugh Masekela. We sang along, we danced. The moment the radio announced that he was walking out with Winnie, that moment was freedom for us. We forgot where we were."

Everywhere Mandela went became a mob scene. But he did not speak the language of the mob. He set off on a long march around South Africa in the weeks immediately following his release, and everywhere he went vast numbers of people turned out, hungry to catch a glimpse of him, dreaming they might receive a smile, touch a fingertip when he reached out – from the start he was a bodyguards' nightmare – into the crowd. Black South Africa reacted to him as if he were a cross between Napoleon and Jesus Christ. Yet while the subtext of what he said was interpreted by Christians like Archbishop Tutu as an entreaty to "love thine enemy," his arguments were hard-nosed.

To convince the militants who provided the ANC with its political energy, he had to appeal to more than morality; he had to use the tough language of political necessity, and leave sectors of his audience to believe, if they so chose, that there was nothing he would like more than outright revolution the Castro way. So he spoke of the need to reach an accommodation with white South Africa, not its desirability, and he did so in uncompromising language that acted persuasively on the militants, reiterating the non-negotiability of basic principles. He reminded the government that if they did not accede to full-on, one-person-one-vote democracy, if they thought – as De Klerk did think for a while – that they could come up with some legalistic compromise that continued to entrench white privilege, then they would have a fight on their hands. Nobody of the millions who saw or heard Mandela in those first days after his release would have mistaken him for a Gandhian pacifist.

Mandela had been famous but faceless for many years, but now his image had spread to every corner of the world, and in South Africa he seemed to be everywhere at once. His long march had the air of a giant party, a royal pageant that went from city to city. The first of these mass rallies was two days after his release at Soweto's "Soccer City" stadium before 120,000 people. It was Mandela's coronation as king of black South Africa. At every stop from then, the same ceremony was re-enacted. In Durban, the biggest city in Natal Province, a similar number of Zulus paid homage to him. In Bloemfontein, the seat of South

Africa's highest court, 80,000 turned up. In Port Elizabeth, capital of the Eastern Cape region where Mandela was born, 200,000.

In each case the frenzy of a pop concert and the passion of a cup final combined with the solemn fervor of high mass. Raptures accompanied his first appearance onstage flanked by Sisulu and other high priests of the struggle. But then a strange order would descend on the proceedings, and there would follow a liturgy whose rituals everybody knew.

First came the cry from the master of ceremonies onstage, "Amandla!" which meant "power" in Xhosa. To which the assembled throng replied, "Awethu!" – "To the people!" – repeated three or four or five times, in crescendo.

Then came what black leaders had always called the "national anthem", "Nkosi Sikelele", whose dirgelike cadences the audience infused now, right fists raised, with a triumphant note never quite heard before. They sang this anthem with the polish of a professional choir, as if they had been practising for the event all their lives, which in a sense they had, in one protest rally after another for years. Not only did everyone, all 120,000 or 200,000 people, know all the words, but the men knew where to keep quiet and let the women sing, and the women knew when to let the deeper voices of the men ring through.

Then more "Amandla! Awethus!" then "An injury to one!" which brought the reply, "Is an injury to all!" followed by "Viva ANC, Viva!" "Viva!" and "Viva ANC, Viva!" and then "Long live Nelson Mandela!" "Long live!"

Then followed more singing and then dancing, a teeming mass disco, and then more "Long live Nelson Mandela!" and then finally the man himself would stand up, seeming taller than his six feet one inch, raise his fist high, and necks would crane and elated faces would turn toward him as if in worship and he would cry, "Amandla!" and receive in reply the loudest "Awethu!" roar of the day and people would point and exclaim and scream, because they had glimpsed him, at last, in the distance, which was what they had come for. And then he would speak. But he was not a good orator, his voice had a metallic monotone quality that never captivated his audiences the way the naturally histrionic Archbishop Tutu did. And in time the crowd would start to fidget, as they did during sermons in church, but when he finished they sprang once more into life, belting out the "Amandlas!" and the "Vivas!" back to another devastatingly moving rendition of "Nkosi Sikelele" and then back home, the coronation over. But the feeling lasted beyond the ferment of the mass rally. Mandela embodied the predicament of all black South Africans. In him they invested all their hopes and aspirations; he had become the personification of an entire people.

CHAPTER VII

THE TIGER KING

"Hang Mandela!" and "Mandela Go Home – to Prison" and "Traitor de Klerk" were some of the politer banners on display at a rally of the white right in Pretoria five days after Mandela's release. The setting was Church Square, a quadrangle in the heart of South Africa's capital city dominated at its centre by a grey, bird-spattered statue of the Boer patriarch Paul Kruger, dressed up in presidential sash, coat, top hat, and cane. Some 20,000 people attended, as big a percentage of the white population as the 120,000 gathered in Soweto had been of the black.

Feelings were as intense as they had been at Soccer City four days earlier, but the mood could not have been more different. In Soweto the smell of victory had been in the air; at Church Square, quiet despair underlay the defiance. These people feared they were about to lose everything. They were government bureaucrats who feared they would lose their jobs, small businessmen who feared they would lose their shops, farmers who feared they would lose their land. And all feared they would lose their flag, their anthem, their language, their schools, their Dutch Reformed Church, their rugby. And beneath that, colouring everything, was the dread of a vengeance commensurate with the crime.

They had gathered in the South African capital at the behest of the Conservative Party, the political branch of right-wing extremism. The CP, the main opposition party in the all-white parliament, was an off-shoot of the National Party, from which it had broken eight years earlier because its leaders considered P. W. Botha to be suspiciously left-wing, and now viewed De Klerk as the devil himself.

The Afrikaner right has its own liturgy, if not quite as elaborate or practised as the ANC's. They began by shutting their eyes, opening their hands in supplication, bowing their heads, and raising a prayer. Then they sang "Die Stem", the lugubrious official national anthem, which praises God and celebrates the triumphs of the Boers as they marched on their wagons northward in the mid-nineteenth-century Great Trek, eating up black-owned land along the way. Brown-shirted men mingled among the crowd like school bullies. They were members of the Afrikaner Weerstandsbeweging (Afrikaner Resistance Movement), the best known of a fragmented collection of far-right-wing groups. Better known as the AWB, their red-and-black insignia consisted of three sevens arranged in such a fashion as to resemble the Nazi swastika.

But it was not the brownshirts, this time, who defined the event. More sinister, and a more ominous measure of the challenge that lay ahead for Mandela, was the outward normality of most of the people, a cross section of the human spectacle you would see any day of the week in the centre of Upington, or Vereeniging, or anywhere else in white South Africa. There were youths in jeans and Springbok jerseys, eager-eyed young couples with babies, potbellied men in khaki shorts and long socks, old gentlemen in tweed jackets, and ladies dressed as if they were going to the annual bowling club dance. They were the white middle class anywhere in northern Europe or Middle America. And they did not want blacks to rule over their lives. They all shared the nightmare of a black hand emerging from under the bed in the middle of the night, of gangs of marauding young black men crashing into their homes.

It was never immediately obvious, but if you looked closely you found that there was a vulnerable softness at the core of white South Africa, among Afrikaners and English speakers, city and country people, poor and rich. The difference lay in the degree to which each individual managed to disguise it. But because acknowledging that vulnerability did not fit with the rugged survivor image that Afrikaners, in particular, chose to have of themselves, some strove to mask their fears behind the rhetoric of resistance. Which was not to say that they did not believe what they said. Fear made them dangerous. Dr. Andries Treurnicht, the Conservative Party leader, got the biggest cheer of the day at the Church Square rally when he cried, "The Afrikaner is a friendly tiger, but don't mess around with him!" The hard, simple certainties of the past were beginning to crack, but here was a truth, they chose to believe, that neither Mandela nor the now legalized "Communists" of the ANC could ever dent. The Afrikaner was a tiger and any beast that tangled with it was doomed. "As long as the ANC operates as a militant organization, we will hit them as hard as we can," roared Treurnicht, a theologian and former minister of the Dutch Reformed Church. "As far as we're concerned, it is war, plain and simple."

Some in the ANC still believed they actually could beat the tiger. Mandela knew they could not. The enemy had all the guns, the air force, the logistics, the money. Mandela's chief principle of political action was the one he had come to understand in prison a long time ago: that the only way to beat the tiger was to tame him. These people snarling under the shadow of Paul Kruger's statue were the same people he had subdued to his will on Robben Island.

Mandela's first priority was to prevent civil war. And not just between whites and blacks, but between whites and whites too. The liberal Dr. Woolf types, who had got where they did after swimming courageously against the currents of white orthodoxy, would be in the sights of the right-wing warriors. They already were. Dr. Woolf himself had received threats from right-wing organizations after the story of his family's encounter with Mandela was published in a Durban newspaper. They put him on a death list. The Arrie Rossouws of the Afrikaans press also paid a price for having run ahead of the times. Poison mail poured into the Johannesburg office of his newspaper, *Beeld*, and the switchboard was jammed with abusive phone calls. At a right-wing rally in the Orange Free State two weeks after Mandela's release a white *Beeld* photographer was beaten up.

No two people better encapsulated the rift between South African whites than the Viljoen twins. The story of Braam and Constand Viljoen is not quite Cain and Abel, nor the Prodigal Son, but it has elements of both. Indistinguishable physically, the brothers set off on radically divergent paths, in their late teens and then barely communicated with one another for forty years. When they did eventually reconnect, destiny played a hand. If the brothers hadn't made peace, South Africa would have made war.

Born in 1933 into an upper class rural Afrikaner family that traced its roots back to the seventeenth-century settlers, among the first to arrive from Europe in Africa's southern tip, the Viljoens (pronounced "Fill-yewn") had a reason other than politics to live their lives apart. Together they ran the risk of being seen as the identical twins of stage farce, but separately each was imposing. They were both grave men, who took themselves and their roles in society seriously, and were taken seriously by others. The only other things they had in common were their religious devotion and their love of farming, to which Constand dedicated himself on and off in the family farm in the Eastern Transvaal, and Braam – more on than off – on another farm 250 miles away in the Northern Transvaal.

In terms of temperament and worldview they could not have been more different. Braam, the reflective type, embarked on a career in the church. Constand, the man of action, joined the army. But whereas one course might have seemed more placid than the other, it was Braam who struggled and, in strict career terms, failed, while Constand rose, with admirable smoothness, to the pinnacle of his profession. While Braam took on the system and lost, Constand not only joined the system, he *became* it. He made it not just to the rank of general, not just to head of the army, but to overall commander of the South African Defence Force – navy and air force included. P. W Botha appointed him to the job after he became prime minister in 1980. Viljoen remained there, apartheid's last line of defence, until his retirement in 1985. He commanded the force in whose absence apartheid would have crumbled overnight. He risked his own life and he took the lives of others in support of a political system based on and defined by three of the most perverse laws ever devised: the Separate Amenities Act, the Group Areas Act, and the Population Registration Act, all of them passed in parliament when he and his brother were seventeen, eighteen, and nineteen years old – when each was deciding which course to take in life.

The Separate Amenities Act was the one that banned black people from stepping onto the better beaches and parks, and black nannies from travelling in white train compartments with the white babies of the "madams" they served. The other two laws Constand Viljoen enforced were equally unjust and absurd.

The Population Registration Act compartmentalized the racial groups. There were four main categories. In descending order of privilege they were: Whites, Coloureds, Indians, Blacks. Once each South African had been placed into the corresponding racial box, all the other apartheid laws could follow. Without the Population Registration Act it would have been impossible to enforce, for example, the Immorality Act, whereby it was illegal not only for people to marry across the race barriers, but to engage in anything resembling sexual contact. It was in part to accommodate the amorous incontinence of a small minority of morally weak souls – in part to satisfy people's desire for material improvement – that the government included a clause in the Population Registration Act allowing individuals the biologically perplexing right to try to change their race.

What one had to do was apply to a body in Pretoria called the Race Classification Board and stipulate from which race to which race one wished to metamorphose. Interviews would be conducted and in the trickier cases petitioners would appear before the ladies and gentlemen of the all-white board. The board members would ask the race changees to walk up and down before them, allowing them to peruse their postures and buttock shapes. In the event that the matter remained unresolved, the pencil test was the most scientifically reliable dispeller of doubt. A pencil would be poked inside a person's hair: the tighter the hair's natural grip, the darker the classification. The Ministry of Home Affairs's figures for 1989 show that 573 Coloured people applied to become White, of whom 519 were successful, and that 369 Black people applied to become Coloured, of whom 327 made it. In these cases the impulse was clearly the improvement of one's material circumstances. But the record also shows that fourteen Whites applied to become Coloured, of whom twelve succeeded; that three Whites applied to become Indian and two to become Chinese, all five succeeding. Such miracles were evidently not wrought by cold reason, but by the Race Classification Board's sympathy for the petitioners' admirably self-sacrificial romantic impulses.

The Group Areas Act was the law by which black and white people were legally prohibited from living in the same parts of town, that made physical apartness between white town and black township compulsory. But in the eyes of apartheid's ideologues it was, in fact, more than that. It was divinely ordained. The God-fearing *volk* would never have set about anything as far-reaching as a system that condemned the vast majority of the inhabitants of their country to fourth-class citizenship had they not been quite certain that they had a biblical justification for what they were doing. Like other fundamentalists before and after them, they dug deep into the Old Testament and came up with theological arguments in support of casting black people into outer darkness. According to a book titled *Biblical Aspects of Apartheid*, published in 1958 by an eminent theologian of the Dutch Reformed Church, Group Areas legislation applied in the afterlife too. The book offered comfort to those white South Africans who might have feared they would have to mix with black people in heaven. Not to worry. *Biblical Aspects of Apartheid* assured them that the Good Book said that there were "many mansions" in "our Father's house".

Constand Viljoen dedicated his life to defending these laws against the forces led by his enemy-in-chief, Nelson Mandela. Braam Viljoen, who from early on regarded the apartheid laws as an abomination, became one of Mandela's unofficial foot soldiers.

If Constand's problem was that he thought too little, Braam's was that he thought too much. A little bit of reassurance from the pulpit that the apartheid laws were all God's work and Constand cheerfully threw in his lot with the defence of the fatherland. Braam, an astoundingly independent-minded teenager for an Afrikaner raised on a farm 150 miles from the nearest city, heard the same words as his brother from the local Dutch Reformed Church *dominee* and found them deeply troubling. On going to university in Pretoria to study theology, with a view to becoming a *dominee* himself, he became intrigued by the work of a subversive little group of theologians who were questioning the reigning orthodoxies. This prompted him in turn to take an interest in the ANC. He read their Freedom Charter ("South Africa belongs to all who live in it, black and white") with keen attention when it came out in 1955, the year his brother completed university and became an officer in the army.

While Constand eased up the ranks, impressing his superior officers, Braam was impressed by the Christian seriousness of Mandela's predecessor as head of the ANC, Albert Luthuli. In the early sixties, by which time he had made the grade as a professor of theology, Braam signed a declaration stating that it was heresy to identify apartheid with the will of God. The wording of the declaration was solemn and respectful. In private, Braam seethed. "I came to detest the naïve, infantile biblical justification of apartheid, based as it was on a literal reading of Genesis," he said. "I detested also that fundamentalist way of thinking, stating dumbly that this was the word of God, admitting of no debate. Naturally, I came into conflict with my family. With my brother, who was now a major in the SADF, we simply did not talk politics, full stop." And into conflict he came too with the Dutch Reformed Church, who dubbed him a dissenter and prevented him from earning the salary due him as a theologically qualified *dominee*. He carried on teaching at the university until the 1980s, but was obliged for financial reasons to go back to farming part-time.

On the farm, he stepped up his political involvement as he began to become aware of what apartheid meant for the lowest of the low: black people in the rural areas. By the early 1980s, as black protest escalated all over the country, he became actively involved with what he found himself describing as "the freedom struggle", conspiring with the very same black political leaders that his brother, as head of the SADF, was committed to defeating. He was also up to his neck with the South African Council of Churches, a body that the security forces considered a front for the terrorists of the ANC. The more powerful his brother became, the keener Braam's understanding of the brutal methods that Constand's boss was sanctioning. He had known the system was evil, but he had not realized until now how murderous it could be. "I was shocked and horrified. My brother's very own people killing and torturing people!" In fact, Braam was lucky not to be tortured and killed himself. After Mandela's release, he discovered that he had been on the hit list of the CCB, the secret military intelligence unit that had assassinated Anton Lubowski.

"I do not think my brother knew about that," he insisted with conviction. But Constand must have suspected that something was up. "He got a message to me via our mother," Braam recalled, "warning me that 'if I knew what was good for me' I would quit the committees of the South African Council of Churches."

Braam did not quit. Throughout the eighties, he continued to work with the SACC. In 1987, he even went with fifty other open-minded Afrikaner intellectuals to Dakar, Senegal, for a pioneering meeting with the exiled leadership of the ANC. One of the key figures behind that meeting was Frederik van Zyl Slabbert, Morné du Plessis's first political hero. After Braam Viljoen returned from Dakar, Niël Barnard's NIS interrogated him, but still he kept going, That same year he joined the small but plucky Progressive Federal Party (another link with Morné du Plessis, for this was the party Morné supported). He even stood for parliament for the PFP, before throwing in his lot with a borderline legal anti-apartheid think tank called the Institute for Democracy in South Africa that Van Zyl Slabbert, who had now quit active politics, had set up.

Despite their profound disparities ("we lived in different worlds" was how Braam put it), Braam and Constand shared many qualities. Both were honest and scrupulously dedicated to their work. Constand was an upright, no-nonsense, soldiers' soldier who spent his professional life inside a moral bubble, convinced that it was as honorable to serve in the SADF as in the army of New Zealand. He was greatly admired by those who'd served under him, as millions of white South

Africans had during his long tenure as head of the army and then all the armed forces. He cemented his reputation during the mid-seventies as the senior officer in charge of South Africa's expeditionary Angolan war, fighting on the side of Jonas Savimbi's UNITA guerrillas against Angola's Marxist government. It was one of dozens of proxy Cold War conflicts going on around the world. The Angolan government received help from Cuba and the Soviet Union, and UNITA from the United States. South Africa joined the fray because its rulers were as anti-Communist as the ones in Washington, and because the Angolan government gave help to the ANC.

On taking over as head of the SADF in 1980, Constand found himself obliged to pay more attention to the ANC itself, now active in neighbouring countries like Zambia and Mozambique, and to their increasingly rebellious surrogates whom his brother was associating with inside the country. A government document a year earlier had said that the political and military threat against South Africa was intensifying at "an alarming rate". Determined to couch the war against the ANC in more internationally palatable geopolitical terms, the document described the enemy's "total onslaught" as part of a plan by Moscow to use South Africa "as a stepping stone to world conquest". The language convinced American conservatives and British prime minister Margaret Thatcher, who publicly agreed with President Botha that the ANC was a Communist-inspired "terrorist" organization. Encouraged, Botha ordered the army into the townships. Viljoen thus became the first head of the South African Army to see his remit expand beyond the protection of the country against a foreign enemy to protection of the state against its own people. The army suddenly found itself working hand in hand with the security police, carrying out joint raids in neighboring Mozambique, Botswana, and Lesotho that killed as many innocent civilians as ANC operatives.

Constand was never comfortable in this role. His moral vision may have been less ample than his brother's, but he was not without scruples. In May 1983 an SADF raid inside Mozambique mistook a number of private homes, a nursery, and a fruit juice factory for an ANC missile site, training centre, and logistical base. Six people were killed, none of them ANC personnel, prompting a furious internal memo from Viljoen to the chief of the army in which he declared himself not just disappointed, but shocked. "If we were to analyse our operational effectiveness and to make the results public we would be ashamed," Viljoen wrote.

The results were not made public and, with the aid of a pliant press, the best possible gloss was put on the exploits of the SADF. A raid on Gaborone, the capital of Botswana, in which South African soldiers killed a boy of six and a man of seventy-one, was reported in glorious terms in the South African press, one newspaper headlining the epic "the Guns of Gaborone". When Constand retired, after a military career spanning thirty-one years, he had become a living legend – in the Afrikaner popular imagination, almost a white Mandela – and, more to the point, a brave, principled, no-nonsense general in keeping with a nineteenth-century Boer tradition of soldier-politicians like Andries Pretorius and Paul Kruger – the perfect antidote, in other words, to that distinctly un-Boerish shifty, slippery, deal-making F. W de Klerk. Constand Viljoen's decision to do the time-honored Boer thing and go back to farming only increased the devotion of his admirers. He imagined back in 1985 that he was returning to the land for good. Five years later, as he sat stewing in front of the television watching Mandela's release, he would not have guessed that the *volk* would soon call on him to abandon his farm and lead them in their last great freedom war.

CHAPTER VIII
THE MASK

1990–93

Mandela was back in prison within a month of getting out. Of his own free will, this time, he visited the place where he feared in 1964 that he would end up, Death Row in Pretoria. He went to see the Upington 14 and other prisoners who were inside for what he believed to be political reasons. Justice Bekebeke missed him. By a perverse sequence of circumstances related to an unfortunately timed visit by a family member, he was unable to see Mandela. "I didn't want to die on Death Row but I wanted to kill myself!" Justice half-joked. Mandela reassured the Upington contingent that, with his release, things in South Africa had changed for ever. Not only would he persuade the government to accept a moratorium on executions, but he would do all he could to help them gain their freedom. They believed him. In the eyes of the black faithful, Mandela was a miracle worker. "Even though I was not there with him, I shared in the excitement of the others," Justice told me. "We knew then for certain that we would be out."

South Africa had taken a new course, and while De Klerk was formally in control, Mandela was doing the steering. Talks did begin between the ANC and the government. The process that Mandela had started in secret in jail continued openly now. The right wing growled but the ANC and the government got to know each other, discovered to their surprise that, as one senior ANC official put it, neither side had horns, and set about building the mutual confidence on which progress in negotiations always depends. "The process", as insiders called it, began formally in May 1990 and advanced as well as Mandela could reasonably have hoped. One of the important concessions Mandela secured early on was, as promised to the Upington 14, a cessation of all legal executions. Political prisoners started to trickle out as part of the horse-trading of negotiations. The Upington group, none of them officially members of the ANC, did not enter into those calculations, however. The law would take its course and they would wait to be exonerated on appeal.

Delegations of the government, the ANC, and various smaller parties met from Monday to Friday, gathering in smoke-filled rooms, like rival lawyers, at a conference building near Johannesburg Airport known, with exaggerated grandeur, as the World Trade Centre. Some of the delegates got along so well after a while that they began to wonder whether they were racing too far ahead of their constituencies; whether there would be problems, especially for the government, when the time came to ask their people to go along with the deals they had struck. The chief negotiator of the ANC, a former trade union leader called Cyril Ramaphosa, and the chief negotiator of the government, Defence Minister Roelf Meyer, became such good friends that they often debated the issues during weekend fishing trips. Mandela and De Klerk never got on as well, but while they had their tense moments, they stayed in permanent touch, sometimes meeting late into the night. There was no longer any need to beg for a meeting: the former prisoner could get the president on the end of a phone line any time he chose.

In this rapidly changing climate, in May 1991 the highest appeal court in South Africa overturned twenty-one out of the twenty-five original murder convictions in the Upington case, and dismissed all fourteen death sentences. Bekebeke was one of the four whose convictions stood. He would leave Death Row, but the court had ruled that he had a ten-year sentence to serve. He took the news with good grace, responding to the verdicts by reaching out and embracing the old man Gideon Madlongolwana who, with his wife Evelina, was free to go. Within eight months, having served a total of six years and one and a half months in prison, he too was free. On January 6, 1992, he rejoined his family and friends and his girlfriend, Selina, in Upington. It was a happy time but Bekebeke was impatient. He had a lot of time to make up, and a pledge to keep. He had made it to himself and to his fellow inmates on the day when Anton Lubowski was killed.

Until then, he had been clear about his life's ambition. He wanted to become a doctor. "But that day I changed my plan. From that day on I knew there was only one thing I wanted to be: a lawyer. I would pick up his spear. I would follow in his footsteps. I would fill the vacuum he had left. I would become another Anton."

It was an amazing thing for an angry young black man like Bekebeke to say, but prison had mellowed him as it had mellowed Mandela. Within two weeks of his release he had acted on his grandiloquent rhetoric. Down in Cape Town, the place where he had had his inspirational child's fantasy of visiting Mandela and the other "leaders" in their island prison, he was now going to start, aged thirty-one, his university career. Bekebeke excelled at the University of the Western Cape. He got top marks in his exams and obtained a scholarship. He was, he said, a student possessed. "All along the spirit of Anton drove me and I knew that however tough it got I would never wilt, I would never fail him. I told my comrades in Death Row that this is what I would do. I made a vow, and I fulfilled it."

Mandela was well on the way to fulfilling his old vow to bring freedom to South Africa, but there were storms ahead, phenomena of political nature that he had not anticipated and that initially escaped his control. For, with the negotiations at the World Trade Centre proceeding at their stately pace, the right-wing war to scupper them was already under way. It was a war that took different forms, and one of them – the bloodiest – had a black face. For there was not only a white right wing in South Africa but also – far more difficult for an outsider to under-stand – a black right. And their interests converged.

The Zulu right-wing movement Inkatha and in particular its leader, Mangosuthu Buthelezi ("crazy like a fox", as a foreign ambassador described him), were as fearful as the white right that if the ANC came to power it would exact dreadful retribution on them. For Buthelezi had gone along with apartheid, while pretending, when the occasion demanded it, that he did not. His rhetoric often aped the ANC's, lash-ing the government's racism and so forth, but the fact was that he had taken the apartheid shilling. Hendrick Verwoerd's "grand apartheid" plan had been to divide South Africa into a series of tribal homelands, which he conceived of as internationally recognized sovereign states. The Dr. Strangelove of apartheid ("I never suffer from the nagging doubt," Verwoerd once declared, "that perhaps I might be wrong") imagined that each of South Africa's nine tribal groups would have its own mini-state, while the white tribe would bag the mineral and farm-rich lion's share, the big cities included. Buthelezi went along with the plan, accepting a little fiefdom financed entirely by Pretoria and named KwaZulu. Here he lived a grand life as "chief minister", complete with a cabinet and ministers and a police force headed by an Afrikaner brigadier (in this terrain Pretoria called the shots) who was a former chief of white South Africa's security police.

Buthelezi's statelet might have been comical had it not been a tool of Botha's counter insurgency. Guided by Pretoria's in-house brigadier, Buthelezi dispatched his *impi* (Zulu for "battalion") forces against the town-dwelling, English-speaking, ANC-supporting half of the Zulu population, resulting in battles between the two sides that caused thousands of deaths. The ANC and its supporters came to detest Buthelezi as much as Botha, if not more. Buthelezi feared that if Mandela ever took power he would lose the political and economic privileges derived from his complicity with the apartheid state. He also feared bloody revenge, as the white right did, which was why neither saw any benefit in a negotiation process whose end was majority rule.

Within six months of Mandela's release, Inkatha's spear-wielding warriors had extended their war beyond Zulu country to the townships around Johannesburg, mounting assaults on the community at large, knowing that the vast majority were going to be supporters of the ANC. Hundreds died – shot, speared, knifed, or burned – every month. In their attacks, which continued for the first three years after Mandela's release, Buthelezi's thugs counted on the overt assistance of the uniformed police, whose armoured cars escorted the Inkatha impis in and out of battle. Covertly, elements of the security police and military intelligence were providing the Inkatha terrorists with guns. The objective was quite clear: to provoke the ANC into a series of mini-civil wars in the townships and render the planned new order ungovernable.

For all Mandela's calculation and charm, he had moments of towering indignation, in most cases precipitated by the slaughter in the townships and by De Klerk, whom he now regretted having called "a man of integrity" and accused of passive complicity in the violence. Tokyo Sexwale, the former Robben Island prisoner and now member of the

ANC's top decision-making body, the National Executive Committee (NEC), said that there came a moment when Mandela wanted to break off relations with the government. "So we remonstrated. 'If we do that, what do we do? Go back to armed struggle?' Mandela was an angry man, but we had to defeat him, and we did. But he was very affected by the amount of blood flowing throughout the country." Mandela let off steam by denouncing De Klerk. "If it were white people dying," he raged, "I know that he would be addressing the matter with a great deal more urgency."

Buthelezi, who knew that the limits of impunity guaranteed him by the apartheid state did not extend to killing white people, found himself drawn ever closer to the far-right Conservative Party and their assorted storm troopers, who cheered on the Inkatha impis, celebrated their massacres, and looked forward to the day when they might forge a Zulu-Boer alliance against the ANC. Mandela, meanwhile, was receiving more and more reports from his own intelligence people, as well as from friendly foreign governments, of right-wing mobilization.

By early 1992 there was no sign of the township bloodbath abating and every sign that the far right would violently show their hand. Danger loomed, and Mandela had to dispel it. He needed to appease whites' fears, to give them some incentive to accept the impending new order. The NEC met and the idea came up to consider converting the political stick that sports had provided them into a carrot: offering to ease up on, or drop altogether, the boycott on rugby. Arnold Stofile, the man jailed in 1985 for his part in stopping an All Black tour, was an active participant in the debate. "This is no ordinary carrot we would be offering white South Africa," the effervescent Stofile told his colleagues, not all of whom grasped the significance of rugby in the Afrikaner soul. "This is not politics. This is not ideology. It is something much more powerful and primal, and personal! Offering to restore the international rugby games is a way of saying to whites, 'If you play along with us you will be able to go to Europe and the U.S. and Australia to visit your friends and not be seen at the airport when your passport is checked as pariahs. And they will see it as good for business too and, above all, it would mean being liked again. That's the bottom line. That will mean so much to them. They'll be able to exclaim, 'They like us! They like us!' In sum, comrades, white South Africa will be able to feel like human beings again, like citizens of the world."

One member of the NEC who understood exactly what Stofile was talking about was Steve Tshwete, a former Robben Islander who had also played rugby. In fact Tshwete had been arguing in favour of using sports more as a tool of positive change since the time of Mandela's release. Arrie Rossouw, the political writer of the Afrikaans newspaper *Beeld*, described how early in 1990 he had flown to Zambia, the ANC's exile base, and had long chats into the night with Tshwete, already the organization's Mr. Sports. "Tshwete understood right from the beginning that the restoration of rugby internationals would prompt Afrikaners to rethink their preconceptions about the ANC," Rossouw said. "He was passionately in favour of using rugby as an instrument of reconciliation."

He and Stofile argued the point before the NEC. Opinion was divided between the pragmatists who believed the time had come to reach out an undeserved hand of friendship and those who found the idea of rewarding the "Boers'" perfidy outrageous. It was the pragmatists who prevailed on Mandela. The idea of using rugby as an inducement for the Afrikaners to board the democracy train could not have been more in keeping with the approach he had rehearsed in prison, most obviously with Major van Sittert in the "hot plate" encounter, and deployed to such valuable political effect since. The whites had plenty of bread, but they had been denied the circus. The ANC would give it back to them; they would allow the Springboks to perform on the world stage once again.

In August 1992 South Africa played its first serious international match in eleven years against New Zealand at Johannesburg's Ellis Park Stadium. A deal was reached beforehand between the rugby authorities and the ANC. We'll give you the game, the ANC said, so long as you stop the event from being used, as the phrase went, "to promote apartheid symbols". There was an inbuilt problem, though: the green Springbok jersey itself. Still a potent apartheid symbol for blacks, it was inevitably associated in white minds with the two other symbols the ANC meant when they set out their conditions: the old South African flag, which was still the official national flag, and the old national anthem, "Die Stem", which was still the national anthem. To ask rugby fans to dissociate one symbol from the others given the inevitable state of inebriation of many by the time they got into the stadium, and their political insensitivity, seemed too much to ask, too soon. And it was.

The old flags flew all around the stadium and Louis Luyt, the big, brash president of the South African Rugby Union, flouted the rules sensationally by ordering the old anthem to be played. The crowd bellowed out the song like a battle cry, converting what the ANC had hoped to be a ritual of reconciliation into a ceremony of defiance. *Rapport*, the Afrikaans newspaper most anchored in the past, waxed sentimental about "the soft tears of pride" spilled by the *volk* at Ellis Park, before switching to heroic mode to applaud their uncompromising spirit. "Here is my song, here is my flag," rhapsodized *Rapport*. "Here I stand and I will sing my song today."

Enlightened Afrikaners like Arrie Rossouw, the government's chief negotiator Roelf Meyer, and Braam Viljoen, the brother of the general, hung their heads in despair. ANC officials lined up to express their indignation. Arnold Stofile felt betrayed. "We were never dogmatic about isolation," he said. "We turned the stick into a sweet, juicy carrot.

But not everybody chewed on it. So when the fans let us down the way they did, singing the apartheid anthem and all the rest of it, our people were really pissed off."

Yet once the Ellis Park dust had settled, Mandela argued forcefully at NEC meetings for persisting with rugby as an instrument of political persuasion. The case was difficult to make among a group of strong-minded people who had had it with indignities at the hands of white people. But he made it anyway. "Up to now rugby has been the application of apartheid in the sports field," he told his ANC colleagues. "But now things are changing. We must use sport for the purpose of nation-building and promoting all the ideas which we think will lead to peace and stability in the country."

The initial response was "very negative," Mandela recalled. "I understood the anger and hostility of the black population because they had grown up in an atmosphere where they regarded sport as an arm of apartheid, where we supported the foreign teams when they came to play against South Africa. Now suddenly I come out of jail and I'm saying we must embrace these people! I understood their reaction very well and I knew I was going to have a tough time." The ANC leadership thrashed out the matter over several meetings. Mandela's most powerful argument was that rugby was worth, as he put it, several battalions. "My idea was to ensure that we got the support of Afrikaners, because – as I kept reminding people – rugby, as far as Afrikaners are concerned, is a religion."

In January 1993, just five months after the fiasco at the game against New Zealand, Mandela gave white South Africa the biggest, best, and least-deserved gift they could have imagined – the 1995 Rugby World Cup. Not only would South Africa be allowed to take part for the first time, but South Africa would stage the competition. Walter Sisulu

headed a small delegation that met at ANC headquarters in Johannesburg with the top people of the International Rugby Board. All
emerged from the meeting to declare their "elation" at the ANC's decision unconditionally to support a proposal unthinkable only three years
earlier, when Mandela was still in jail.

But instead of responding with the gratitude that Mandela had
expected, the white right stepped up their resistance rhetoric and their
plans for war. They saw that negotiations between the ANC and
the government were inching towards democracy. De Klerk had
announced just a few weeks later that he had set a target date for
multirace elections, April 1994. The fears that prospect held outweighed Mandela's sporting blandishments.

Within days of the rugby announcement, all the talk in political
circles was of civil war. Even President de Klerk, a lawyer who generally tried to keep noise levels down, felt compelled by the intelligence
information he was receiving to declare that the alternative to negotiations was "a devastating war". A member of his cabinet said, "We are
concerned by events in Yugoslavia – more so than most people realize."
So was the ANC. Mandela and his lieutenants openly worried about
their dreams of democracy "drowning", as Mandela himself put it,
"in blood".

On April 10, 1993, they nearly did. An odd couple emerged from
the motley far-right crew to carry out the closest thing to regicide
South Africa had seen since the assassination of Verwoerd in 1966, but
with incalculably more dangerous consequences. Verwoerd had been
stabbed to death by a half-mad parliamentary messenger. It was a shock
to his family and supporters, but not to the political system, which carried on regardless. The assassination of Chris Hani was something else
altogether.

Hani was, next to Mandela, black South Africa's greatest hero. Had
Mandela never been born, or had he died in prison, Hani would have

been the leader of black South Africa by acclamation. Like Mandela, his myth preceded him. In exile for nearly thirty years, his face was unknown to the general public until the ANC was unbanned and he returned home shortly after Mandela's release. The myth rested on two powerful arguments: he had led the two organizations the white regime feared most, Umkhonto we Sizwe and the South African Communist Party. The general rule among black militants was that the more an ANC leader was reviled by the government, the more he was admired. Hani, Mandela's heir as "terrorist-in-chief" in white eyes, had been a legend whose dimensions were compounded by tales of derring-do and survived assassination attempts that filtered back to the townships; by the rumour – entirely true – of the extreme poverty into which he had been born in the black, rural Eastern Cape.

The photographs and TV images of April 10, 1993, foreshadowed big trouble: the fallen idol lying face down in a pool of blood, the spontaneous nationwide demonstrations and the forests of black fists raised in anger, the burning barricades, the torched cars, the white riot policemen clutching their shotguns protectively to their chests. The scale of the peril was contained in the words Archbishop Tutu used to restrain the blacks from doing what natural justice demanded. "Let us not allow Chris's killers success in their nefarious purpose of getting our country to go up in flames," Tutu pleaded, "because now it could easily go up in flames."

Hani's assassin, the man who gunned him down outside his home in the previously all-white working-class suburb of Dawn Park, in Johannesburg, was a Polish immigrant, a foot soldier of the white resistance struggle, a member of the AWB called Janusz Walus whose anti-Communist zealotry was matched only by his desire to be admitted into the right-wing Boer fold. Walus's comrade in arms, the nearest thing to a brain behind the plot, shared the Pole's need to be welcomed into the volk's embrace. He was called Clive Derby-Lewis and he looked and sounded exactly as one would expect someone with a name like that. A member of parliament for Dr. Treurnicht's Conservative Party, he wore blue blazers and cravats, sported an exuberant mustache, and spoke English with a plummy upper-crust accent: he looked and sounded like an actor playing the part of a British pantomime cad.

These two wannabe Boers brought South Africa closer than ever to race war. *Beeld* understood it perfectly. The paper of the Afrikaans establishment warned, "One rash outburst now, one stray bullet, one act of vengeance can bring down the delicate structure of negotiations and unleash satanic forces."

Mandela received the news by phone in Qunu, the village in the Transkei, by the Eastern Cape, where he was born. Richard Stengel, who co-wrote Mandela's autobiography, was with him at the time, watching him have his typical breakfast of porridge, fruit, and toast. Mandela's face turned to stone – or, as Stengel put it, fixed "in the frown of tragedy". He was devastated. He felt a father's affection for Hani as a man, huge respect for him as his political heir. Yet, weighing up instantly the gravity of the moment, he saw that he couldn't afford to indulge his own feelings now. He switched instantly from grieving father to calculating politician.

"He put the phone down," Stengel recalled, "his mind was already spinning and working, and thinking what's going to happen? What would this do for the nation? What would it do for the peace? What would this do for the negotiations? And he began a series of phone calls to aides and he saw immediately this could be the match that ignites the tinder, the revolution, God knows what. And he was completely the master of the political moment. And I almost felt I could see inside of this head and see all of these different gears whirring. He was the consummate political animal, thinking through all of the consequences of this and what it meant."

What it meant was that he had never had greater power than in that moment to define the course his country took. The easier option would be to make war. The difficult one was the call to restraint, an appeal to the angry masses to set aside the emotions of the moment in favour of the bigger goal.

Jessie Duarte, his personal assistant, had phoned him with the news, and she greeted him, after he had travelled to Hani's village to offer the family his condolences, when he arrived that afternoon at the ANC's headquarters in Johannesburg. "He was so sad," Duarte recalled. "He really loved Chris. Yet he knew also that there was not time to lose, that this was no time to give in to his private feelings. The assessment he made was that the potential for violence around Chris's death was immense, and as difficult a time as this was for everybody, the responsibility that he carried was to calm people down."

Duarte worked with Mandela for four years. They shared an office and he rarely travelled anywhere without her. She was a short, intense, bundle of energy whose fiery political activism had earned her a reputation in ANC circles as an angry young woman. But Mandela brought out a cheery side in her and she became, among many other things, a sort of surrogate daughter to him. As such, she was one of the few people whom he let see his sad face, before whom he occasionally let slip his composed politician's mask. Jessie Duarte understood as well as anyone that his life had been happier, richer, and generally more satisfying in politics than in the personal sphere, which had been filled with failure, disappointment, and tragedy.

Duarte was close by him on the day in April 1992 when he decided to announce his separation from his second wife, Winnie. She was struck by the black gloom that descended on him as he took on board the enormous disappointment Winnie had been to him. She had carried on an affair with a much younger man even after Mandela left prison, she never shared his bed when he was awake, she swore with a vulgarity that Mandela could not stomach, and she drank to ugly excess.

As he would say in the divorce trial three years later, describing his two years of post-prison marriage, "I was the loneliest man," all the lonelier for the dream of love that had sustained him in prison, and that she had helped nourish on her visits to him. A letter he wrote to her early on in his time in prison revealed the longing, as well as his perception of the need not to let those around him detect his vulnerability. "My Darling Winnie," Mandela wrote, "I have been fairly successful in putting on a mask behind which I have pined for the family alone, never rushing for the post when it comes until somebody calls out my name. I am struggling to suppress my emotions as I write this letter."

He announced the end of his marriage at ANC headquarters in Johannesburg. In a room far too small for the occasion, packed stiflingly with more than a hundred journalists from all over the world, Mandela sat down at a table, Walter Sisulu by his side, slipped on his reading glasses, and read out a brief statement. Then he looked up, greyer and graver than they had ever seen him, and said, "Ladies and gentlemen, I am sure you will appreciate how painful this is for me. This conference is now over." Usually an announcement of this magnitude prompts reporters to fire a barrage of questions in hopes of provoking an unguarded, quotable outburst. But as he got up, slowly and stiffly, and turned towards the door with a mournful look on his face, the journalists stood, all of them, in silence.

Never before and never again would they be offered such a harrowing glimpse of the regret he felt at his failure as a family man. It was the only time he let the mask slip, allowing the world to see the sorrow written on his face; the cumulative sorrow of decades, for he felt responsible for the hardships that Winnie endured during his absence in jail, and for the drunken acts of criminality to which she was eventually reduced, unable to cope on her own with the combination of fame and relentless police persecution to which she was subjected. He felt just as responsible for the waywardness, and in some cases bitterness towards him, displayed by some of his children (two with Winnie, four – two of whom died – with Eveline). "He never shook off the idea that if he hadn't gone to prison his entire family would have been very different people," Jessie said.

But that was the risk he consciously took the day in 1961 when he founded Umkhonto we Sizwe. He had made his choice then to be father of the nation first, paterfamilias second. Partly to cover the pain of the choice he made, partly in a measure of how complete his dedication to the cause had been, the political mask became his real face; Mandela the man and Mandela the politician became one and the same.

Hani's death rivalled the divorce for the heartache it caused Mandela. He had lost a wife then; now he had lost a surrogate son. But this time he could not afford to let the mask slip. The audience, live on prime time, was the entire country, via the state-run channels of the SABC. De Klerk could have objected, but he did not because he grasped that in the light of the looming catastrophe he was powerless, irrelevant. He had as much ability to influence the angry black masses as Mandela had to influence the AWB, probably less. Mandela, not De Klerk, was now the keeper of the peace. It was as de facto head of state that he addressed the nation on TV and radio that night.

"It was a father talking about a son who had just been murdered and asking people to be calm," Jessie Duarte said of Mandela's performance. Pitched in that way, how could anyone disobey? If the father himself was not baying for revenge, then what right had anybody else to go and seek it? For once, Mandela's flat public speaking style was of a piece with the message he sought to convey. This time the challenge wasn't winning over the whites; it was to persuade his own people. To do this he had to reroute the river of their anger, which was headed straight for hostile confrontation with white South Africa. To succeed he had to appeal not to their resentment, but to what remained of their generosity. That was why in his televised address he drew his audience's attention to the fortuitous fact that an Afrikaner had been, amid the tragedy, the hero of the hour. Janusz Walus was arrested almost immediately due to an Afrikaner woman, a neighbour of Hani's, who had the presence of mind to note down the numberplate of the getaway car.

"A white man, full of prejudice and hate, came to our country and committed a deed so foul that our whole nation teeters on the brink of disaster," Mandela said. "A white woman, of Afrikaner origin, risked her life so that we may know, and bring to justice, this assassin."

If Mandela exaggerated her heroism, he did it with a clear political purpose. "This is a watershed moment for all of us," he said. "Our decisions and actions will determine whether we use our pain, our grief, and our outrage to move forward to what is the only lasting solution for our country, an elected government of the people . . . I appeal, with all the authority at my command, to all our people to remain calm and honour the memory of Chris Hani by remaining a disciplined force for peace."

It worked. Mass rallies erupted all over the country but the people did not allow their grief to spill over into violent anger. "That time in 1993, it was really touch and go," Tutu reflected much later on those perilous days. "What I know for sure is that if he hadn't been around the country would, in fact, have torn itself apart. Because it would have been the easiest thing to have released the dogs of war. That is what maybe many of the younger Turks would have wanted. It was one of the most devastating moments and the anger was palpable. Had Nelson not gone on television and radio the way he did . . . our country would have gone up in flames."

CHAPTER IX
THE BITTER-ENDERS

1993

For General Constand Viljoen, following events from his farm, the spectacle was exasperating. Throw what you might in its way, the Mandela juggernaut just kept going. Not that Viljoen had conspired in the assassination of Chris Hani. He didn't belong to the murderous wing of the SADF. But as a member of the *volk* and as a hard-nosed student of counterinsurgency warfare, he'd figured that Hani's killing would have knocked the process of democratic change off course. Bill Keller, *New York Times* bureau chief in South Africa at the time, described the surprisingly steadying impact of Mandela's address, and the fact that the government had broadcast it, as signs "of the tacit partnership that has developed between the Government and the African National Congress". Keller continued, "It is a quarrelsome but remarkably durable working relationship that amounts almost to an informal government of national unity. As a result, the process of peaceful change has become, if not quite inexorable, at least amazingly resilient."

Viljoen understood this as well as Keller did, but he didn't like it at all. What was worse, he and the rest of the right-wing *volk* chose to interpret Hani's funeral – a massive affair that ended with a thrilling call for peace and unity from Desmond Tutu – as a coming-out party for vengeful blacks. Rather than listen to the words of Mandela and Tutu calling for calm, they tuned in to the discordant messages emitted from the podium by young, third-ranking ANC officials who, doing the exact opposite of what Mandela always strove for, appealled to the crowd's baser instincts by leading them in a song popular among the angry township youth. The drumbeat refrain, repeated in a rising, hypnotic crescendo, went, "Kill the Boer! Kill the farmer! Kill the Boer! Kill the farmer!"

That sentiment was always there among the politically energetic black youth. The obvious thing would have been to seize on that energy and transform it into scorched-earth, Ayatollah revolution. The fear and prejudice and guilt in white hearts was such that it was impossible for many to conceive of the changes Mandela had in mind in anything other than vengeful terms.

The cries of "Kill the Boer", which Mandela tolerated as a means of allowing the youth to blow off their anger, were the sideshow, not the main event. Failing to understand that, Constand Viljoen decided that he had been seething silently in his farm long enough, that the time had come to answer the call of nationalist duty. On May 7, 1993, he entered the fray, turning up at the biggest right-wing rally to date in Potchef-stroom, a town seventy-five miles south-west of Johannesburg. There, a mini-Nuremberg was enacted, complete with flags, imitation Swastika insignias, parade drills, long-bearded Boer "bitter-ender" warriors in brown shirts, and barking orators like Eugene Terreblanche of the AWB. An ample and varied host of malcontents gathered there, united all by their expectation that on the day the blacks came to power they would treat the whites as the whites had treated them. An AWB offshoot called the Boer Resistance Movement (Boere Weerstandsbe-weging, or BWB), was there, an outfit called Resistance Against Communism, the Afrikaner Monarchist Movement, the Foundation for Survival and Freedom, Blanke Veiligheid (White Security), Blanke Weerstandsbeweging (White Resistance Movement), the Boer Republican Army, Boere Kommando, Orde Boerevolk (Order of the Boer People), Pretoria Boere, Volksleër (People's Army), Wenkommando (Victory Commando), the White Wolves, the Order of Death, and even the Ku Klux Klan. They might have been dismissed as a bunch of wackos in fancy dress, were there not 15,000 of them, and were this not the mental swamp that had spawned Hani's murderer, Janusz Walus.

Constand Viljoen was treated with reverence by the first Boer patriots to spot his arrival. At the pageant's climax, he was called up onstage and invited to assume the leadership of the *volk*. He did as he was bade, Eugene Terreblanche ushering him up the steps and declaring that he would be "proud, proud" to serve as "a corporal" under a Boer hero like Viljoen. Entering into the spirit of the occasion, Viljoen denounced the "unholy alliance"that had emerged between Mandela and De Klerk and declared himself ready and willing to lead the Boer battalions. "The Afrikaner people must prepare to defend themselves," the general cried. "Every Afrikaner must be ready. Every farm, every school is a target. If they attack our churches, nowhere is safe. If we are stripped of our defensive capacity we will be destroyed. A bloody conflict which will require sacrifices is inevitable, but we will gladly sacrifice because our cause is just."

The crowd roared their approval. "You lead, we will follow! You lead, we will follow!" they chanted. Terreblanche offered good theatre but the serious-minded Viljoen, who still commanded much respect within the officer class of the SADF, was the redeemer the *volk* had been waiting for. The leaders of the AWB, the BWB, the Wenkommando, and all the rest of them took turns to pledge their fealty, as

Terreblanche had done, to the general, who was anointed there and then the leader of the new "Boer People's Army".

A political wing was created too that day, the Afrikaner Volksfront, a coalition of the Conservative Party and all the other assorted militias. The Volksfront's platform: the creation of an independent Afrikaner state – a "Boerestaat" – carved out of South Africa's existing borders. "An Israel for the Afrikaner", Viljoen called it, making almost explicit a new vision of himself, shared by his ecstatic followers, as the Boer Moses.

Journalists were sometimes tempted to mock these Old Testament naysayers. But the arrival of Viljoen, who brought in four other retired generals as his aides-de-camp, made the white right a serious threat. Within two days of the Potchefstroom rally De Klerk sounded his strongest warning yet, declaring that the possibility had increased of "a bloody Bosnia-like civil war".

Viljoen set about his new mission with the dedication and thoroughness that had characterized his military operations in Angola. Within two months he and his generals had organized and addressed 155 clandestine meetings nationwide. "We had to mobilize the Afrikaners psychologically, start our propaganda campaigns," Viljoen would later reveal. "But as importantly, we had to build a massive military capability." In those first two months the Volksfront recruited 150,000 secessionists to the cause, of whom 100,000 were men-at-arms, practically all of them with military experience.

That still left another three million-plus Afrikaners, and a total of five million white South Africans if you included the "English," who were not openly aligned with the separatist cause. Where were they? There was a Lubowski minority that actively supported the ANC. There was a large minority, about 15 per cent of the whites, who might not vote for the ANC in an election but were sufficiently alert politically to see apartheid for what it was and give their support to the Democratic Party, the new offshoot of the Progressive Federal Party for which Braam Viljoen had stood in the 1987 election. Roughly 20 per cent of whites, mostly Afrikaners, quietly went along with the general thinking of the Volksfront, or at least with its fears. And then there was the rest, the large rump of middle-class white South Africa to which François Pienaar and his family belonged, about 60 per cent of whom tended to believe that the long-ruling National Party could be relied upon to look after their interests. They did wake out of their torpor, but only sporadically, when events like Hani's assassination caught their eye and the thought occurred that there might be consequences for their daily lives.

But this very same rump was also susceptible to Mandela's appeals. Unfixed in their views, their identities less dependent on ancient prejudices than those of the Volksfront faithful, they responded with pleasant surprise to Mandela's praise of the Afrikaner lady who noted down numberplate of Hani's assassin. And they liked his position on rugby, the first fruits of which they would taste on June 26, 1993, when the Springboks kicked off their long and deliberate preparations for the World Cup, still two years away, by playing an international at home against France. It was the game in which François Pienaar made his Springbok debut.

Pienaar, then twenty-six, reacted to the news of his selection as if he were living in a normal country. In his autobiography, *Rainbow Warrior*, he makes no mention of the charged political context against which he achieved "the over-riding ambition" of his life. The continued killings in the townships, the preparations for right-wing war, the possible imminence of all-race elections: none of it impinged seriously on his consciousness, none of it had any more bearing on his life than the Sharpeville blacks had done when he was growing up. A new era was dawning in South African rugby and the national team needed a new captain. Pienaar was overwhelmed to learn at his first Springbok training session that, in a break with all precedent in all sports, he would be leading South Africa out onto the field against France in his debut game. The game was to be played on a Saturday at Durban's King's Park Stadium. On the Thursday before, Pienaar arranged for his parents to fly to Durban, the first plane flight of their lives, and in the evening he drove around to their hotel in a Mercedes-Benz the Springboks' sponsors had loaned him. As he posed for family photographs in his green Springbok kit, fit and ready for battle, he was as happy as any Afrikaner had ever been.

That very evening thousands of Volksfront soldiers were polishing their weapons in preparation for the first military action since General Constand Viljoen had been made bitter-ender-in-chief. In a well-organized logistical operation, they began converging overnight by road on Johannesburg, aiming to arrive at dawn at the gates of the World Trade Centre, the site of negotiations between the ANC and the government. They came from all over South Africa, from the Western Cape and the Northern Cape, the Eastern and the Northern Transvaal. Eddie von Maltitz headed a contingent from Ficksburg in the Orange Free State, five hours away. "We organized ourselves a bus and we crammed into it, strong men only, all heavily armed," as he would recall. "We expected blood. We didn't just have to stop the ANC, we had to stop De Klerk. We had to stop those negotiations. They were leading us to Armageddon. It was the storming of the Bastille all over again; the start of a revolution, we thought."

Von Maltitz's bus was composed mainly of members of the AWB, which he had joined back in that eventful year, 1985. Why did he join? "God spoke to me," he replied. "He urged me to fight to stop the Communists from taking over my country." A dedicated Christian, Von

Maltitz was of German origin but considered himself an honorary Boer. The AWB manifesto struck a chord with him. It defined the resistance movement's mission as "assuring the survival of the Boer nation" that "came into being through Divine Providence". To this end they proposed secession and the creation within South Africa's boundaries of "a free Christian republic".

The biggest draw for most of the AWB brownshirts was not the manifesto, however, so much as their leader, Eugene Terreblanche, whose speeches contained such pearls as "We will level the gravel with Nelson Mandela!" and "We will govern ourselves with our own superior white genes." Even better was how he said it. The beefy, white-bearded Terreblanche was a rousing public speaker. His rallies could always be depended upon to stir the passions of Boers, anxious to mask their fears in blustery defiance. He was good in part because he was a natural actor, whose most treasured prop was the white horse he rode, in part because he had a poetically rich sense of the cadences of language, in part because a propensity for drink loosened his tongue, and in part because he had made a point during his youth of studying the oratorical techniques of Adolf Hitler.

Von Maltitz was less of a demagogue than Terreblanche, but he was just as driven. His zeal saw him rise quickly in the AWB to become Terreblanche's chief lieutenant in the Free State, South Africa's geographical heart. If he was not Boer by blood, he was one in spirit. His grandfather had fought alongside the Afrikaners in the war against the British, but, more important, he felt as pure and passionate an attachment to the land as any of the *volk*. Raised on the family farm, which he inherited from his father, he saw himself as a true son of Africa, proud of having milked his first cow at the age of three. Militarily, he felt he brought a measure of Prussian professionalism to Boer ranks that some of Terreblanche's blowhards lacked. He had done his military service in the elite paratroop regiment, knew how to handle all sorts of weaponry, and had a black belt in karate.

But he became disaffected with Terreblanche, in particular by his heavy drinking. (More than once the leader, drunk, fell off his white horse, to the delight of journalists and black passers-by.) Terreblanche, alert to the possibility that he might lose his best man in the Free State, phoned him one night and said, "Herr von Maltitz, are you with me or against me?" Von Maltitz replied ambiguously, "I am with you in the cause."

Soon after (this was in 1989), Von Maltitz left and formed an outfit he named the Boer Resistance Movement, or BWB, which he left shortly thereafter to form another group calling itself Resistance Against Communism. Sinewy and straight-backed, with strong farmer's hands, he never left his home in anything other than full military camouflage gear and he always had a gun strapped to his hip. Von Maltitz believed that God spoke to him – often – and this might have been funny had he not converted his farm, in response to Mandela's release, into a part-time military training camp. At least once a week, he would gather like-minded Christian soldiers and prepare them for what he called "full military resistance" against the ANC. "The enemy is now at my back door. I must fight him," was Von Maltitz's reasoning. As many as seventy aspiring "kommandos" at a time were schooled in the use of shotguns, Magnum pistols, and guerrilla warfare.

Von Maltitz's name was on the list of right-wing radicals being watched by Niël Barnard's National Intelligence Service. For the intelligence people, as well as to a handful of journalists who kept tabs on the far right, the name Eddie von Maltitz had by now acquired a sinister resonance.

The Boer Warriors stormed the World Trade Centre on the morning of Friday, June 25, 1993. Inside the two-storey glass and concrete building prominent officials had gathered, including Joe Slovo, legendary head of the Communist Party, and Foreign Minister Pik Botha. Before the attack, some three thousand armed Volksfront loyalists found themselves facing down riot police who formed a protective perimeter around the building. One side wore brown, the other grey-blue, but otherwise they were the mirror image of each other. They spoke the same language, they had the same surnames, they had been taught the same white supremacist propaganda all their lives, they had learned to hate and fear the ANC. These policemen belonged to the riot squad, apartheid enforcers programmed to crush "black unrest". Today, here at the World Trade Centre, they confronted something new and bewildering. This was white unrest. Their training – their upbringing – hadn't prepared them for this. What were they supposed to do? Would one among their ranks imitate the example of the soldier guarding the Bastille who refused to fire on his own people, and turned his gun on his officer instead? And if so, then what?

The standoff lasted four hours, the two sides a hundred yards apart, neither daring to make the first move. The government understood that if people died here, if Boer martyrs were created, the consequences were potentially catastrophic. The ANC's supporters were numerous, but few were armed. These people were armed to the teeth and in Constand Viljoen they had a leader now capable of tearing the country apart. So the police were ordered to behave with the utmost restraint, not to respond with the force customary in the more familiar environment of a crowd of stone-throwing black youths. Also, the authorities' respect for Viljoen led them to hope that restraint might yield a reasonable response from their opponents and avoid a bloodbath.

Whether Viljoen actually supported the order to attack was not clear. But it began when Terreblanche ordered his storm troopers, the "elite" unit of the AWB, to advance. Known as the "Iron Guard", they stood out from the rest on account of their black, SS-style uniforms. There were about thirty of them. The police stepped gingerly aside and let them pass. Eddie von Maltitz, in his camouflage uniform, joined in with them, trotting alongside a tank-sized four-wheeled "bakkie" headed for the building's main entrance. It smashed through the glass, creating a breach through which Von Maltitz charged. "I led the first group in," he recalled, triumphant. "We had flak jackets and were ready to shoot. I had an R1 machine gun."

In no time, four hundred warrior-farmers were marauding inside the building, brushing past heavily armed policemen who didn't know how to react. At one point a group of four Volksfronters surrounded a black journalist from the Reuters news agency. He was wearing a jacket and tie, which seemed to make them especially angry. "Uppity kaffir," muttered one. As they pondered whether to do him some damage, a white journalist intervened. "You're a disgrace to the white race," one of the armed invaders told him. Eddie von Maltitz suddenly appeared. "Leave this man alone," he shouted. "We have no quarrel with the black man. The problem's our white government. Let's shoot those traitors. Let's shoot Pik Botha."

Von Maltitz boasted afterward that he had "stopped a bloodbath". Viljoen stopped a bigger one. The general stepped in through the broken glass and went upstairs, flanked by a solemn guard of AWBers, to confer with the ANC and government delegates, and the police officers in charge. He had made his point. Like a terrorist who places a bomb but then warns the police in time to defuse it, he had shown his people's potential to cause harm. All he wanted for now was safe passage out and agreement that none of his men would be arrested on their way home. Agreement was granted and, save for some rude graffiti on the walls, some urinating on the carpets, and much broken glass, no harm was done. For the second time in two months, South Africa had flirted with catastrophe, but managed to avoid it.

. . .

Real life carried on regardless. Half a mile away from the World Trade Centre, people were working at offices and factories as usual. A mile farther away, passengers checked in for flights at Johannesburg Airport and airplanes continued to take off and land without interruption. The city bustled on as usual, the traffic lights turned red and green, the coffee shops were full. And Pienaar's Springboks trained like demons, 375 miles away in Durban, for the game the next day against France.

The ANC had had by now ample reason to say, "Enough is enough, we're taking the carrot away now and never giving it back." But they did not. Again Mandela, supported by Steve Tshwete, prevailed, arguing that it was not the Viljoens and Terreblanches and the Von Maltitzes they were appealing to, for they were a lost cause for now, but to the ordinary Afrikaners. Like ordinary people everywhere when a country is poised between war and peace, they put safety and prosperity before ideology, watched what way the wind was blowing, tried to judge which option would best serve the interests of their families. For those people, rugby remained an inducement; taking it away would cause them pain, tempt them to lean closer to the Viljoen camp. Mandela understood that rugby was the opium of apartheid, the drug that dulled white South Africa to what their politicians were doing. It might well be useful to have on hand a drug that could anesthetize white South African minds to the pain of losing their power and privilege.

The game against France, a powerhouse in world rugby against whom South Africa had not been allowed to play in thirteen years, was the proudest moment in François Pienaar's twenty-six years. Played before an exuberant full house of 52,000, it eclipsed, in the popular imagination, the events at the World Trade Centre twenty-four hours earlier. The game ended in a 20–20 draw, but to Pienaar, and to most of white South Africa, it tasted like victory.

CHAPTER X

ROMANCING THE GENERAL

In 1838, the Boer general Piet Retief led a thousand ox-wagons laden with men, women, and children deep into Zulu country. Dingaan, the Zulu king, eyed the trekkers with apprehension. He had received reports that they were gobbling up land wherever they went, but he had also heard that they had inflicted terrible losses on the black tribes that had tried to oppose them. Dingaan's first instinct was to stand and fight. The Zulus were, after all, the bravest, most disciplined, and most feared warriors in southern Africa. Earlier generations of his people had swept all before them the way the Boers appeared to be doing now. But this enemy had horses and rifles, and the Zulu king reckoned he might be better off trying to strike a deal than pitting his spear-wielding impis against them. So he sent out emissaries to General Retief and invited him to his royal kraal, proposing they come up with a formula to allow them to live side by side in peace.

Retief, whom history holds to have been an honorable man, accepted the invitation, despite warnings from some of his people not to trust the Zulu king, who had ascended to the throne after murdering his half-brother, Shaka. Retief calculated, however, that Dingaan would not be so rash as to do the same to the leader of a large contingent of heavily armed white men.

On February 3, Retief arrived at the Zulu capital of uMgun-gundlovu, which means "the secret place of the elephant," with a party of sixty-nine men and gifts for Dingaan of cattle and horses. Things went well. Before the end of the next day the two sides agreed to a treaty whereby Dingaan ceded large tracts of land to the Boer pioneers. To celebrate the deal the king invited Retief and his party to a feast two days later featuring traditional Zulu dances. They received instructions, which they politely obeyed, to leave their guns outside the royal kraal. They went in, sat down, and then, as the dancing reached its frenzied high-stepping climax, Dingaan leapt to his feet and cried, "Bambani aba thakathi!" – "Kill the wizards!" The king's warriors overpowered Retief and his men and took them to a nearby hill where they butchered them.

The story of Piet Retief and Dingaan was known by every white South African schoolchild. For traditionalists like Constand Viljoen who were steeped in Boer lore and who saw themselves following in the proud tradition of Boer heroes like Retief, the memory of Dingaan's treachery lurked always as a reminder of what could happen if you chose to trust the black man.

That was pretty much what Mandela was doing to F. W. de Klerk in the eyes of the Volksfront faithful. Braam Viljoen, Constand's twin brother, understood the way of thinking of the far right better than practically any other person, aligned broadly, as he was, with the ANC camp. What the right had chosen to learn from history was that "our blacks" responded not to rational persuasion, but to intimidation and force. Braam Viljoen wrote a paper for IDASA, the think tank for which he was working, that influenced Mandela and the ANC to start taking the far right as seriously as De Klerk, who possessed better intelligence, had been doing for some time. In his paper, Braam said that the new calibre of leadership "had transformed the mood of the right wing from doom to militant activism and made it possible for the most diverse Afrikaner groups to unite under the new Volksfront umbrella". Braam, who did not exclude the possibility of significant sectors of the serving SADF answering his brother's call, warned that the far right had to be given a hearing. "Sometimes I think that the classic elements of tragedy are constellating here: the past inescapably determining the future; heroism and valour combining strangely with utter foolishness to bring about ultimate – but inevitable – disaster."

In order to find out whether the far right might countenance the "hearing" he advocated, meaning talks with the ANC, Braam decided the time had finally come to break the ice with his brother. Four months short of their sixtieth birthdays, in early July 1993, Braam and Constand Viljoen sat and talked politics for the first time either of them could remember.

Braam began by asking Constand a simple, blunt question. "What are your options?"

"I am afraid," Constand replied, "that we have only one option. We will have to sort this out with military action."

Braam, who was expecting him to say that, said, "There might be one more option. Would you consider a high-level bilateral meeting with the ANC? As a last attempt to prevent a civil war?"

Constand reflected for a moment, then he said, "I will put it to my board at the Volksfront."

A few days later Constand reported back to his brother. Constand was familiar with war; he wished to avoid it. He was in favour of meeting Mandela, and the Volksfront leadership, military types who deferred naturally to their leader, had agreed. "The answer is yes," Constand told his brother. "We are prepared to meet with the ANC." Braam set to work immediately. He contacted a former theology student of his called Carl Niehaus who had become one of the most high-profile Afrikaners in the ANC. He ran the day-to-day operations in the organization's communications department.

Braam Viljoen told Niehaus that since his brother had been made head of the Volksfront, he had been travelling the country rousing the faithful for war. They hoped to derail the negotiations process and stop all-race elections from taking place. Constand, in league with senior SADF officers sympathetic to his cause, was seriously entertaining the prospect of mounting a coup. "Braam told me they had it in them to break the the SADF's loyalty to the negotiations process and force government out of power in classic coup style," Niehaus later recalled. "He told me they believed they had enough firepower and people at their disposal to make it happen."

Braam told Niehaus that the Volksfront would not participate, as numerous small political groups had done, in the World Trade Centre negotiations. For them, sitting with the ANC was bad enough, but sitting with the De Klerk government was unthinkable. The only faint possibility of finding a peaceful way out of the looming crisis lay in direct talks between the ANC and the Volksfront leadership. Did Niehaus think this might be feasible?

Niehaus immediately contacted a senior ANC intelligence officer, Mathews Phosa, and asked him whether talk of a coup should be taken seriously. Phosa confirmed that, according to his sources, it should be taken very seriously indeed. Phosa was in favour of a meeting with the Volksfront, as were other senior ANC figures Niehaus talked to. "When Nelson Mandela heard about the proposal, he did not hesitate. He immediately saw the value of the meeting," Niehaus recalled. "He believed in the personal contact and he was convinced that he would be able to connect with Constand Viljoen and persuade him to think again."

Niehaus conveyed the ANC's positive response back to Braam, who

reported back to his brother. Constand said he was satisfied the meeting should go on, but he had two basic preconditions. Guarantees had
to be given, first, for the safety of the Volksfront delegation and, second, that the meeting would be held in absolute secrecy. Constand, who
may have had Piet Retief in the back of his mind, was unwittingly following in Mandela's footsteps. Back in the late '80s, it would have been
disastrous for the imprisoned Mandela if the ANC rank and file had
found out he was talking to the enemy. Bafflement would have given
way to damaging divisions in the ranks. Viljoen feared the same, or
worse, if his soldiers found out that he was meeting with Mandela.

Braam reassured his brother on the ANC's behalf, and on August 12,
1993, just four days after that first contact with Niehaus, Braam and
Constand Viljoen stepped through the front door of Nelson Mandela's
home in Houghton. Waiting for them, hand outstretched, and offering
them his beaming smile, stood Mandela himself. It was a mutually stu-
pefying encounter. Mandela was so much taller than the two brothers,
so physically imposing generally. And he was so warm; so apparently
delighted to see them. Mandela, looking from one brother to the other,
saw two middle-height, middle-sized men with identically bulbous
noses, jutting chins, boyishly lush white heads of hair, and solemn, sea-
blue eyes. It was only when he ushered the brothers inside, and saw
them walk, that he perceived a difference between the stiff, straight-
backed step of the military man and the more shambling gait of his
theologian brother.

Constand brought with him the three retired generals who made up
his Volksfront high command; Mandela had the top two people in the
ANC's military and intelligence wings. Braam and Carl Niehaus, the
peace brokers, completed the group. The person most at ease during
the otherwise awkward introductions was Mandela, who might as well
have been welcoming a group of European ambassadors. Yet here were
two sets of people who were on the brink of an inversion of their

decades-long relationship, while maintaining the same violent enmity. Viljoen was doing what Mandela had done back in 1961: set up an armed resistance movement designed violently to challenge the status quo. Mandela wanted to give the would-be terrorists the peaceful alternative he himself had not been offered until nearly thirty years after he had founded Umkhonto.

As the two delegations eyed each other, unsure whether to be fascinated or appalled to find themselves all in the same room, Mandela gently invited General Viljoen to take a seat next to him in the living room. Formal discussions around a large conference table would start presently, but first Mandela paid P. W. Botha the compliment of replicating with Viljoen the elegant manners the big crocodile had shown him four years earlier in Tuynhuys. He offered Constand a cup of tea, and poured it himself. "Do you take milk, General?" The general said he did. "Would you like some sugar?" "Yes, please, Mr. Mandela," said the general.

Viljoen stirred his tea in a state of quiet confusion, thrown by Mandela's show of courtly respect. This was not at all what he had expected. Long-cemented stereotypes were crumbling. What he did not – and by his upbringing could not – see at that moment was that in political terms he was out of his class. Mandela, as a man of the world rather than a man of one *volk*, had a capacity the general lacked to penetrate the minds of people culturally different from himself. He knew when to flatter and soothe (Niël Barnard spoke of Mandela's "almost animal instinct for tapping into people's vulnerabilities and reassuring them"); he knew also when he could go on the offensive, without causing offence, thus conveying an impression of directness that he knew the general would take to, as P. W. Botha had done. Years later, Mandela said, "I have worked with Afrikaners ever since I was in training as a lawyer, and I found them to be simple and straightforward. And if he doesn't like you, an Afrikaner, he'll say '*gaan kak*'" – "Get lost" would be a polite translation of the Boer original. "But if he likes you, then he agrees with you. They have the ability to stick to what they have undertaken."

Mandela – polite but decidedly not mincing his words – worked on making Viljoen like him. "Mandela began by saying that the Afrikaner people had done him and his people a lot of harm," General Viljoen recalled, "and yet somehow he had a great respect for the Afrikaners. He said that maybe it was because, though it was hard to explain to outsiders, the Afrikaner had a humanity about him. He said that if the child of an Afrikaner's farm labourer got sick, the Afrikaner farmer would take him in his bakkie to the hospital and phone to check up on him and take his parents to see him and be decent. At the same time the Afrikaner farmer will treat his worker hard, expect him to work hard. He will be a demanding employer, Mandela said, but he was also human and that aspect of the Afrikaner was something Mandela was very impressed by."

Viljoen was amazed at Mandela's ability to get past the surface caricatures and reach such a deep understanding, as he saw it, of the true nature of the Afrikaner. Just how many black farm labourers Mandela might have found to validate his assessment of the "baas" is another matter. The point was that Mandela knew that his portrait of the Afrikaner as rugged Christian would conform absolutely with Viljoen's own vision of his people.

Viljoen was as intrigued as Botha had been when Mandela proceeded to point out the similarities between the histories of the blacks and the Afrikaners, both of whom had fought freedom wars. And, of course, Mandela was doing something that Viljoen had not expected. He was doing the general the courtesy of speaking to him in his own language.

Mandela had gauged the mood just right, establishing his bona fides with Viljoen as a man with whom he could talk and expect to be understood. But the real substance of the encounter came at the end of their conversation over that same cup of tea. Braam and Niehaus were eavesdropping at just the right time.

"I hope you understand how difficult it is for white people to trust that things are going to go right with the ANC in power," Constand Viljoen said, adding, "I am not sure if you realize it, Mr. Mandela, but this can be stopped."

By "this", Viljoen meant the peaceful transition to black rule. He stopped short of saying it in so many words, but he was clearly indicating to Mandela that there would be military intervention and the right wing, aided by the SADF, could take over if the Afrikaners were not given a chunk of sovereign territory inside South Africa's borders.

Gravely, Mandela replied: "Look, General, I know that the military forces you can muster are powerful and well-armed and well-trained; and that they are far more powerful than mine. Militarily we cannot fight you; we cannot win. If, however, you do go to war, you assuredly will not win either, not in the long run. Because, one, the international community will be totally behind us. And, two, we are too many, and you cannot kill us all. So then, what kind of life will there be for your people in this country? My people will go to the bush, the international pressure on you will be enormous and this country will become a living hell for all of us. Is that what you want? No, General, there can be no winners if we go to war."

"This is so," General Viljoen replied. "There can be no winner."

And that was it. That was the understanding on which the far right and the black liberation movement built their dialogue. That first meeting in Houghton laid the basis for three and a half months of secret talks between delegations of the ANC and the Volksfront. The Volksfront wanted to establish the constitutional principle of an Afrikaner Israel, to which the ANC never quite said no, and never quite said yes, their main concern having been to keep Viljoen's people talking, dangling before them the possibility of future talks on the constitution of their own longed-for "Boerestaat".

These contacts continued apace despite a potentially destabilizing sequence of events during the last three months of 1993. First, negotiators at the World Trade Centre announced that South Africa's first all-race elections would be held on April 27, 1994. Then they set up a committee to decide on a new national anthem and flag. Then Mangosuthu Buthelezi unmasked himself by forming a coalition with the white far right, a body incorporating the Volksfront and Inkatha that called itself the Freedom Alliance. (Viljoen's followers, impressed by Inkatha's willingness to back up their rhetoric with force, cheered this development.) Then Chris Hani's killers, Janusz Walus and Clive Derby-Lewis, were condemned to death. Then a black woman was crowned Miss South Africa for the first time. Then, rubbing still more salt into the wound, Mandela and De Klerk were awarded the Nobel Peace Prize. And, most important of all, Mandela and De Klerk presided over a ceremony at which the country's new transitional constitution was solemnized. The outcome of three and a half years of negotiations was a compromise whereby the first democratically elected government would be a power-sharing coalition, lasting five years: the president would belong to the majority party but the configuration of the cabinet would reflect the proportion of the vote each party won. The new arrangements also provided guarantees that white civil servants, the military included, would not lose their jobs and that white farmers would not lose their land. Neither would there be any Nuremberg-style trials.

Despite the fact that he made this historic deal with De Klerk, Mandela always had more personal regard for Constand Viljoen – and indeed for

P. W. Botha – than for the president who had let him free. In Mandela's eyes, Viljoen was, like him, a patriarchal leader who, within the confines of his unworldly Boerness, had a big heart. Mandela saw mirrored in Viljoen qualities of his own – honesty, integrity, courage – that he liked.

In De Klerk, by contrast, Mandela saw little that he would wish to emulate. Never forgiving him for what he perceived to be his disregard for the loss of black life in the townships, he came to see the president as a lean-souled, slippery lawyer who dwelt in detail and lacked the temperament and conviction of a true leader. This was unfair in the view even of some of his own colleagues in the ANC's National Executive Committee, but if there was one thing the proper Victorian gentleman in Mandela detested it was the sense that someone had betrayed his good faith.

Yet it was with De Klerk that Mandela received his joint Nobel Prize. This infuriated him, not because he judged it to be premature, which it was since nobody knew yet what the outcome of the race between peace and war was going to be, but because he believed, according to his old friend and lawyer George Bizos, that De Klerk did not deserve it, that it should have been awarded to Mandela and to the ANC as a whole. "When De Klerk gave his acceptance speech," said George Bizos, who travelled to Norway with the Nobel delegation, "Mandela expected him to acknowledge that an injustice had been done by the cruelties of apartheid to the people of South Africa. There was no such statement in De Klerk's address." As if believing the propaganda, as if buying into the evening's tacit half-truth that he had earned a position of moral equality with Mandela, all De Klerk said was that "mistakes" had been made by both sides. "I looked at Mandela. He just shook his head."

That evening Mandela and De Klerk were standing by Oslo Cathedral watching a torchlit procession. Part of the ceremony involved a rendition of "Nkosi Sikelele". Mandela noticed that, as the liberation anthem was sung, De Klerk chatted distractedly with his wife. Mandela's patience finally snapped at a dinner hosted that night by the prime minister of Norway before 150 guests, members of his government and the diplomatic corps. Bizos was as shocked as everyone else present by the venom that left Mandela's lips when he stood up to speak. "He gave the most horrible detail of what had happened to prisoners on Robben Island," Bizos recalled, "including the burying of a man in the sand with his head out and urinating on him . . . he told the story as an example of the inhumanity there had been in this system, though he did actually stop short of saying, 'Look, here are the people who represented that system.'"

Clearly, Mandela retained some residue of bitterness toward his jailers, contrary to his own claim in the press conference on the day after his release, and to the perception that his admirers worldwide wished to have of him. He was human after all; he was not a saint.

CHAPTER XI
"ADDRESS THEIR HEARTS"

1994

A simple, low-fat diet, vigorous exercise, fresh sea air, plenty of sleep, regular hours, practically zero stress: prison did have its compensations. It helped explain why Mandela's doctors confirmed the evidence of those who watched him in action during his spectacularly eventful seventy-sixth year: he had the constitution of a fit man of fifty.

Nineteen ninety-three had been eventful; 1994 was shaping up to be more arduous still. Mandela was getting up at 4:30 every morning as a matter not only of routine, but of necessity. The black and white right were still refusing to sign up for the elections, and threatened war if they went ahead without them; in the event that the first ever multiracial vote did go ahead on April 27, as scheduled, there was the matter of a national election campaign to occupy himself with, and assuming that passed off successfully, he would then have a country to run – one that would present all the usual problems faced by countries everywhere, plus the certainty that the fundamental problem of stability, the prospect of counterrevolutionary terrorism of some sort, would not be going away.

The good news was that Constand Viljoen was losing his enthusiasm for war. Since his call to arms at Potchefstroom he had developed – with Mandela's prodding – a sharper sense of the bloodbath he might unleash, and he was beginning to see that a black-led government mightn't be as apocalyptic as he had first imagined. Yet Viljoen continued to urge his people to mobilize for war. "If you want to argue with a wolf, make sure you have a pistol in your hand," was his motto. The problem was that he was not entirely certain anymore whether the wolf was a wolf, or a hound that could be tamed. He liked Mandela but had his doubts about the ANC; he worried that the leaders he was meeting with, like the ANC's wily number two, Thabo Mbeki, might be abusing his bona fides, might seek to trick him into selling out his people. And there was another thing. If the ANC was playing an elaborately deceitful game, if they really did mean to convert South Africa to communism and exact terrible vengeance on whites but were pretending not to, the SADF high command had fallen for it completely. General Georg Meiring, Viljoen's successor as head of the armed forces, had come out with a speech just before Christmas 1993 in which he had pledged his support for the new constitution. (One inducement to do so was a threat from the progressive-minded chief of the air force that he would bomb him if he turned the army against the new order.) Viljoen now knew that if the Volksfront went to war they would probably face the might of the same military he had served with such distinction and pride. Certain sectors of the SADF might still be relied upon to fight alongside the Boer resistance, but short of a progressively less likely coup at the top, the institution appeared to be aligned with Mandela and De Klerk.

General Viljoen felt more uncertain and uncomfortable than ever before. As the chances of victory for the Volksfront became more remote, his soldiers clamoured more loudly for war. Mandela heard those cries too, and felt for Viljoen. He knew that Viljoen's constituency needed something to cheer. The rest of the ANC leadership were not so clear on this point. At a meeting of the movement's National Executive Committee early in 1994, the issue on the table was, what should the position of the new government be on the delicate question of the national anthem? The old anthem was clearly unacceptable. A part of "Die Stem", a sombre martial tune, was an acceptably neutral entreaty to God to "guard our beloved land"; but another part of it – and this was the part black people heard – celebrated the triumphs of Retief, Pretorius, and the rest of the "trekkers" as they drove upward through South Africa in the nineteenth century, crushing black resistance, their "creaking wagons cutting their trails into the earth". The unofficial anthem of black South Africa, "Nkosi Sikelele", was the richly soulful expression of a long-suffering people yearning to be free.

The meeting had just got started when an assistant walked in to inform Mandela that he had a phone call from a head of state. He left the room and the thirty or so men and women of the ANC's supreme decision-making body carried on without him. The consensus was overwhelmingly in favour of scrapping "Die Stem" and replacing it with "Nkosi Sikelele". The NEC members were revelling in their decision and all it symbolized for the new South Africa when Mandela returned. They told him what they'd decided and he said, 'Well, I am sorry. I don't want to be rude, but . . . I think I should express myself on this motion. I never thought seasoned people such as yourselves would take a decision of such magnitude on such an important matter without even waiting for the president of your organization."

And then Mandela sternly set forth his point of view. "This song that you treat so easily holds the emotions of many people who you don't represent yet. With the stroke of a pen, you would take a decision to destroy the very – the only – basis that we are building upon: reconciliation."

The ladies and gentlemen of the National Executive Committee of the ANC cringed with embarrassment. Mandela proposed instead that South Africa should have two anthems, to be played one immediately after the other at all official ceremonies, from presidential inaugurations to international rugby matches: "Die Stem" and "Nkosi Sikelele." Quickly convinced by the logic of Mandela's argument, the freedom fighters unanimously caved in. Jacob Zuma, who had been chairing the meeting said, "Well, I . . . I . . . I think the matter is clear, comrades. I think the matter is clear." There were no objections.

The NEC capitulated in the face of Mandela's wrath because they realized that his response to the anthem question was the correct one in tactical terms. He had in fact lectured the NEC on the business of winning over the Afrikaners, on showing respect for their symbols; on going out of one's way, for example, to employ a few words of Afrikaans at the beginning of a speech. "You don't address their brains," he told them, "you address their hearts."

With Constand Viljoen, Mandela addressed both head and heart, but it was the heart that won out in the end. It helped a huge amount that on March 11 the Volksfront met its Waterloo, shoving the general in the direction towards which Mandela had been gently pushing him.

With the elections barely six weeks away, Viljoen responded to a call from one of his black allies in the Freedom Alliance. It was not Buthelezi this time, but the leader of another of the tribal statelets that the ideologue-in-chief Hendrick Verwoerd had devised as part of his "grand apartheid" strategy, a man by the name of Lucas Mangope, whose rule over Bophuthatswana was under threat from the majority of his ANC-supporting citizens, who found his dependence on Pretoria offensive. Viljoen mobilized a force of over a thousand men to go to the capital of "Bop", a town called Mmabatho. The whole thing turned

Nelson Mandela, the first of thousands to burn his apartheid pass book during the ANC's 1952 Defiance Campaign. *(Eli Weinberg, UWC-Robben Island Museum Mayibuye Archives)*

Mandela, political activist and trial lawyer, sporting one of the suits made for him by Johannesburg's finest tailor, in 1958. *(Jürgen Schadeberg)*

Nelson and Winnie Mandela in the happy early days of their marriage. *(Eli Weinberg, UWC-Robben Island Museum Mayibuye Archives)*

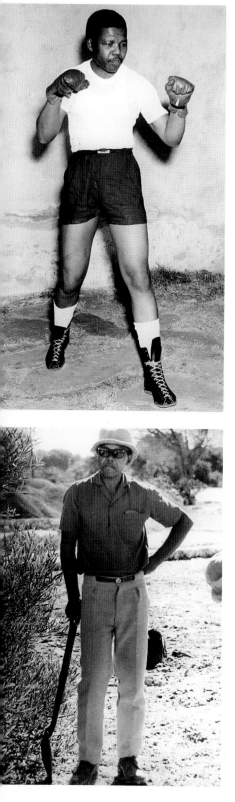

Mandela, the amateur boxer and physical fitness fanatic, striking a pose. *(Eli Weinberg, UWC-Robben Island Museum Mayibuye Archives)*

ABOVE: Mandela, posing in tribal robes at a friend's house while on the run from the police in 1961. *(Eli Weinberg, UWC-Robben Island Museum Mayibuye Archives)*

Mandela in prison in 1977, looking surly as an apartheid-friendly photographer grabs a shot of him in Robben Island. This image was the first public glimpse of him since his arrival fifteen years earlier. *(South African National Archives. Courtesy of The Nelson Mandela Foundation)*

Kobie Coetsee, Minister of Justice who initiated the apartheid government's talks with the imprisoned Mandela, at his desk. *(Terry Shean, Sunday Times/ PictureNET Africa)*

Mandela meets secretly with President P. W. Botha at Tuynhuys, the presidential residence in Cape Town. In attendance are, FROM LEFT: General Willie Willemse, the commissioner of prisons; Mandela; Niël Barnard, head of state intelligence; Botha; and Kobie Coetsee, the Minister of Justice. *(Ters Ehlers)*

Nelson Mandela smiling
sunnily in his office at
ANC headquarters in 1992,
as negotiations with the
government continued
and the country drifted
between peace and war.
(Gisèle Wulfsohn)

Mandela at his presidential inauguration in Pretoria on May 10, 1994, his daughter Zenani
to his left, to her left, deputy president F. W. de Klerk and to Mandela's right, the joint
deputy president, Thabo Mbeki. The taller uniformed man behind Mandela and Zenani is
Georg Meiring, head of the South African military.
(David Sandison, Sunday Times/PictureNET)

Mandela addressing a crowd at Cape Town's parade, amid scenes of jubilant pandemonium, on the day of his release from prison, February 11, 1990. *(Chris Ledochowski)*

Mandela's example and the Springboks' unlikely rise helped transform Justice Bekebeke from the ultimate angry young man – in prison for murder – into a widely respected lawyer.
(Independent Electoral Commission South Africa)

After secret negotiations with Mandela, General Constand Viljoen decided to abandon war against the government and take part in South Africa's first democratic elections. He is shown here at the opening of the new parliament on May 24, 1994.
(Shaun Harris/PictureNET)

Mandela meets the Springbok players for the first time at their training camp. He is shaking hands with James Small, the most emotional member of the team. *(Getty Images)*

Morné du Plessis, the Springbok team manager who worked hard to raise the political consciousness of the players, at a Rugby World Cup game in June 1995. *(Sunday Times/PictureNET)*

Chester Williams, the sole non-white player in the Springbok team, scoring during a World Cup game on the way to the final. *(Paul Velasco/PictureNET)*

ABOVE: Mandela in Springbok shirt acknowledging the crowd before the start of the Rugby World Cup final at Ellis Park, Johannesburg, on 24 June 1995. Behind him in dark glasses is his "number one" bodyguard, Linga Moonsamy; in profile to his right is the rugby chief Louis Luyt.
(Paul Velasco/PictureNET Africa)

RIGHT: François Pienaar, the Spingbok captain, raising the World Cup in triumph on the Ellis Park field. *(John Parkin, AP Photo/PictureNET)*

François Pienaar celebrates with the player who scored all the points for the Springboks in the final match, Joel Stransky.
(Paul Velasco/PictureNET Africa)

Ecstatic South African rugby fans at Ellis Park after the Springbok victory. *(AP/PictureNET)*

Nelson Mandela, retired from politics at eighty-nine, savors victory again with the Springbok team after they won the Rugby World Cup in 2007. *(Getty Images)*

into a fiasco when Eugene Terreblanche's AWB entered the fray and went on what the Afrikaans papers were to describe as a "kaffirskiet-piekniek" – a kaffir-shooting picnic. Mangope's security forces revolted, turning their guns on the Volksfronters, and when the SADF arrived late in the day in a column of armoured vehicles, Viljoen's forces fled the field in disarray.

What happened at Mmabatho is often given as the sole reason why Viljoen decided to abandon the Boer resistance struggle. He confided that there was more to it than that. Once rid of the AWB hooligan element, it would have remained within his means to carry on leading an effective "military" campaign, even if everybody else would have described it as terrorism. "We had a plan in place. We could have stopped the elections from taking place, and not with the SADF, but on our own. We had the means, we had the arms, we had the tactics, and we had the will. Not to take power, not to defeat the SADF, but yes, to prevent the elections from taking place successfully, no doubt about that."

Arrie Rossouw, perceived four years after Mandela's release as a heavyweight of Afrikaner journalism, a man who would go on to become editor-in-chief of both *Beeld* and *Die Burger*, agreed. "No question, he could have caused terrible damage to this country," Rossouw said. "He could easily have placed four hundred highly trained former members of the Reconnaissance regiments [Special Forces] under his command, and with them, well armed, he could have blown up airports, train stations, bus stations, assassinated people. They would not have managed to overthrow the government – that was the lesson of Mmabatho – but they could have paralysed the economy and caused absolute political chaos. And they could have gone on for years and years."

They could have done, in other words, what the IRA did in Northern Ireland for thirty years, but with far more catastrophic impact. This was partly because they disposed of more arms and more men with more sophisticated military experience, but mainly because South Africa was a fragile, volatile, infant democracy, with a brittle economy, susceptible in a way neither Ireland nor Britain had been to chaos and collapse. The alarming thing was that it fell not to a collective but to one man to decide which of the two it would be, peace or war.

"Yes, it was entirely my decision. Entirely," Viljoen solemnly confirmed. "During those final weeks before the election, opinion was divided in the Afrikaner Volksfront, fifty-fifty between those who wanted the violent option, disrupting the elections and the whole democratic process in South Africa, and those who wanted a negotiated solution." So how did he reach his decision? "I always took the view that war or violence is not an easy option. I know war. So I told my supporters that I would take it upon myself whether to go to war or not to go. It was the most difficult decision I had to take in my life.

"In the military you must understand that before making up our minds on a question like this we weigh up all the factors, we evaluate, we think hard, and it is only after a long process that we decide. I considered that the right option was negotiations, and participation in the elections. I considered that it was best for the country, and best for the Afrikaner people."

But what was the decisive factor? Was it the AWB rabble? Was it Mmabatho? He replied without hesitation, "The character of the opponent – whether you can trust him, whether you believe he is genuinely for peace. The important thing when you sit down and negotiate with an enemy is the character of the people you have across the table from you and whether they carry their people's support. Mandela had both."

Few could withstand Mandela's charm offensives – not even De Klerk, not even when they were campaigning against each other in the run-up to the April 27 elections, not even after they had gone head-to-head in a U.S.-style live TV debate. De Klerk, young enough to be Mandela's son, proved sharper and better prepared than his adversary. Then, as the debate was reaching its conclusion, Mandela reached out and shook the president's hand, praising him as "a true son of Africa". De Klerk, flabbergasted, could only accept the handshake and put on his best smile, though he knew that in so doing Mandela was landing a knockout punch.

"I felt, and everybody felt, that I was winning on points," De Klerk would recall. "Then he really pulled up level again by suddenly reaching out, praising me, and taking my hand in front of all the television cameras. That might have been preplanned. I think it was a political move. But I do think that the majority of his media triumphs were an instinctive reaction from him. I think he has a wonderful talent in that regard." A few days after the debate, De Klerk himself made a gracious public statement. During his very last press conference before the election, he was asked his opinion of his opponent. "Nelson Mandela," replied De Klerk, spreading out his hands as if in surrender, "is a man of destiny."

As part of the election campaign Mandela went on a nighttime talk show on Johannesburg's Radio 702 to answer callers' questions live. Eddie von Maltitz, the first Volksfront warrior to enter the World Trade Centre during the raid, was down on his farm with some of his "kommandos", listening to 702. Urged by his comrades to call in and give the "kaffir" a piece of his mind, Von Maltitz obliged. For a full three minutes he ranted and raved at Mandela – communism that, terrorists the other, the destruction of our culture, civilized standards, and norms. He ended with a brutally direct threat. "This country will be embroiled in a bloodbath if you carry on walking with the Communist thugs."

After a tense pause, Mandela replied, "Well, Eddie, I regard you as a worthy South African and I have no doubt that if we were to sit down and exchange views I will come closer to you and you will come closer to me. Let's talk, Eddie."

"Uh . . . Right, okay, Mr. Mandela," Eddie muttered in confusion. "Thank you," and he hung up.

At his farm three months later, while Eddie still wore a green military jumpsuit, light green camouflage boots, and a 9mm pistol tucked into his waist, he was a changed man, He had stopped training his kommandos; he had abandoned his preparations for war. The exchange on Radio 702 had changed everything. "That was what got me thinking," he said. The new ANC premier of the Orange Free State, where he lived, was the man who pushed him over the edge. The premier's name was "Terror" Lekota, known as such because of his lethal goal-scoring on the soccer field. Lekota, who had spent time on Robben Island during Mandela's later years there, had many of Mandela's instincts. He made it his first mission on coming to power to win over the Free State's Afrikaner farmers. If he roped in Von Maltitz, he would go a long way towards corralling the rest. Lekota himself called Von Maltitz and invited him to his birthday party at his residence in the state capital, Bloemfontein. Von Maltitz said no, but Lekota insisted. He called again. "Please, Eddie, I'd really like you to come." Von Maltitz said he would talk to his men and get back to him. "We talked and figured, what could we lose?" Von Maltitz recalled. "So when he called back the next time I said yes."

Von Maltitz turned up at what he called "the big house" in Bloemfontein fully armed. "I did not want to do a Piet Retief with Dingaan," he said. He went into the house and joined the party, where black people predominated, without being searched. "Terror Lekota saw me across the room and he came over and gave me a big hug. He must have felt my guns but he said nothing. He just kept smiling. I liked him. He was genuine. Like Mr. Mandela, a genuine man. So that's why I figured, Let's give them a chance; they deserve it."

Why? Because Mr. Mandela, and his new friend Terror had treated him with respect – Walter Sisulu's "ordinary respect". "I never got that respect from De Klerk and the National Party, you know. But from Mr. Mandela, yes . . . I believe, I really do, that we must give them a chance."

. . .

The ANC had won the elections with just under two-thirds of the national vote, and nearly 89 per cent of the black one. Of the rest, one per cent went to the openly anti-white PAC – whose "one settler, one bullet" slogan ANC supporters jeeringly translated into "one settler, one per cent"; and 10 per cent went to Inkatha. (Abandoned by Viljoen, Chief Mangosuthu Buthelezi was left with no option but to join the election process.) The National Party got 20 per cent, which meant four seats in cabinet, including the deputy presidency for De Klerk, in the new coalition government over which Mandela would preside. And Viljoen's party, which he named the Freedom Front, got 2 per cent of the vote, which meant a not unrespectable nine seats in the new, multi-coloured parliament.

No sooner had the results come in than John Reinders, chief of presidential protocol under both De Klerk and P. W. Botha, contacted his former employers, the Department of Correctional Services. Botha had dragged him out of the prison bureaucracy in 1980, when he had occupied the rank of major, but Reinders found to his relief that, yes, they had a job for him.

His last job before leaving was to organize Nelson Mandela's presidential inauguration on May 10, 1994. It was a logistical nightmare compared to De Klerk's inauguration, to which no foreign delegation – save locally based diplomats – had thought fit to travel. This inauguration would be quite different. Four thousand people gathered at Pretoria's seat of power, an early-twentieth-century pile called the Union Buildings atop a hill overlooking the city. Among the guests were figures otherwise unimaginable in the same room, such as Hillary Clinton, Fidel Castro, Prince Philip, Yassir Arafat, and the president of Israel, Chaim Herzog. The two national anthems – "Nkosi Sikelele" and "Die Stem" – – were played side by side as the brand-new national flag fluttered. It was the most multicoloured flag in the world, a sort of crazy quilt in black, green, gold, red, blue,' and white, combining colours associated with black resistance with those of the old South African flag. Mandela took his oath of office before a white judge flanked by his daughter Zenani, and surrounded by black former prisoners and white SADF generals standing to attention in full-dress uniform. ("A few years earlier they would have arrested me," he joked later.) The ceremony closed with the spectacle of South African Air Force jets soaring overhead painting the colours of the new flag in the sky.

Mightily relieved that the ceremony had passed without catastrophe, John Reinders arrived at his office in the Union Buildings early next morning, May 11, with a couple of large cardboard boxes under his arms. He was a large man, but he had the deferential manner of some-one much slighter, as well as the good judgment to know when he was beaten.

"I came in early that morning to collect my things," Reinders recalled. "All we whites had applied for jobs elsewhere, sure we would be asked to leave. Quite a few meant to go and work for Mr. de Klerk in the deputy presidency."

Reinders was packing away his mementos of seventeen years spent running the presidential office, organizing ceremonial dos, bumping into famous people on official trips, when suddenly he was startled out of his reminiscences by a knock at the door. It was another early riser. Mandela.

"Good morning, how are you?" he said, stepping into Reinders's office with outstretched hand.

"Very well, Mr. President, thank you. And you?"

"Well, well, but . . ." Mandela said, puzzled, "what are you doing?"

"I am collecting my things and getting ready to go, Mr. President."

"Oh, I see. And may I ask where you are going?"

"Back to correctional services, Mr. President, where I used to serve."

"Mmm," said Mandela, pursing his lips. "I was there twenty-seven years, you know. It was very bad." He grinned as he repeated, "Very bad!"

Reinders, flummoxed, offered him a half-smile back. "Now," Mandela continued, "I would like you to consider staying here with us." Reinders examined Mandela's eyes with astonishment. "Yes. I am quite serious. You know this job. I don't. I am from the bush. I am ignorant. Now, if you stay with me, it would be just one term, that is all. Five years. And then, of course, you would be free to leave. Now, please understand me: this is not an order. I would like to have you here only if you wish to stay and share your knowledge and your experience with me."

Mandela smiled. Reinders smiled, wholeheartedly now. "So," Mandela continued, "what do you say? Will you stay with me?"

Amazed as he was, Reinders did not hesitate. 'Yes, Mr. President. I will. Yes. Thank you."

At which point his new boss gave him his first task: to gather together all the presidential staff, including the cleaners and the gardeners, at the cabinet room for a meeting. The new president walked among them, shaking hands with each one of the hundred or so people assembled, saying a few words to each, in Afrikaans where appropriate. Then he addressed them all. "Hello, I'm Nelson Mandela. If any of you prefer to take the [severance] package, you are free to leave. Go. There is no problem. But I beg you, stay! Five years, that is all. You have the knowledge. We need that knowledge, we need that experience of yours."

Every single member of the presidential staff stayed.

Two weeks later, on May 24, four hundred newly elected delegates converged on Cape Town for the opening of South Africa's first democratic parliament, held at the very same National Assembly building where the whites-only parliament used to gather. Until now it had been a dull, heavy, monochrome sort of place. On the May morning when the same chamber opened its doors to Mandela's non-racial democracy the scene underwent a Technicolor transformation. The sight from high up in the visitors' gallery suggested a cross between the United Nations General Assembly, a pop concert, and an end-of-term college party. A glance at the roster of new members of parliament told it all. Before they were called Botha or Van der Merwe or Smith. Now they were called those names, but also Bengu and Dlamini and Farisani and Maharaj and Mushwana and Neerahoo and Pahad and Zulu. And a third of the MPs, including the new speaker, Frene Ginwala, were women. More striking was the proportion of MPs who had spent time in prison, or had been on the run from the police. Practically every ANC MP had broken the law; now they would be making it, led by the longest-serving prisoner of them all, the last man in today, Mandela.

As word spread of his arrival, the MPs rose to their feet, the buzz gave way to a roar, to freedom songs and swaying dances from the younger, more exuberant members of the ANC contingent. Amid the Rainbow Nation hurly-burly, General Viljoen cut an anomalous figure. Sober as ever, in a dark suit and tie, he stood in the middle of the oval chamber at ground level, as befitted the leader of the honorable Freedom Front opposition. Mandela emerged, also at ground level, straight-backed and beaming, to a cheer from the assembly.

Viljoen was staring at Mandela with a mixture of awe and affection. On seeing him, Mandela broke parliamentary protocol and, crossing the floor, shook his hand and said with a big smile, "I am very happy to see you here, General."

Some voices from high up in the gallery shouted, "Give him a hug, General! Go on, hug him!"

In recalling the moment, Viljoen let a small smile pass his lips, nodded, then turned solemn again. "But I did not do that. I am a military man and he was my president. I shook his hand and I stood to attention."

. . .

And that could have been the end of that: order restored, old enemies reconciled, the good king crowned, all players exeunt – exuberantly – stage left. But it was not the end. It was not over yet, neither for Mandela nor for General Viljoen. There was still one more act to be played out before Viljoen could hang up his sword with peace of mind, one final set of challenges to be overcome before Mandela could consider his life's quest complete.

As Viljoen pointed out, "Forty or fifty per cent of my people did not take part in the voting." Some of them placed bombs at bus stops and other places where black people gathered in large crowds during the week before the election. They also set off a bomb at Johannesburg International Airport. Twenty-one people were killed and more than a hundred badly injured. Mandela's speeches during his first month in power were consistently upbeat, deliberately trying to set an optimistic, energized mood. But he could not refrain from pointing out at the closing of that first session of parliament that the security forces would have to remain on full alert. "The problem of politically motivated violence is still with us," he said.

Mandela had a lot on his plate during his five-year term in office: providing houses and schools, water and electricity for black people. But his overwhelming priority was to cement the foundations of the new democracy, render it bombproof. He knew that attempts would be made to subvert the inevitably fragile new order. It could not be that all of white South Africa would surrender its ancient powers, and a fair number of its privileges, without a fight.

As for General Viljoen, he was torn, the way Niël Barnard had been four and a half years earlier on the morning of Mandela's release. Despite having met Mandela sixty times in prison, Barnard could not entirely dispel that alarm bell going off deep inside his head, warning him, however irrationally, of the Ayatollah factor. Viljoen felt similar misgivings, as if he could not quite believe that life could be as good as Mandela made it seem, as if he had not been able entirely to shed his ancestral misgivings about the black man. A part of him worried as he sat there on that opening day of parliament, and throughout the year ahead, that he might have done the right thing by himself – Mandela always had the door open to him, always treated him with respect – but not the right thing by his people. He confessed that his conscience nagged at him. "I was troubled. Very troubled," he said. "A lot of fine things had been said, but where was the proof that I could show my people once and for all?"

The answer lay in Mandela's proving to Viljoen's people that they were his people too; in widening his embrace beyond Constand Viljoen and John Reinders and Niël Barnard and Kobie Coetsee to include all Afrikaners. Mandela's legal adviser and close confidant in the presidential office, a white lawyer called Nicholas Haysom, who had been jailed three times during the anti-apartheid years, defined the mission in appropriately epic terms.

"We called it nation-building. But Garibaldi has a quote that exemplifies it more eloquently," said Haysom, referring to Giuseppe Garibaldi, the soldier-patriot who unified Italy in the mid-nineteenth century. "When he had finished his military mission Garibaldi said, 'We have made Italy, now we must make Italians.'" Actually, the challenge Mandela faced was tougher than Garibaldi's. "Italy was divided but homogeneous. South Africa in 1994 was a country that was split historically, culturally, racially, and so many other ways," Haysom added. "No amount of negotiations, speeches, constitutions would suffice in themselves to 'make South Africans'. You needed something else to bring people together. You needed Mandela to do what he did best: rise above our differences, be bigger than those things that divided us and appeal to that which bound us together."

CHAPTER XII
THE CAPTAIN AND THE PRESIDENT

1994–95

"You looked at him," Mandela said, recalling his first meeting with François Pienaar, "you considered where he came from, and what you saw was a typical Afrikaner."

Mandela was right. If the apartheid ideologues had had the same inclination for putting art to political use as their Soviet counterparts, they would have chosen Pienaar to depict the model specimen of Afrikaner manhood. Six foot four, he carried his seventeen stone of muscle with the statuesque ease of Michelangelo's David.

If then, as Mandela said, you considered where he came from, you pictured a boy growing up to manhood in Vereeniging in the seventies and eighties and what you saw, with almost cinematic clarity – as Mandela did – was a faithful representation of 90 per cent of the Afrikaner *volk*: a people conditioned by the particular time and place in which they happened to be born to be straightforward, uncomplicated, hard-working, tough, secretly sentimental, churchgoing rugby fanatics who related to their superabundant black neighbours with a mixture of disdain, ignorance, and fear.

Yet if there was one thing Mandela had learned in his dealings with the Afrikaners it was to see past appearances. "He did not seem to me at all to be the typical product of an apartheid society," Mandela said. "I found him quite a charming fellow and I sensed that he was progressive. And, you know, he was an educated chap. He had a BA in law. It was a pleasure to sit down with him."

Pleasure was the last thing on Pienaar's mind as he stood on the stone steps of the giant Union Buildings on June 17, 1994, preparing to go inside for a meeting to which President Mandela had invited him. Pienaar, now twenty-seven years old but suddenly feeling an awful lot younger, confessed to waiting reporters that he had never been more nervous in all his life; that the prospect of meeting the president was more daunting than any rugby game.

Dressed in dark suit and tie, Pienaar entered through a small door at the buildings' west wing, ducked through a metal detector, and presented himself before two policemen waiting for him at a desk behind a green-tinted window of thick bulletproof glass. Both being Afrikaners, they immediately started engaging him animatedly on rugby. One of them led him out into a courtyard and down a corridor lined, though he barely noticed the anomaly, with watercolours of scenes from the Great Trek, ox-wagons and men on horses against a background of brown, yellowy *veldt*. The policeman dropped him off at a small waiting room, bare save for a table and some leather chairs, into which stepped Mandela's personal assistant, a tall, imposing black lady called Mary Mxadana who asked him to take a seat and wait a moment. He sat in the room alone for five minutes, his palms sweating. "I was incredibly tense as the moment arrived when I would meet him," he recalled. "I was really in awe of him. I kept thinking, 'What do I say? What do I ask him?'"

Then Mxadana reappeared, asked him if he would like tea or coffee – he said coffee – and bade him follow her. She stepped out of the waiting room into the corridor with the pictures of the ox-wagons, stopped at a tall, dark brown door, knocked sharply, and, in one move, stepped in. She held open the door for Pienaar, whose stage fright only worsened at the sight of the vast room before him, oceanically empty, as at first it seemed, till he crossed the threshold and spotted to his right a tall grey-haired man jumping out of his chair. Mandela was seventy-six but he headed toward Pienaar with the alacrity of a rugby opponent charging in for a tackle – except that he stood erect, had a big smile on his face and his hand outstretched. "Ah, François, how very good of you to come!" Pienaar muttered, "No, Mr. President, thank you so much for inviting me." Mandela shook his hand warmly, Pienaar registering with surprise that Mandela was almost as tall as he was. "So, how are you, François?" "Oh, very well, Mr. President, and you?" "Ah, very well. Ve-ry well!"

Mandela, smiling all the time, clearly happy to have this big young Boer in his new office, gestured to him to sit down on a sofa at right angles to his own, as he congratulated him on a Springbok victory over England, a convincing 27–9, in a game down in Cape Town six days earlier.

There was a knock at the door and a lady came in carrying a tray of coffee and tea. She was a white woman, middle-aged, wearing a floral dress with shoulder pads. Mandela saw her appear at the door at the other end of the room – a distance six times greater than the length of the cell that had been his home for eighteen years of his life – and immediately stood up, remaining standing as she placed the tray on a low table before the two men. "Ah, thank you very much. Thank you ve-ry much," smiled Mandela, still standing. "And, ah, this is François Pienaar . . . Lenoy Coetzee." Pienaar reached out and shook hands with her, and before she turned to go away, Mandela thanked her again and did not sit down again until the Afrikaner lady had exited the room.

Pienaar looked around the large wood-panelled office, vaguely registering a blend of decor old South African and new; ox-wagon watercolours side by side with shields of leather hide and wooden African scupltures. Mandela broke in. "Do you take milk, François?"

In less than five minutes Pienaar's mood had been transformed. "It's more than just being comfortable in his presence," Pienaar recalled. "You have a feeling when you are with him that you are safe." So safe that Pienaar had the audacity half-jokingly to ask him whether he would accompany the Springboks on a tour to New Zealand the following month. "Nothing would please me more, François!" he smiled. "But most unfortunately I have these people here in this building who drive me very, very hard and I know they will give me orders to remain here and work!"

To Pienaar's relief, Mandela simply took charge from there, launching into a sequence of reminiscences and stories that made Pienaar feel, as he put it, like a little boy sitting at the feet of a wise old man. One of the stories concerned the theft of a chicken in Qunu, the village in the Transkei where Mandela had been raised and to which he still returned to dispense his ancient chiefly duties. One day when Mandela was visiting, a lady came around to his home to tell him that a neighbour had stolen her chicken. Pienaar picked up the story: "Mandela summoned the neighbour, who confessed he had done it, but only because his family was hungry. Then Mandela called both of them to his house and he ruled that the man had to pay the lady back two chickens. But she argued, she bargained, she wanted more, and they settled on more. But it was a lot for this guy, so Mandela helped him out with the repayment."

Mandela chuckled throughout as he told the story, a peculiar one for him to choose to tell the Springbok captain at a meeting he had called with the clear purpose of forging a relationship with him in preparation for the following year's Rugby World Cup. It was peculiarly light and inconsequential, too, given the solemnity of the surroundings, a room where, as Mandela had put it during an interview here a few days earlier, "the most diabolical plans were hatched". Yet the story of the stolen chicken worked, in that it helped forge precisely the sort of complicit intimacy Mandela wished to establish with the young man. In sharing with him what had been something of a private confidence, a story Pienaar would not have read about in the newspapers, Mandela had found a way to the heart of the overawed rugby captain, making him feel as if he were in the company of a favourite great-uncle. Pienaar would not have guessed it at the time, but winning him over – and through him, enlisting the rest of the Springbok team – was an important objective for Mandela. For what Mandela had reckoned, in that half-instinctive, half-calculating way of his, was that the World Cup might prove helpful in the great challenge of national unification that still lay ahead.

Mandela never made his purpose overt in that first meeting with Pienaar, but he did edge closer to the main theme when he switched the conversation to his memories of the Barcelona Olympic Games, which he had attended in 1992 and recalled with great enthusiasm. "He talked about the power that sport had to move people and how he had seen this not long after his release in the Barcelona Olympics, which he especially remembered for one particular moment when he said he stood up and he felt the whole stadium reverberating," said Pienaar, in whose mind Mandela was seeking to plant the first seeds of a political idea. Pienaar did not register it as such, but in Mandela's version of the encounter, warm as it had been, the subtext was crystal clear.

"François Pienaar was the captain of rugby and if I wanted to use rugby, I had to work with him," Mandela said. "I concentrated in our meeting on complimenting him for the role which he was playing and which he could play. And I briefed him on what I was doing about sports and why I was doing so. And I found him a highly intelligent person." The time had come, as Mandela explained to his guest, to abandon the old perception of the Springbok rugby team as "enemies" and see them as compatriots and friends. His message was, "Let us use sport for the purpose of nation-building and promoting all the ideas which we think will lead to peace and stability in our country."

Pienaar had become the latest Afrikaner to be "enveloped", as he himself put it, in Mandela's aura; but he did not become an overnight evangelizer. He was a straightforward rugby man, for whom big words like "nation-building" carried little meaning. The message he took away from that meeting was a straightforward one: Get out there and win, wear that shirt with pride, certain of my support. Mandela bade Pienaar good-bye as if they were already the best of friends.

Mandela returned to his job, Pienaar to his, neither realizing the uncanny similarity between the enterprises each faced. Pienaar, new to the captain's job, viewed with some reservation by a sector of the rugby fraternity that questioned his character and his ability, had a tough task ahead: consolidating his authority and uniting the rugby team. This required a significant measure of political skill, for the Springboks were big men with big egos drawn from provincial teams accustomed to see each other as fierce enemies in the big domestic competition, the Currie Cup.

The Afrikaans–English divide presented another challenge. Handling James Small, one of the most talented "Englishmen" in South African rugby, proved an early test of Pienaar's leadership. Small, a relatively short and light member of the team at six feet and just over fourteen stone, was one of the team's fastest sprinters – and most volatile characters. Pienaar's joy at beating England the week before he met Mandela had been tarnished by the memory of something Small had said to him on the field during the game. A lapse by Small had led to England being awarded a penalty kick. Pienaar rebuked him with a gruff "Come on, James!" to which Small replied, "Fuck off!" Pienaar was shocked. The role of captain in other sports often has a token or ceremonial quality to it, but in rugby it carries real weight. Not only does the captain exercise a great deal of tactical authority during a game, calling moves, he also carries, by rugby tradition, a special mystique. The rest of the team is expected to relate to him with something of the deference schoolchildren regard a school principal, or soldiers a commanding officer. Small's "Fuck off!" was an act of insubordination so serious that, unchecked, it could have ended up corroding Pienaar's influence over the entire team. After the game, Pienaar, who towered over Small, took him to one side and firmly informed him that he would never, ever swear at him on the field again. Small had a reputation as a barroom brawler way beyond Pienaar's, even, but he heard his captain loud and clear. He never did swear at him again.

South Africa, making up for the lost years of isolation with a sudden blur of international games, travelled to New Zealand for the first time in thirteen years in July 1994, losing one game narrowly and drawing another against the New Zealand All Blacks, already regarded widely as favourites for the following year's World Cup. In October the Springboks played two games at home against Argentina, another strong rugby nation, and won both. Small starred in the second game but in the nighttime celebrations that followed found himself caught up in yet another drunken fight. The incident, sparked when a woman in a bar pinched Small's behind, received much media coverage. He was banned from a tour the following month to Britain, in which the South Africans convincingly beat Scotland and Wales, intimidating all who saw them with the uncompromising ferocity of their play.

The tunnel vision of the Springboks was now total. The only thing in their minds was the World Cup, which began at the end of May next year. Neither Pienaar, nor Small, nor anyone else on the team was paying any attention at all to South African politics, where there was plenty going on.

November 1994 had been the diciest month yet of Mandela's half-year in power. He left to his ministers the tough business of providing housing, education, electricity, and water to those whom apartheid had deliberately denied the basics of a dignified modern life. His job was to try to become the father of the whole nation; to make everybody feel that he symbolized their identity and values. That was why a part of him always kept a wary watch on the most recalcitrant members of the new family he was seeking to create, the Afrikaner right. This meant also worrying about the police. Mandela was fairly relaxed about the

South African Defence Force, whose Afrikaner generals had been joined at the top of the military by former commanders of Umkhonto we Sizwe. The SADF generals were disciplined. The police were looser cannon, and most of the top people from the apartheid era remained at their posts. The government intelligence services, hitherto deployed to monitor the left, concentrated their energies now on that 50 per cent of General Constand Viljoen's former supporters who had not taken part in the April elections, and from whose discontented midst the pre-election terrorist bombers had sprung.

The prevailing view among white South Africans in the aftermath of Mandela's inauguration was one of relief. The apocalypse had come and gone and life remained much as it had been. The guillotine blocks had not gone up and the civil servants remained, for the most part, in their jobs. But white people did not shake off their inbred mixture of guilt and fear overnight. They began to worry whether this might not be the calm before the storm, whether there might be an overnight change of policy on public service jobs for white people, precipitated by the inevitable clamour whites expected from blacks for instant economic gratification. In a measure of how whites continued to underestimate the intelligence of their black neighbours, stories began to do the rounds about black "cleaning girls" and "garden boys" striding into their "madams'" and "masters'" sitting rooms and demanding the keys of their homes.

The truth was that black South Africans were, for the most part, sufficiently shrewd and sufficiently patient to know that Rome would not be built in a day. They trusted their government eventually to deliver but understood that to drive the whites into the sea would not do anyone any good. That was why they had voted for the ANC instead of the PAC.

The generosity implicit in that choice eluded a large chunk of the white population, few of whom had the slightest sense of what was going on in the minds of black South Africans. General Viljoen, the accidental politician, kept worrying too, still unsure whether he had done the right thing by his people in shelving the Boerestaat option and going along with the bonafides of Mandela's ANC. He worried also about the potential for violence his well-armed and, in some cases, half-crazed former allies might pose. Mandela, who talked about these matters with Viljoen, with whom he regularly had tea, saw his fears confirmed on the evening of November 5.

On this day, the Springboks had annihilated a Welsh team with such style and passion that the team's coach, Kitch Christie, declared himself convinced that the Springboks could win the World Cup. Quite possibly Johan Heyns, in common with many other Afrikaners, had formed the same opinion too. But he did not live to see the day. That evening, as he sat at his home in Pretoria playing cards with his wife and his two grandsons, aged eight and eleven, he was shot dead. A gunman outside killed him with one bullet to the back of the head.

Professor Johan Heyns, who was sixty-six, had been a pillar of the apartheid establishment, serving as moderator of the Dutch Reformed Church between 1986 and 1990. But he had also been a motor for political change, having ended thirty years of conflict with Braam Viljoen and the small group of dissenting theologians who thought like him by acknowledging that it was wrong to believe that apartheid enjoyed biblical justification. That was in 1986. His own parting shot as head of the Afrikaners' biggest church had been boldly to declare in 1990, soon after Mandela's release, that apartheid was a sin. He had undergone his private conversion during a protracted stay in Europe in the early eighties. "I had grown up with the idea that blacks were culturally inferior to whites," Heyns had once confessed. "Exposure in Europe to black people of high academic standing had a profound effect on me."

In 1990, when the first spasms of right-wing resistance were being felt, he had said, "What we're experiencing now are the birth pangs of the new nation. And – have no doubt – the new nation will be born. But birth is usually accompanied by pain, even death."

Heyns's assassination was not in the same order as Chris Hani's in terms of the immediate dangers that it posed, but it did fill people with foreboding. Who had done it and who might be next? Could it have been a former member of one of the old police or army death squads? It had certainly been a professional job. The murder weapon had been a high-calibre rifle fired through a window from some twenty feet away. No one doubted that it had been an action of the far right. But nobody knew who had done it, or why.

Mandela was outraged. Heyns, whom he had met many times, had been his favourite kind of Afrikaner. Morally and physically brave, honest to the core, he'd had the courage late in life to admit to the error of his ways. Mandela mourned his "loss to the South African nation as a whole, both black and white". But then, three days after Heyns's death, he went on the offensive. He announced a crackdown on the far right, accusing the previous government of having not done nearly enough to defuse the right-wing threat. And he began his crackdown by wielding the axe on the police, from whose ranks he suspected complicity in Heyns's killing, as well as an unwillingness to seriously uncover the culprits. Mandela had hitherto trod gingerly with the police. He had deliberately not done what his heart asked him to do, cut heads at the top. Now he did.

One man who had remained in place six months into the Mandela presidency was the nation's top cop, Commisioner Johan van der Merwe, a former security police chief who had been suspected of colluding in dirty tricks operations against the ANC, including murder. Mandela was prepared to swallow a lot for the cause of peace, going so far as to name the Inkatha leader, Mangosuthu Buthelezi, minister of home affairs. But Heyns's death had stretched his patience. "We cannot allow a police force to develop in opposition to government," he declared, going so far as to accuse segements of the police of "declaring war" on the ANC. Singling out Van der Merwe, who had been chief of the notorious security police in the eighties, he accused him of failing to support the democratic government. A few days later, he acted on his threats and fired him.

Expecting a backlash, Mandela received reports two months later of what sounded like a serious plot against his government. "I discovered that there was a plan amongst the right-wingers to link up with the Inkatha Freedom Party to attack the ANC. Now, when that happened I went to Pretoria. I did not even tell the ANC. I went to Pretoria because this debate was going on in Pretoria. I checked and cross-checked with the intelligence people and this was what I found: One group of right-wingers was saying, 'Let us join with Inkatha and attack the ANC. The United Nations would not interfere because it would be blacks attacking blacks. They won't interfere. And we must topple this government because it's a communist government.' But other right-wingers were saying, 'No you can't do that! Look at what they have done for rugby, look at the international rugby they have given us.'"

The conservative paper *Rapport* soon published an article that confirmed what Mandela's sources had told him. The right-wing coalition was hatching a plot to kill the Zulu king, which was supposed to spark a black rebellion against the ANC. Mandela immediately put his intelligence people and his most trusted police officers on the case. He also went on the political offensive, with rugby once again as his instrument, his carrot. But there was a problem.

Everybody in the ANC leadership, by far the dominant party in the coalition government Mandela was heading, had come around to the idea that staging the Rugby World Cup in South Africa was a good thing. But what many could not stomach was the notion of preserving the Springbok name. They had got rid of the old flag, they had half got rid of the old anthem, and this, the third great symbol of apartheid, could not be allowed to remain the badge of a team that represented the new South Africa. Word leaked out of the desire of the ANC's national executive to change the name, and the rugby-loving Afrikaner fraternity was up in arms.

Mandela said he had initially agreed to do away with the Springbok. But the tensions precipitated by the death of Heyns and the sacking of the police chiefs, followed by this latest news of a right-wing plot, made him pause. Looking at the bigger picture, he decided that he had to do something to placate the restless right.

"I decided to act. I made a statement. I suggested that we must retain the Springbok."

The ANC leadership had responded meekly a year earlier to his chiding on the matter of the anthem, but this time the response was openly rebellious.

"You would not believe it! People like Arnold Stofile! They came out and attacked me! So I called them in one by one and I briefed them. I explained to them the situation." For Mandela the Springbok was a matter of ultimately cosmetic interest; for the likes of Stofile it was close to their hearts – a source of much accumulated indignation. They could not see the funny side of the argument, as Mandela did.

Mandela phoned Stofile and asked him to stop by his house. "I would like us to talk about this animal," he said.

"I don't follow you," replied Stofile.

"You know, this sports animal."

They met the next day, and after some hand-wringing, Stofile, informed by Mandela that there was a matter of national security involved, caved in. "In the end," Stofile said, "we agreed to disagree." As did the rest of the ANC's rugby rebels. Mandela had imposed his will once again. In time for the World Cup, the Springbok had been saved.

CHAPTER XIII
SPRINGBOK SERENADE

The question now was whether the Springboks would save Mandela. He had stuck his neck out for the rugby people and now it was up to them to pay him back in kind. Stofile and other members of the ANC National Executive Committee still smarted at the memory of the rugby authorities' response three years earlier to their decision to allow them to play international rugby again. At the game against New Zealand in 1992, Louis Luyt, the president of the South African Rugby Football Union, had deliberately encouraged the crowd to flout the conditions imposed by the ANC and wave the old flags, sing the old anthem. Luyt, a huge former rugby player himself, had risen from relative poverty in childhood to become a phenomenally rich fertilizer and beer magnate. Humility was not this self-made man's most immediately striking trait. Now sixty-two years old, he was brash, loud, and bossy. He hated being told what to do by anyone, let alone a black man. Hence his reaction to the rules the ANC had tried to impose on him back in 1992.

But much had changed in South Africa in that short time, and Luyt had changed too. Softened by Mandela the way all Afrikaners seemed to be ("He was so nice, respectful, and charming at the same time, the first time we met," he said), Luyt had learned a new sense of political responsibility from the international rugby authorities, who did not want the World Cup to become a racially fraught global fiasco. Responding to this need, Luyt made two enlightened appointments. He named Edward Griffiths, a liberal-minded former journalist, as CEO of the rugby federation, and Morné du Plessis, the former Springbok captain who had gone to see Mandela at the Cape Town Parade on the day of his release, as manager of the World Cup team. Griffiths earned praise for the deftness with which he ran the World Cup operation, but his most enduring and valuable contribution came in the form of the slogan he invented for the Springbok campaign. "One Team, One Country" not only captured the imagination of South Africans, it conveyed Mandela's purpose to perfection.

If Griffiths was the brains behind the scenes, Morné du Plessis was the guiding spirit, his job to put theory into practice, to persuade the team to behave in such a way as to convince the country at large, but black South Africa in particular, that the slogan was not just hollow words. Being manager meant a lot of other things too. The job differed from that of the coach, Kitch Christie, who was in charge of everything that had to do with the game itself, with what happened on the field, starting with team selection. Du Plessis's duties covered everything that happened off the field of play, something along the lines of team administrator: ensuring the travel arrangements were right, the playing equipment was in place, the bills were paid. But in this case, at this time in South African history, the job came to mean a great deal more. It was an opportunity for Du Plessis not only to forge a winning team but also to atone for what he increasingly understood to have been his failure ("one of my life's greatest regrets", he later confessed) to rise to the occasion when he had been Springbok captain and do or say something that might have helped improve the lot of black South Africans.

Du Plessis believed his new role to be about more than logistics. He wanted his team to strike the right national chord, get the political atmospherics right, make the players realize that they were playing not just for white South Africa but for the whole country. The one great thing he had going for him was his credibility. A giant of a man, he remained a legend among white South Africans, who never forgot his record as Springbok captain, most famously the leadership and talent he displayed in a famous victory over the old enemy, New Zealand, in 1976.

Luyt's choice of Du Plessis impressed the ANC, for his liberal political leanings were now well-known. But it was a delicate task he had ahead of him, and he knew it. "I understood almost immediately on taking up the job how easily one could slip up, how one could ruin everything with one silly mistake, by saying the wrong thing, striking the wrong note."

It was precisely out of his desire to strike the right note that Du Plessis came up with the idea of teaching the Springboks to sing the "black" half of the new national anthem, "Nkosi Sikelele". He and Mandela shared the same mission impossible: persuading black South Africans to perform a historical about-face and support the Boks. Mandela was doing his bit within the ANC, sending word out to his people that now "they" were "us". Du Plessis did his bit by urging the players to behave respectfully in public. He knew that things could go terribly wrong if before the start of each World Cup game black people were to see the Springboks singing the Afrikaans and English words of "Die Stem" with gusto but making no effort to sing "Nkosi Sikelele". If that happened, Mandela's and Du Plessis's enterprise would be doomed; the notion of "One Team, One Country" would become a laughing stock. It was clear to Du Plessis what had to be done. The players had to be seen singing the old liberation protest song. This image would upend the conventional black view of the Springboks as Afrikaner louts who sang violent racist songs.

Du Plessis had not talked politics with any of the players but he had no reason to believe that they were anything but run-of-the-mill Nat-voters, with the ignorance and prejudice that entailed. "We had some real through-and-through Afrikaners there and this ["Nkosi Sikele"] was in Xhosa and it was the language of what, for many white South Africans, if not most, had been the enemy. It was quite a thing to ask these guys to sing a song that carried that kind of associations." Quite a thing too to teach them to pronounce the Xhosa words. Only two players in the team spoke the language. Mark Andrews, six foot seven and seventeen stone, had been raised in the rural Eastern Cape, Xhosa country, and he had been exposed to Mandela's language from birth. Hennie Le Roux, smaller and faster and also from that part of the world, spoke some Xhosa too. As for the other twenty-four players in the squad, not a clue.

Fortunately Du Plessis had a friend who could help, a neighbour in Cape Town called Anne Munnik. She was a trim, attractive, bubbly English-speaking white woman in her thirties who earned her living teaching Xhosa. She had learned the language as a child, also in the Eastern Cape, and had perfected it at the University of Cape Town, where she now taught. She was staggered when Du Plessis suggested she give the Boks a lesson on how to sing "Nkosi Sikelele" and then doubtful, once she thought about it, about the kind of response she would get from those hulking great Boers. But Du Plessis insisted, and, with some misgivings, she agreed.

An evening was fixed in the third week of May 1995 at the hotel in Cape Town where the team was staying in preparation for the opening game of the World Cup against world champions Australia, just days away. The players were ordered to gather after training in what had become known as the Team Room, an anodyne space where typically local banks or marketing companies would hold seminars for their staff, and where now Kitch Christie would lecture the players on strategy and tactics. This time, waiting for them at the head of the room, were Du Plessis and Anne Munnik.

Du Plessis, towering over the choirmistress, introduced her to the freshly showered Springboks as an old friend whom he had known for twenty years. The players reacted like teenagers. Nudges, winks, knowing nods. "When Morné said he had been out to my farm a number of times, that was it," Anne Munnik recalled. "It was 'Oohs' and 'Aahs' and giggles and laughter and innuendos and teasing generally."

But the teasing was good-natured. They quieted down when Du Plessis, turning serious, said, "Come on, guys, by singing the song loudly and with pride you'll be bringing alive the slogan 'One Team, One Country'." Anne Munnik gawked at the spectacle before her. She was keen on rugby but nothing that she had seen on TV had prepared her for the size of these men in the flesh. Huge and muscular, they were Hollywood central casting's overenthusiastic response to a request for twenty-six Roman gladiators. She had seen their classically guttural Afrikaans names on a list that Du Plessis had given her – Kobus Wiese, Balie Swart, Os du Randt, Ruben Kruger, Hannes Strydom, Joost van der Westhuizen, Hennie le Roux – and she sensed that politically too they had to have more in common with the far right than with the ANC, with "Die Stem" than with "Nkosi Sikelele". But she went ahead and gave each of the players a piece of paper with the words of the song on it, and made them go over it, repeating the difficult ones, having a crack at the Xhosa clicking sounds, almost impossible for people who had not learned them from birth. "Then when the time came to sing," she said, still surprised, years later, "they did so with great feeling."

Some more than others. Kobus Wiese, Balie Swart, and Hannes Strydom were naturals. Wiese and Strydom were both six foot six and nearly eighteen stone; Swart was three inches shorter but as wide as a barn door. They were all extraordinarily fit, as they had to be to play the brutally high-voltage kind of rugby that the Boks were famous for. And they loved to sing. Wiese (pronounced "Veessuh") was one of the team's funny guys, a man whose sharpness of mind belied his bulk, but whom no one had ever accused of being a progressive thinker. Mandela's release had moved Du Plessis, had inspired his teammate Joel Stransky, had shaken Pienaar, but, by Wiese's own admission, it had left him cold. Swart was one of the quietest members of the team, but because he was older than most, as well as bigger, he demanded and inspired respect. Wiese and Swart were best friends. Not only were they both forwards physically bound to each other during games in the frenzied human pileups that are rucks, mauls, and scrums, but they had been performing together in a choir for years.

Wiese was amazed at how quickly the music of "Nkosi Sikelele", the very first time he had ever sung it, swept away all political scruples. "I'd heard the song before, of course," he said. "I'd seen those television images of huge masses of black people marching and singing and danc-ing through the streets with sticks and burning tyres; throwing stones and burning down houses. And you always had 'Nkosi Sikelele iAfrika' playing over the images. For me, and for just about everyone I knew, that song was synonymous with 'swart gevaar' – the black danger. But, you know, I love singing. Always have. And suddenly I found, to my aston-ishment, that I was caught up in it; that this song was so lovely."

Os du Randt, the baby of the team, aged twenty-two, but the heavi-est at six foot three and eighteen and a half stone, sang shyly, as if trying not to be seen. Known as "the Ox", he had served in the army in a tank regiment, though it was a mystery to anyone how he would ever have managed to get into a vehicle so confined. Ruben Kruger, six foot two and weighing a measly sixteen stone, was one of the smaller players in the forward engine room but as strong as a wildebeest, having built up his muscles from an early age in a family business whose chief activity consisted of carrying vast bags of potatoes over the shoulders. Pienaar sought as always to lead by example, and joined in gamely, yet he struggled badly with the pronounciation of the words, and the song itself had registered in his mind far less – "few of us even knew the tune, to be honest" – than it had on the politically unenlightened Wiese.

Wiese, Swart, Kruger, Pienaar, Du Randt, Mark Andrews – these were some of the star players in the forward pack. The players who filled the fast-running three quarters positions seemed at first sight to belong almost to a different species. Anne Munnik was struck by the contrast. Not only were they more normal-sized, but their faces were less fearsome, their noses less misshapen, their ears not deformed by hours and hours of rubbing against thick, hairy thighs in the sweaty, heaving meat factory of the scrum. They were the Springboks' matinee idols, rugby's David Beckhams.

James Small, who modelled clothes when he was not playing rugby, was the bad boy among them, the one who had been banned from the previous year's tour to Britain after a barroom brawl. But, Munnik noticed, no one sang the song with more feeling than he did. "He was close to tears the whole time," she said. The ordinary South African rugby fan, aware of his off-field shenanigans, would have struggled to believe it, but his teammates did not. Everybody who knew him had the sense that he lived perilously close to the edge, that had it not been for the partial escape valve rugby provided for his overwrought emotions, he had an uncontrolled, violent personality that could have landed him behind bars. He himself was the first to say so. "I'm so fortunate," he said. "I was a hard guy, I could have ended up in prison. I'd go to those rough Johannesburg clubs late at night. I could easily have taken a bullet."

But there was another reason why he got so emotional when he started singing the old black anthem. He had felt what it meant to be marginalized. Apartheid existed within rugby too, among whites. "I know what it's like to be on the receiving end too," he said. "I was an Englishman playing a Dutchman's game. When I began in the game at provincial level I got fucked around badly by the Afrikaner players. I was made not welcome both by my own team and by the rival. Players in my own team tried to get their Afrikaner mates ahead of me in the team

selection. They ostracized me, and I was badly beaten too. At my Springbok initiation, they fucked me up so badly my dad wanted to report
them to the police. The point was that, for them, it was an Afrikaans
game and there was no room for an Englishman. The Englishman was
an interloper." Pienaar had viewed "the Englishmen" precisely as such
when he grew up, as shown by his pride in the fact that when he was a
teenager his team never lost against a side from an "English" school.
"But I used all that to spur me," Small said, "and I got my way in the end.
I became a Springbok. Yet the whole experience taught me an apprecia-
tion for the outsider, a sympathy for those in my country who did not
have the opportunities that I'd been so lucky to have."

One Afrikaner who never showed Small anything other than kindness and respect was Morné du Plessis. His influence told too in Small's
response to learning the black anthem. "I saw things a lot differently a
year earlier. As we approached the 1994 elections, I was swept along by
the fear so many white people had that it was going to be chaos and violence and vengeance. That was why I bought a gun for the first time in
my life. I was afraid. And yet, a year later, this . . . Singing 'Nkosi
Sikelele'! But it wouldn't have happened without Morné. He was the
one who impressed on us that we needed to represent South Africa as a
collective, that we had to have a true understanding of being a South
African in a South Africa that was just one year old. It was through him
that I understood that learning 'Nkosi Sikelele' was a part of that."

Chester Williams was less moved than Small was by the liberation song.
Like Small, Williams was a chunky, speedy player who played on the
wing. Unlike Small, he was a quiet man whose timidity made him seem
cold. Williams was the only non-white player in the team, but that didn't
mean he had any greater facility for Xhosa or Zulu than Small did. He
was a "Coloured", according to the rules of the recently defunct Popula-

tion Registration Act. "Coloureds" – or as the politically correct appella-
tion had it, "so-called Coloured" – were the least politically engaged of
the four main apartheid subgroups, the others being Black, White, and
Indian. Being a blend of races, they were also the most physically varied.
The majority corresponded more to people's ideas of black African than
white European, yet the ethnic group to whom Coloureds typically felt
closest to were the Afrikaners, chiefly because at home they spoke the
same language as them. It was in this general category that Chester
Williams belonged: African-looking, Afrikaans-speaking, non-political.

Not that the Afrikaners gave Coloureds any special respect. F. W.
de Klerk's wife, Marike, ventured some celebrated thoughts on
"Coloureds" in 1983 that came back to haunt her later, when her husband was seeking to assume a degree of "non-racial" respectability.
"You know, they are a negative group," the First Lady-to-be had said.
"The definition of a Coloured in the population register is someone
that is not black, and is not white and is also not an Indian, in other
words a non-person. They are the left-overs. They are the people that
were left after the nations were sorted out. They are the rest."

The evolution in the way Williams was treated by his fellow Springboks between becoming a Springbok in 1993, the year the Volksfront
was formed, and the World Cup two years later mirrored the abrupt
change in the way white people generally, and Afrikaners in particular,
engaged with their darker-skinned compatriots. "It was a difficult time
for me," Williams said, referring to his first days as a Springbok.
"People did not accept me. You tried to make conversation but you
were left on your own."

In a book Williams co-wrote, he went further, claiming that James
Small, among others, would call him "kaffir" and suggest he was in the
team not on merit, but because he was "a token black". Small was hurt
by these claims and Williams went some way to retracting them. According to Small, Williams apologized later in front of the whole team and

the two eventually made up. In an interview some time after the dust had settled, Williams looked a little sheepish about some of the things that had appeared in the book, conceding there might have been some exaggerations. But he did insist that he had been discriminated against. "It was only as time passed that I found that people changed, that they included me more and more, and by 1995 I had been fully accepted as a member of the team, on merit."

The team, in a way, was left with little choice, Chester Williams having been selected by South African rugby's marketing people as the Rainbow Nation's face of the tournament. It was an odd situation for him to find himself in, given his retiring character, but to his astonishment, and that of his teammates, everywhere they went in South Africa his face stared down at them from huge roadside billboards. It would have been a little confusing, and not entirely convincing, to black South Africans too – not only because Williams was a "Coloured" (like it or not, and the ANC did not, these labels often persisted), but because he was a sergeant in the South African Defence Force, an institution he had served during apartheid. Williams, whose relationship with black South Africans would have been minimal, whose languages he did not understand, would have understood all this better than the marketing people, whose ploys made more impact on whites than on blacks, on foreign visitors than on South Africans generally. At an auction in early May, Williams stared in bafflement as he saw a portrait of himself selling for what was then the equivalent of $50,000. South Africa was selling an image of itself to the world that the world wanted to buy.

The dream Joel Stransky had had, when watching Mandela's release on TV in a French bar, of South Africa being welcomed back into the global fold had been fulfilled, and indeed surpassed. Not only was he playing for his country at rugby, he was playing in a World Cup. And he was in the pivotal position of fly half, which in his case also included the vast responsibility of taking the penalty kicks on which the outcome of big games so often turned. He needed steely nerves to do what he did, in addition to physical fearlessness, for at five foot ten and thirteen and a half stone he had to endure the most brutal charges from men far bigger than he. Yet he was anxious going into the singing class, wishing he could be somewhere else. "I'm one of those people who hates singing," he said. "It's almost a phobia." But he surprised himself. "We all knew the politics behind that song and we'd heard about it so often and then there I was learning the words and it felt really special."

Hennie le Roux, one of the more serious-minded members of the team, and a close friend of François Pienaar's, applied himself earnestly to Anne Munnik's lessons. A talented jinking runner, the most versatile of the Springbok backs, Le Roux was no more political than anyone else on the team but for him the national imperative to learn "Nkosi Sikelele" was now clear. He had seen it, as other Springboks had, on arrival at their Cape Town hotel a few days earlier when the mostly black staff came out to greet them in the lobby. "They were singing songs and dancing and carrying on, just so happy to see us, so welcoming. It was something we had never seen in our careers, black people right there in front of us, welcoming us with as much excitement as we got from the wildest white rugby crowds. It was a big moment for all of us." James Small put it more bluntly. "We looked at each other and thought, 'Fuck, there's something going on here!'" For Le Roux it was the moment he understood he had to give something back. "If they were so willing to stand with us the least we could do was make an effort to learn their song. Remembering those scenes at our arrival when we were there learning the song made it all so much more moving for me."

Pienaar was as moved as his friend, but his motivation was even more personal. He was the only Springbok to have sat down with Mandela one-on-one, and he was particularly anxious that his team project an image that would please Mandela. But he was also thinking, as he did always with relentless detail, what the team did off the field might improve their performance on it. And as he heard himself and his teammates singing, his rugby brain clicked into action. He understood that victory in a top-class rugby game was 50 per cent psychology, and saw a sporting value in the song, beyond the politics. "I made up my mind right there and then that this was an unexpected plus that Morné had given us; that it could give us something special going into a game, if we respected it and felt the energy of it," Pienaar said, before adding, with a smile and a shake of the head, "but . . . it's amazing to think about. The Afrikaans boys singing that anthem!"

Anne Munnik was about to wrap up the lesson when the team's three largest players, Kobus Wiese, Hannes Strydom, and Balie Swart, made a request: could they sing the song one more time, just the three of them? "I said, 'Of course!' And then they began, like three giant choirboys, softly at first, rising, rising to the high notes. They sang it so, so beautifully! The other players just stood there with their mouths open. No laughing, no jokes. They just stood and stared."

For the big men, singing this song had the power of an epiphany. "That was my innocent ignorance shattered!" Wiese exclaimed. "When I learnt the words of that song, doors opened for me. Ever since then, when I hear a whole group of black people sing 'Nkosi Sikele', it's, like, stunning, man. It's so beautiful."

You could be as dubious about the Springboks as Justice Bekebeke or as generous-minded as Mandela, but any black South African who walked into that room at the moment when this Boer trio burst into song would have been stunned too.

CHAPTER XIV
SILVERMINE

On May 25, 1995, the Springboks would meet the reigning world champions, Australia, in the first match of the World Cup in Cape Town. The day before, the team was gathered at Silvermine, an old military base inside a mountainous nature preserve on the Cape Peninsula, where they had established a temporary training camp. On the eastern half of the peninsula's narrow waist, Silvermine was one of the most beautiful spots in South Africa. Looking north, you saw the totemic monolith of Table Mountain. Looking south, you saw the rocky extremity where the Indian and Atlantic oceans met. All around were cliffs, forests, valleys, and sea.

The team had just finished an afternoon training session when they looked up and saw a big military helicopter throbbing down from the sky. Morné du Plessis, who had been tipped off about the visit, had put on a suit and tie. As they gawked up at the flying machine descending towards the field, he announced that this was Mandela on his way to see them. They continued to stare as Mandela himself stepped out from under the rotor blades in a bright red and orange shirt, worn loose below the waist, in what had become his trademark presidential style. As Mandela strode smiling towards them, the players crowded forward, jostling each other like photographers at a press conference, craning their necks to get the best view.

Mandela made some light remarks, raising some laughs, and then Du Plessis called for quiet so that the president could address the team.

Somewhat to their surprise, Mandela started by taking up the same lofty themes he generally did when addressing white people. (His audience was all white that day, as Chester Williams was away nursing an injury.) He reminded them that the ANC had promised that the new government would keep the commander of the army, the national commissioner of police, the Reserve Bank governor, and the minister of finance. He then pointed out that, a year after the elections, his government had remained true to its word. As Afrikaners, they had nothing to fear from the ANC. Nor, Mandela added, breaking into a grin, from their opponents the next day.

"You are playing the World Cup champions, Australia. The team who wins this match will go right through to the end," he predicted, before returning to a solemn tone. "You now have the opportunity of serving South Africa and uniting our people. From the point of view of merit, you are equal to anything in the world. But we are playing at home and you have got an edge. Just remember, all of us, black and white, are behind you."

The players cheered and applauded, then Mandela took turns to chat with them one by one. "He asked me why I had dressed so formally to see him," Du Plessis remembered. "But what was amazing was the chemistry. The players were drawn to him immediately." Kobus Wiese admitted, "I can't remember why we laughed, but I remember we were laughing with Mandela the whole time he was there."

Hennie le Roux, the chunky centre three quarter, decided out of the blue to offer Mandela a token of his gratitude for taking the trouble to come and visit them. When the president got to him, he handed him his green Springbok cap and said, "Please take it, Mr. President, it is for you." Le Roux paused and added, "Thanks a lot for being here. It means a lot to the team."

Mandela took it, smiled, and said, "Thank you very much. I shall wear it!" He put the cap on right then and there.

François Pienaar put the seal on the mountaintop ceremony with a brief message of farewell to Mandela. Referring to the next day's game, he declared, "There's one guy that now we understand we have to play for, and that's the president."

The Silvermine encounter redefined the Springboks' feelings for their president and their country. Describing the scene as Mandela boarded his helicopter and flew off, Du Plessis was almost lost for words. "I looked at the players as they looked up at the helicopter and they were like young boys waving, so full of this . . . excitement. These guys had all seen a million helicopters before but Mandela . . . well, he had won their hearts."

And he did them some good as a rugby team too. Pienaar had been worried about the tension among his teammates on the day before play began. He would usually try to find a way to break it, with a song maybe or a film, but this time Mandela had done his job for him. A year earlier, Mandela had put Pienaar at his ease in the presidential office. Now he had done the same for the team as a whole. "He relaxed the guys. His interaction with the team was jovial, always smiling, always cracking little jokes. And he always has time for everyone. He'd stop and chat, and put the players at ease. That was very special before the opening match."

Mandela may have lowered the Springboks' stress, but he couldn't banish it entirely. Few people actually died on a rugby field, but no sport – in terms of pain endured and brutality of collision – was closer to war. Rugby players took and gave hits without any helmets, shoulder pads, or other protective gear. And rugby demanded far more stamina than did American football. Each rugby match was played in two forty-minute halves with only a ten-minute break between them and no timeouts except for injury. But physical fear weighed less heavily on the players than the burden of national expectation. In less than twenty-four hours they would face Australia's Wallabies, one of the five teams with a serious chance of winning the World Cup, along with France, England, New Zealand, and South Africa. Mandela might have made them feel special, but what still remained to be seen was whether the Springboks could channel that pressure in their favour during the game itself, or be crushed under its weight.

It also remained to be seen how much support black South Africans would really give the Springboks, how effective Mandela had been in his efforts to persuade his people that the old green-and-gold jersey was now theirs too.

The Presidential Protection Unit provided as good a barometer of the national mood as any. They were one group of South Africans who went to bed on the night before the game against Australia feeling as tense as the Springboks themselves. But for different reasons. "For that first game against Australia the security challenge was huge and the security arrangements enormous," said Linga Moonsamy, the former ANC guerrilla and a member of the PPU since Mandela's inauguration. "We spent weeks planning for that day. We went up and down examining every high-rise around the stadium. We placed snipers on rooftops at strategic points, we placed people at the points of weakness inside the stadium."

The PPU was united in its sense of mission but split down the middle between blacks and whites, between former members of Umkhonto we Sizwe, like Moonsamy, and former members of the security police. "The Umkhonto guys and the police guys: people who'd been each other's mortal enemies, literally – we had wanted to kill each other for years," Moonsamy said, "though they succeeded, it should be said, more than we did."

The split extended to rugby. Being in Mandela's presence day in, day out for a year had smoothed Moonsamy's sharper edges. But he was still some way from actively supporting the Springboks or, for that matter, understanding what the game was about.

"There had been plenty of rumours that the white far right would use the competition to stage a terrorist act against the new democracy, against Mandela himself," Moonsamy recalled. "Our white colleagues were as aware of that possibility as us, and they were prepared, like us, but the big difference was that they were, if anything, even more nervous about the outcome of the game itself. We looked at them, smiled, and shook our heads. We just didn't get it."

At the event, the PPU's preparedness paid off. The South Africa–Australia game went without a hitch. Mandela was helicoptered from the presidential residence in Cape Town to a tall building near the stadium. From the building he travelled in a silver armoured BMW to the stadium, with Moonsamy, who was number one bodyguard on the day, sitting in the passenger seat before him. Amid all the excitement, Mandela had not forgotten Hennie le Roux's cap. He wore it at the tournament's opening ceremony, where the sixteen teams taking part in the tournament went on parade there at Newlands Stadium alongside 1,500 dancers (or 1,501, Mandela himself joining in and performing a lively jig), before the inaugural game itself. And he wore it when he went out onto the pitch to shake the hands of the two teams, to a warm cheer from the overwhelmingly white 50,000-strong crowd, among whom new South African flags abounded. He kept wearing it when the Springboks sang the twin national anthems, into which they now invested equal emotion, if in the case of "Die Stem" they still showed more familiarity with the words.

The game itself was a triumph for the Springboks. All the pressure had worked in their favour, in the end, and they beat Australia, whom none had beaten for fourteen months, more comfortably than the score – 27–18 – suggested. Joel Stransky was the man of the match, scoring 22 of the Springbok points, 17 of them from kicks, plus a try. As the game neared the end a hastily painted banner emerged from the crowd that read, "Forget the Rhino. Save the Wallaby!" The Australians, themselves ferocious competitors in every sport they played, were gracious in defeat. "There's no doubt that the better team won," Bob Dwyer, Australia's coach, said. "Any other result, if we had sneaked it, would have been unfair."

That night the Springbok players celebrated as rugby players do, drinking until four in the morning, being feted – carried high aloft – everywhere they went. Kitch Christie, the coach, did not spare them their daily run at nine the next morning, from the heart of the city out to the seashore, but the throbbing pain of it was eased by the passers-by who cheered them every step of the way.

A day later, their heads still rather the worse for wear, they found themselves on a ferry bound for Robben Island. It had been Morné du Plessis's idea. Du Plessis had begun to see just how enormous the impact of this "One Team, One Country" business was, not only in terms of the good it would do the country, but the good it would do the team.

"There was a cause-and-effect connection between the Mandela factor and our performance in the field," Du Plessis said. "It was cause and effect on a thousand fronts. In players overcoming the pain barrier, in a superior desire to win, in luck going your way because you make your own luck, in all kinds of tiny details that together or separately mark the difference between winning and losing. It all came perfectly together. Our willingness to be the nation's team and Mandela's desire to make the team the national team."

Robben Island was still being used as a prison and all the prisoners there were either Black or Coloured. Part of the day's event involved meeting them, but first the players took turns viewing the cell where Mandela had spent eighteen of his twenty-seven years in captivity. The players entered the cell one or two at a time; it couldn't hold any more than that. Having just met Mandela, they knew that he was a tall man like most of them, if not as broad. It required no great mental leap to picture the challenges, physical and psychological, of being confined in a box so small for so long. Pienaar, who had done a bit of reading on Mandela's past, also knew that it was in this cell, or at any rate in this prison, that much of the energy and planning behind the boycott of the Springbok international tours had come. Morné du Plessis had a similar reflection, all the more powerful since he had been one of the Springbok players affected by it. Steve Tshwete, now the minister of sport, had told Du Plessis that, in these cells, they listened on the radio to the Springboks' games against the British Lions in 1980. The guards yelled at the prisoners to stop their cheering, but they cheered on. "And you know," Du Plessis told me, "looking around those cells, seeing what we put them through, you know what? I would have cheered for the Lions too."

After Mandela's cell the Springbok players went outside to the yard where Mandela had once been obliged to break stones. Waiting for them was a group of prisoners.

"They were so happy to see us," Pienaar said. "Despite being confined here they were so obviously proud of our team. I spoke to them about our sense that we were representing the whole country now, them included, and then they sang us a song. James Small – I'll never forget this – stood in a corner, tears streaming out. James lived very close to the sword and I think he must have felt, 'I could have been here.' Yes, he felt his life could so easily have gone down another path. But," Pienaar added, recalling the bruising fights he would get into when he was younger, the time he thought he had killed a man, " . . . but mine too, eh? I could have ended up there too."

Small remembered the episode. "The prisoners not only sang for us, they gave us a huge cheer and I . . . I just burst into tears," he said, his eyes reddening again at the recollection. "That was where the sense really took hold in me that I belonged to the new South Africa, and where I really got a sense of the responsibility of my position as a Springbok. There I was, hearing the applause for me, and at the same time thinking about Mandela's cell and how he spent twenty-seven years in prison and came out with love and friendship. All that washed over me, that huge realization, and the tears just rolled down my face."

CHAPTER XV
DOUBTING THOMASES

"My own supporters: they booed me! They booed me down when I said these boys are now ours, let us embrace them!" Mandela frowned at the recollection. "Oh, it was very difficult . . ."

He was recalling a particular incident near the end of the World Cup competition, an ANC rally deep in rural KwaZulu, that captured for him the daunting difficulties he had faced in persuading black South Africans to get behind the Springbok team. Persuading them actively to embrace a symbol so redolent of the pain and indignity they had endured for so long was an exercise in political persuasion almost as implausible as the one he had pulled off with Constand Viljoen. Justice Bekebeke, for one, was not going to roll over easily on this one. As he said, "These Afrikaner rugby people, they were the ones – the very ones – who treated us worst. These were the guys who kicked us off the pavement onto the streets. These were the guys – the big white thugs – who said, 'Give way, kaffir.'"

But his present circumstances, in line with the new spirit in the country, had changed. Having escaped the rope, he was on his way in

May 1995 towards obtaining his BA degree in law by the end of that year. He approved of the historic compromise Mandela had made, was in favour of his black and white power-sharing government, but there were limits.

"I was a loyal member of the ANC," he said, "a believer in the philosophy of non-racialism, and an admirer of Mandela. The example Anton Lubowski left me was a rock-solid guarantee I would never be a racist. But the Springboks, that Springbok emblem those people took such pride in: I hated it. It remained for me a potent and loathsome symbol of apartheid."

That symbol was exactly what ANC supporters at that rally in KwaZulu saw Mandela put on his head in the middle of his address to them. It was the Springbok cap Hennie le Roux had given him. Mandela had come to this town to celebrate the anniversary of the event that sparked the South African revolution, the day in 1976 when Soweto schoolchildren rose up against their apartheid masters. But still they booed.

In choosing this place, Ezakheni, to perform this gesture, Mandela may have been pushing his luck. First, as he pointed out in his speech that day, it was in rural backwaters like Ezakheni that people experienced the old system at its worst. "Here," Mandela said, "apartheid left communities in conditions that defy description." Second, a decade of violence between ANC-supporting Zulus and Inkatha-supporting Zulus continued, despite the rise of the new government, prompting Mandela to declare, "The killing of Zulu by Zulu must stop." Third, the crowd hated the local white farmers, most of whom had been sympathetic to Inkatha.

Buthelezi, the Inkatha leader, was now a cabinet minister in Mandela's government. Mandela's generosity towards him was political pragmatism pushed to moral extremes. But here in Ezakheni the wounds remained wide open and fraternizing with the enemy was not well seen. Asking them to love the Springbok was almost indelicate. Yet that was what Mandela did. "You see this cap that I am wearing," he told his audience, "it does honour to our boys who are playing France tomorrow afternoon."

That was what set the crowd booing. Mandela would have none of it. "Look," he admonished them, "amongst you are leaders. Don't be shortsighted, don't be emotional. Nation-building means that we have to pay a price, in the same way that the whites have to pay a price. For them to open sports to black people: they are paying a price; for us to say we must now embrace the rugby team is paying a price. That's what we should do." As the booing slowly subsided, he continued, "I want leaders amongst you, men and women to stand up and to promote this idea."

When Mandela recalled that rally, he spoke of it in terms almost of a hunter tracking his prey. "Eventually, you know," he said with a victorious smile, "eventually I got the crowd." He had been here before, seemingly on the point of losing a crowd, then winning it back. Once it had happened in territory where Inkatha had inflicted terrible loss of life. Standing up to the crowd's understandable desire for revenge, he appealed to them to take the broader view, to "throw their weapons into the sea". Another time, in a township outside Johannesburg called Katlehong, where Inkatha had also been on the rampage against the civilian population, he silenced 15,000 people incensed by his refusal to give them weapons by asking them if they wished him to continue being their leader. Because unless they did as he asked, and strove to make peace with people whom he described as not so much evil as misguided, he would step down. This they didn't want, and by the end of his address they were singing his name and dancing in triumph – celebrating the successful appeal he had made to the wiser part of their natures.

Almost as difficult was convincing people that the Springboks really could win the World Cup. All rugby experts agreed that it was a vain hope. "When I went to see the team in Silvermine and told them that I was sure they would win I did not want to be proved wrong," Mandela said. "Personally, it was very important for me because I knew that victory would mobilize the Doubting Thomases. That is why I was so keen that South Africa should come out tops! It would be reward for all the hard work – going around the country, being booed down . . ."

He spoke of "hard work"; previously he had used the word "campaign": indications of how deliberately he had set about his objective of using rugby as a political instrument. Nicholas Haysom, Mandela's legal adviser in the presidency, was a lifelong rugby fan and former player who became Mandela's in-house rugby buddy at the Union Buildings. Haysom acknowledged that Mandela had seen quite clearly how powerful an instrument the World Cup would be regarding "the number one strategic imperative of his five-year presidency". But that was not the whole picture. Again, the political and the personal, the calculation and the spontaneity, merged into one. "As the World Cup was getting started," Haysom recalled, "I would hear him talking to me about 'the boys', as in 'the boys are in good spirits', or 'the boys are going to win'. At first I'd ask him, 'What boys?' And he'd look at me as if I had asked a puzzlingly silly question and reply, '*My* boys', by which I soon came to understand that he meant the Springboks." Although Mandela did not enter the World Cup as a man with a great historical knowledge of rugby, he became ever more informed and passionate as the tournament unfolded. "He saw the political opportunity, yes, but it was not something cold because he too, as an individual, got swept away by the fervor of it all and became just another mad-keen patriotic fan."

The black half of Mandela's bodyguard detachment took longer than he did to enter into the spirit of the tournament. That very first game against Australia, Moonsamy recalled, had been a hair-raising ordeal in terms of their professional obligation to keep the president alive. But in sporting terms the game had left them cold.

"After the final whistle went, the white guys were going nuts! We were just looking at them, chuckling, baffled. We did not understand the game, were not interested in it, we were unimpressed. The Springboks were still their team, not ours." Moonsamy said Mandela's campaign to de-demonize the Springboks had made an impact on him, but he had yet to move from indifference to outright support. His evolution, together with the rest of the black PPU members, over the four weeks of the World Cup mirrored the evolution black South Africans underwent in their relationship with the old green-and-gold enemy.

"After the Springbok team won its second game, we started to get a little bit curious," Moonsamy said, referring to a relatively easy game against Romania. "The excitement of our white colleagues inevitably intrigued us and so we started to ask them questions about the game. To our surprise, rugby became a bonding topic between us." Every two weeks the PPU would go away for a training session to freshen old routines and stay sharp. They would practise shooting, unarmed combat, and other skills. At the session after the Australia match, a big white PPU member named Kallis introduced them to touch rugby. That meant rugby with less extreme physical violence, without the usual ferocity in the collision. "Through these sessions," Moonsamy said, "the black bodyguard learnt about the details of the game. But, just as important, we started to get a feel for rugby. We'd play touch rugby but we'd go for each other. Sometimes we'd really take each other out. That way we began to understand and, again, to our huge surprise, started actually to quite like the game."

Images broadcast all over South African TV the day before a game against Canada began to persuade Moonsamy that perhaps he might start to quite like the Springboks too. The entire Springbok squad visited a small township called Zwide outside the big Eastern Cape city of Port Elizabeth. Scenes of huge white men chatting and playing with excited black children moved Moonsamy, as well as everyone else who saw them.

Some three hundred children gathered around a dusty field for a coaching clinic led by Morné du Plessis, who divided the boys up into groups of fifteen, but it was Mark Andrews who attracted all the attention: because he was so huge, and because he also happened to speak Xhosa. Balie Swart was there too, leading the children in passing routines, cheerfully revealing to their flabbergasted elders that big Boers could be friends too. That same evening Du Plessis took a group of players to a rickety stadium where local black teams played. There was a game on and Du Plessis felt it would be appreciated if the Springboks came along to watch. It was, thanks not least to James Small, whose blend of talent and notoriety made him the most recognizable face in the party. Small spent an hour and a half signing autographs, for adults and children alike.

When South Africa beat Canada 20–0 at Port Elizabeth's Boet Erasmus Stadium, the whole of Zwide cheered and so did Linga Moonsamy. The next game, a quarter-final against the tough and talented Western Samoans, big Pacific islander folk fanatical about the game, posed what appeared to be a stiffer challenge. They also presented what ought to have been more of a test to black South African allegiances, since this was a dark-skinned team that they would have really got behind in the old days. Chester Williams took care of that, though, living up to what had appeared until now to be his somewhat inflated marquee billing by scoring four tries, in a 42–14 victory. "Whatever doubts I may have had about myself or the rest of the team or anybody else might have had about me disappeared that day – simple as that," Williams recalled. "I got big support on and off the pitch from François and Morné and from now on I was, in the eyes of everybody, a fully accepted and respected team member. The whole story turned that day. The fact that I wasn't white was now completely irrelevant."

One week later was the semi-final, the one Mandela had mentioned in Ezakheni, against one of the pre-tournament favourites, France. The venue was to be Durban's King's Park Stadium, where Pienaar had made his Springbok debut two years earlier on the day after the Volksfront's attack on the World Trade Centre. The political mood in the days leading up to this game could not have been more different.

As the team drove back and forth between their hotel and the training camps, the roads would be lined with crowds of people, more and more of them black as the days passed. James Small remembered that "we looked at each other and thought, Fuck! President Mandela wasn't kidding: maybe the whole country really was with us."

Hennie le Roux echoed the point Mandela had made about victory mobilizing the Doubting Thomases. "We could see the country really was uniting around us but it was through winning that we would make that bond stronger. The better we did on the pitch, the wider the ripple effect off it."

The adversity and high drama before and during the game against France also helped. There was a distinct chance that the game might be called off and a victory would be awarded to France. The balmy Indian Ocean city of Durban had experienced one of its periodic semi-tropical downpours and the King's Park field was waterlogged. If the game was not played that day, World Cup rules decreed that France would be declared the winner, owing to South Africa having had a poorer disciplinary record in the tournament so far. (One player had been sent off for fighting in a fiercely fought game against Canada.) The whole country paid anxious attention as rugby officials and even the armed forces launched a desperate race to get the field fit for play on time. Military helicopters were recruited to fan the field from above, but the day was saved by a battalion of black ladies with mops and buckets whose heroic labours persuaded the referee to let the game proceed.

Despite the cleaning ladies' efforts, the game itself was a mudbath with a slippery oval ball somewhere in the middle over which large, filthy men violently scrapped. With two minutes to go and South Africa holding on at 19 points to 15, a vast, Kobus Wiese-sized Frenchman of Moroccan extraction called Abdelatif Benazzi thought he had wrested the ball over the line for what would have been the winning try. But instead the referee awarded the French a scrum five metres from the South African line. If the exhausted "Bleus" pushed the exhausted Springboks back over the line, that would be that. France in the final. Show over for the Rainbow Nation. The Springboks were about to go down and take their position in the melee when Kobus Wiese, all six foot six of him in the second-row engine room of the scrum, uttered a battle cry that stirred his team mates. Addressing himself to his best friend Balie Swart, the prop forward in the front row, he said, "Listen, Balie, in this scrum, you are not coming back. You can go forward, you can go up, you can go down or you can go under. But you're not coming back!"

The Springboks did not go back and South Africa were through to the final.

"That game was a battle of wills, more than anything else," Morné du Plessis said. "It was the game in which we really felt that Mandela magic having an impact on us on the field of play. Because we had found out, you see, about Mandela's speech the day before there in KwaZulu. We had heard that at a place where people were dying he had given a speech in which he said the time had come for all South Africa to get behind the Springboks, and he said it wearing his Springbok cap. That really moved the team."

Linga Moonsamy was more moved than he could have imagined. "We were so tense during the game," he recalled. "We were so close at the end of it. The black and white groups in our unit: we were now indistinguishable. All of us going absolutely crazy with relief and joy."

Some years later, Morné du Plessis came across Benazzi, the big French forward who nearly won the game for his side. Inevitably, they talked about that game, and Benazzi insisted that it had been a try, that the ball had crossed the line. But Benazzi also told Du Plessis, "We cried like hell when we lost to you guys. But when I went to the final the following weekend I cried again, because I knew that it was more important for us not to be there, that something more important was happening before our eyes than victory or defeat in a game of rugby."

CHAPTER XVI
THE NUMBER SIX JERSEY

June 24, 1995 – morning

On the day before the Rugby World Cup final against New Zealand, just after the Springboks had finished their final training session, François Pienaar was in the changing room about to take his boots off when his mobile phone rang inside his kit bag. "Hello, François, how are you?" It was Mandela calling to wish the team good luck. Morné du Plessis made a point of relaying the news to the press. Mandela was delighted to read Du Plessis in the papers, that morning of the final, giving his spin on the phone call. "Mr. Mandela told François he was almost more nervous than the team," all the papers quoted Du Plessis as saying. "These calls prove he is now part of our camp and our campaign."

Everything indicated that this day would turn out well, that South Africans had moved on, that a new era of political maturity loomed – but you never quite knew. If he had talked to Niël Barnard, the old Boer spymaster would have told him that in June 1995 "the political situation was still very raw: many whites felt alienated, out of it." It was hard to tell how those alienated, many of whom would undoubtedly be at the stadium, might react. That was maybe why Mandela, recalling the tense eve of the game, popped out with the surprising remark, "I have never been very good at predicting things." It was his way of confessing to the misgivings he felt. What if, for all his best efforts, he had misjudged the mood of the Afrikaners? What if some fans jeered during the singing of "Nkosi Sikelele"? What if people started unfurling the flags of the old South Africa, as they had done in that ill-starred game against New Zealand three years earlier?

Those questions floated through his mind as he sat down to the papaya, kiwi, mango, porridge, and coffee breakfast he always enjoyed at his Houghton home. He was concerned, but it would be a mistake to say that he was consumed by worry. The good news outweighed the bad portents. One of the reasons Mandela dispensed with his 4:30 a.m. walk on the day of the rugby final was to devote more time to the morning papers. Usually he devoured the political pages and skimmed the sports section. This time both demanded his attention. Never had he enjoyed the morning press as much as today. The national consensus he had striven so hard to forge around the Springbok cause was reflected in the celebratory unanimity of the editorials and the political analysts. South Africa was giving itself a huge pat on the back. And while there was caution regarding the game's outcome, reflected in vast respect for New Zealand's All Black rivals (*Die Burger* said, "The All Blacks stand like Himalayas before the Boks"), there was a quiet confidence that destiny would be on South Africa's side. The headline in Cape Town's main newspaper, the *Argus*, trumpeted the exultant national mood. "Viva the Boks!" it read. "Viva" was a war cry of black protest down the decades, borrowed somewhere along the way from the Cuban revolution. But better than the headline was the story immediately below it by the newspaper's "political staff".

"The Rugby World Cup has led to a spectacular upsurge of national reconciliation among all races in South Africa, researchers and social scientists reported this week." The article then quoted a well-known Afrikaner academic named Willie Breytenbach saying that the right-wing terrorism threat had been "virtually annihilated" and that the clamour for a separate Afrikaner state had been substantially weakened. "At the same time the mainly black streets of Johannesburg have become remarkably empty when the Springboks play. Township dwellers flock home to watch the matches on TV. . . . Rugby, the remarkable new nation-building phenomenon, has amazed analysts as all races eagerly seize on the event which has released a wave of latent patriotism through the sport traditionally associated in South Africa with white Afrikaner males."

The *Argus* then listed the five "key factors" that enabled rugby to become "a unifying catalyst": Mandela's vociferous support for "our boys" and his wearing of the Springbok cap; Archbishop Tutu's public support; the rugby team acting in concert with the "One Team, One Country" slogan; the team's success on the field; the singing of the new combined anthem and the waving of the new flag.

Here was the fruit of all Mandela's behind-the-scenes orchestration, and he was thrilled to see patriotic variations on the same points made in all the papers. He was pleased to see black newspapers entering into the spirit of the thing. The big-selling *Sowetan* was especially memorable because it was they who coined a new South African word that would catch the imagination of the whole of black South Africa – "AmaBokoBoko," a new word for the Springboks, one that at last gave black people ownership of them too. But what gave Mandela special satisfaction were the Afrikaans newspapers, for they could barely contain their euphoria at the manner in which black South Africa had embraced the Springboks. *Die Burger* quoted a statement from the famously radical ANC Youth League that said, "Bring the cup home, Boks! We're waiting!" *Beeld* quoted the ANC's chief negotiator in the constitutional talks, former trade union chief Cyril Ramaphosa, declaring, "We're proud of our national team, the Springboks." Mandela especially enjoyed seeing himself quoted on the front pages of both *Beeld* and *Die Burger*. "I have never been so proud of our boys," Mandela read himself saying. "I hope we will all be cheering them on to victory. They will be playing for the entire South Africa."

That word "hope" revealed a glimmer of concern. The crowd he would face today would be the most daunting of all his life. Down at Newlands Stadium in Cape Town, for the first game against Australia, it had been a different matter. The Cape was South Africa's white liberal stronghold. The Afrikaners there were softer, gentler. They were the descendants of those Boers who had decided not to head off on the Great Trek north, who had not taken such grave offence at the British Empire's decision to abolish slavery. But the Transvaalers at Ellis Park, they had Piet Retief and the Battle of Blood River written into their DNA. These were the people, many of them, who would have cheered the attack on the World Trade Centre, for some of whom, as Bekebeke had bitterly observed, the phrase "Give way, kaffir!" had been the habit of a lifetime. These were the people who had "voted Nat" all their lives and who had, in some cases, since shifted their allegiances to the far right. Of the 62,000 at Ellis Park that afternoon, many, if not the majority, would look as if they had stepped straight out of a Boer defiance rally. They'd be sporting their game-warden khaki outfits, their long woolen socks, their big bellies, home to countless Castle lagers and innumerable *boerewors* sausages. Mandela had been the chief attraction at more mass gatherings than anyone alive, but he had never ventured into a crowd like this.

Glancing out of the window of his living room, Mandela caught sight of his bodyguards outside, in the driveway, muscular men, sixteen of them, checking their weapons, filling out forms, looking under the hoods of the cars, and chatting amiably with each other. He'd noticed that, until a few weeks ago, his black and white bodyguards had offered a bleak picture of apartheid separateness. Now he could see them chatting away together, gesturing emphatically, smiling, laughing.

"We were chatting away about what to do to stop the All Blacks, some reckoning we had no chance, others that we'd be better on the day," Moonsamy said, "when in the middle of it all the idea popped out that it would be great if the president wore the green-and-gold Springbok jersey to the stadium." When pressed, Moonsamy admitted it had been he who had come up with the idea. The impact on his colleagues, he admitted, was electric. "We were all really into it. So we agreed that when I went into the house to give him his security briefing, which was always the job of the guy who was 'number one' for the day, I should mention the idea to him and see what he said."

They were due to leave for the stadium at one-thirty. At twelve Moonsamy went inside the house to brief Mandela. The security formalities dispensed with, he said, "Tata" – this was the affectionate name the black bodyguards used with him, meaning Granddaddy – "we were thinking, why don't you wear the Springbok jersey today'?"

Mandela would usually put on his pensive, sphinx face when someone put forward an entirely novel proposal to him, especially one that carried political repercussions and concerned the always important matter to him of his public image. But this time he did not hesistate in his response. He broke, instead, into a radiant ear-to-ear smile. "He just lit up," Moonsamy said. "He thought it was a brilliant idea."

Mandela had grasped the value of the gesture immediately. "I decided on this jersey," he said, "because I thought, 'When the whites see me wearing that Springbok rugby jersey they will see that here is a man who is now completely behind our team.'"

But there was a problem. He did not have a jersey, and there was only an hour and a half left before departure for the stadium. Going straight from Moonsamy to his secretary, Mary Mxadana, he ordered her to phone Louis Luyt, the head of the South African Rugby Football Union, right away. He told her that he wanted not just any jersey but – and this was his own idea – one with Pienaar's number 6 on it, and a Springbok cap too. (He had left Le Roux's cap at his residence in Cape Town.)

An hour after Moonsamy had proposed the idea, the jersey was in Mandela's house, being ironed – at Mandela's bidding – by his house-keeper. Now Mandela turned his attention to the game itself. His concerns, like those of every Springbok fan and player, focused on a very large black man named Jonah Lomu.

New Zealand had a formidable team, one of the greatest ever. In their captain Sean Fitzpatrick and the veterans Zinzan Brooke, Frank Bunce, Walter Little, and Ian Jones they had players who were not only household names everywhere that rugby was played, they were each the best in their respective positions in the world game. But their secret weapon, being touted already as the most formidable rugby player in history, was the twenty-year-old Jonah Lomu.

Of Tongan origin, as dark-skinned as Mandela, he was six foot four and weighed eighteen and a half stone. He was as big as the Springboks' biggest man, Kobus Wiese, and he could run faster than Williams or Small – 100 metres in less than eleven seconds. One newspaper called him "a rhinoceros in ballet shoes". In the All Blacks' semi-final against England, one of the favourites in the tournament, he'd proven himself practically unstoppable. He found his way across the line four times. As the London newspapers put it, he made the England team seem like little boys.

Small's position on the Springbok side meant that he would be the man responsible for keeping Lomu in check. The newspapers produced charts comparing the two players' vital statistics, as if they were boxers about to step into the ring. Small – for once living up to his last name – was four inches shorter and weighed more than four stones less than his opponent.

In the newspapers Mandela read himself opining on what to do about the All Black colossus. "Strategically it would be a mistake to concentrate on him, because they must concentrate on the whole team," Mandela had said, before adding, as if surprised at his temerity in venturing into unfamiliar terrain, "But I am sure the Springboks have worked it out completely."

Few shared his optimistic view, especially among the neutrals. The Australian coach, Bob Dwyer, was all over the sports pages confidently predicting that the "fit and fast" All Blacks would have the hefty Springbok forwards chasing shadows all afternoon; the *Sydney Morning Herald* had said the soon-to-be "bamboozled" Boks would "come nowhere near winning"; a former All Black star, Grant Batty, seemed to summarize the totality of expert world opinion on the game when he said "only an elephant gun" would keep Lomu and company from victory.

An elephant gun – or a superhuman effort of collective will. And something close to that was what the Springbok players discovered they carried within when they awoke that morning at the Sandton Sun and Towers Hotel, a modern five-star complex in an affluent shopping area of Johannesburg, about ten minutes' drive north of Mandela's home.

Big Kobus Wiese was sharing a room with his equally big companion, and fellow choir singer, Balie Swart. Wiese was the one who had uttered that bloodcurdling cry of defiance in the scrum at the semifinal against France, but now he was silent. "The pressure," said Wiese, "was absolutely hectic. It was massive. The night before I had phoned my mother. Nothing specific, just to hear her voice, which helps me switch off. But now I felt fear – fear that we would disappoint all those millions of fans. We had that sense of expectations from knowing for the first time ever that the whole country was behind us, and it was quite overwhelming. It was frightening, but it also gave you energy. I had a profound sense that everything I had done all my life was now coming to a head."

The players had breakfast in an atmosphere of unbearable tension and pressure and expectation. They felt as if they were inside a bubble, suspended in time. Or like astronauts about to lift off. They needed to let off steam or they would explode. That was what "the captain's run" was for. Mid-morning, they all gathered at the foyer of the hotel and, with Pienaar leading the way, they went for a two-kilometre jog around the neighbourhood of the hotel. As François Pienaar recalled, "There was so much nervous tension among the guys but then we turned left out of the hotel, running in a tight group, and I heard noises and shouts, and four little black kids selling newspapers recognized us and chased after us and started calling our names – they knew almost everyone on that team – and the hairs on my neck stood on end. I don't even know if these kids were literate, but they recognized who we were and for them it was their team. It was the moment when I saw, more clearly than ever before, that this was far bigger than anything we could ever have imagined."

Mandela looked at himself in the mirror in his new green jersey, put on his cap, and liked what he saw. Shortly before 1:30, he walked out of the front door of his home, ready to board his grey armoured Mercedes-Benz to the stadium. Kick-off was at three o'clock. Ordinarily, Ellis Park wouldn't have been much more than fifteen minutes away, but given the certainty of heavy traffic, they would leave early. The bodyguards were all brisk, silent, muscular efficiency. As the day had worn on they had became progressively less chatty, more solemnly busy, checking their route on a map – a route they had gone over a dozen times in the previous week, alert to every possible vulnerability. They kept in constant touch with the police, making sure the snipers were all in position around the stadium, checking in with the motorcycle escort cops, checking with the security people at Ellis Park that the entrance would be clear for the arrival of the presidential convoy.

But when Mandela stepped out of the house, the entire sixteen-strong bodyguard detail froze, breaking the flow of their intense prepa-rations to gawk at their charge in his new green jersey. "Wow!" Moonsamy heard himself say under his breath. Mandela chuckled at their surprise and bade them all his customarily cheery good morning, at which point they all mumbled "good afternoon" back and snapped back into PPU mode, all briskness as they ushered Mandela into his car, slammed the doors shut, took their places in the four-car convoy. Moonsamy's place, as "number one", was in the grey Mercedes, stiffly alert, on the passenger seat in front of Mandela. All day long he would never be more than a pace away from the president. The police motor-cycles were waiting outside. They drove out, wheels screeching on the driveway. The PPU men wore their humourless bodyguard faces, but inside they glowed. "We looked at him in that green rugby jersey," Moonsamy said, "and we felt so proud, because he himself looked so proud."

Mandela was not the only black man in an AmaBokoBoko jersey that day. Black people were seen all over South Africa happily sporting the symbol of the old oppressors, as Justice Bekebeke discovered to his bafflement on the morning of the final.

If Mandela had woken up thinking he had the Springboks' black support in the bag, he had not reckoned on the man he had almost met on Death Row five years earlier. Mandela was worrying about the white bitter-enders, unaware that such a thing as a black bitter-ender existed.

"At the start of the World Cup I was rooting for the All Blacks with as much passion as I had in the old days, when I rooted for them as a child that time they came to Upington," Bekebeke said. "I was happy we had made the political deal we had with the whites. I accepted that we had to have a power-sharing government for now, with people like De Klerk in cabinet. Fine. I saw all that. I welcomed it. But, 'Don't ask me to support the Springboks!' was my position. I had no intention of budging. I had forgiven enough."

The puzzling thing for Bekebeke was that there did not seem to be too many other people in Paballelo who shared his view. Not even Selina, his girlfriend, who had stood by him when he was in prison, who had worked to help finance his studies. On paper, she was more politically radical than he was. She belonged not only to the ANC, but to its hard-line ideological ally, the South African Communist Party. Yet she too had gone along with Mandela, abandoned the justified prejudices of a lifetime and chosen to see the Springboks as "our team". The players might be practically all white, most of them Boers, but she was going to support them in this afternoon's game with as much patriotic enthusiasm as if they had been all black, like her.

This presented Bekebeke with a dilemma: how to spend the rest of the day. Selina was dead set on watching the game, but he was not sure what he would do. He might do as he had done all his life: support the visiting team in this case, New Zealand. Or maybe he might make an exception this time and simply not care.

"As the morning wore on, as I saw the papers, heard the radio, saw the gathering excitement in my girlfriend, I began to feel torn. A part of me thought it might be best not to watch the damn game. But then, I thought, well, everyone's going to watch it. My girlfriend is. All my friends are. Even my comrades who were in prison with me. I can't miss it myself."

One thing Bekebeke had clear was that he should not watch the game alone with Selina. "I was worried that if we did, we'd get very tense and fight," he said. "So luckily an opportunity came along to watch the game at the home of some friends. They had organized a braai [a barbecue] for the occasion and so I thought that even if I had to go through this game, there would at least be some compensation in the food." There were going to be four couples, themselves included, at the braai. The other three men had been in prison with Bekebeke; one of them – Kenneth Khumalo, "Accused Number One" – had been on Death Row with him. This was encouraging news to Bekebeke, sure now that he would not be alone in his doubts about all this Springbok business, confident that Selina's enthusiasm would stand out in the group. She had gone ahead of him to help with the preparations, and so he arrived on his own, at more or less the time that Mandela was leaving home for the stadium.

"I have never been more astonished in all my life," Bekebeke said. "The door opens. I go into the house and what do I see? All seven of them, wearing the green Springbok jersey!"

CHAPTER XVII
"NELSON! NELSON!"

June 24, 1995 – afternoon

In the sixty minutes between two o'clock, when Mandela arrived at Ellis Park, and three o'clock, when the game began, everything happened. First there was a song, then a jumbo jet, and finally a shout that shook the world.

The song was called "Shosholoza". Mandela knew it very well indeed, as did practically every black South African. Originally sung by black migrant workers who travelled from the rural areas of southern Africa to work at the gold mines around Johannesburg, it was a bouncy, high-energy tune that sought to mimic the rhythm of the steam train. "Shosholoza" was sometimes translated as "Make way", sometimes as "Move forward", sometimes as "Travel fast". Whatever else it was, it was dynamic – hugely popular at soccer matches among the sport's almost exclusively black fans. Mandela used to sing it along with Walter Sisulu and other inmates when they worked at the lime quarry in Robben Island. He had sung it again only four months earlier when he and a hundred former prisoners made a jolly, ceremonial return to the prison. But now, in yet another sign of the accelerated pace of change in South Africa, Louis Luyt's rugby union had chosen "Shosholoza" as the official World Cup song, and the white fans had cheerfully adopted it as their own.

They needed a bit of help, though, with both the music and the words. They needed, as the Springboks had with "Nkosi Sikelele", a singing coach. This was where Dan Moyane entered the picture. Moyane was born in Soweto in 1959 and grew up with no interest in rugby whatsoever, "save to register," as he said, "that it was a symbol of Afrikaner domination". Following the student riots of 1976, most of his friends went either into exile or into jail. Harassed by the security police, he fled the country, sneaking over the border to Mozambique where in 1979 he joined the ANC. There he worked as a journalist for BBC radio and Reuters, among others, and, having survived the cross-border commando raids General Constand Viljoen's special forces were launching in the early eighties, he returned home in 1991, a year after the ANC was unbanned. Almost immediately he got a job on Johannesburg's Radio 702 (where Eddie von Maltitz would later have his phone-in conversion with Mandela), and soon he was co-hosting a 6 a.m. to 9 a.m. radio show with an Irish-born former rugby player called John Robbie who had played for the British Lions against the Springboks in 1980. The duo were very popular, and their blend of easy banter and serious political discussion was one of the more palpable contributions that emerged from civil society to help precipitate South Africa's political changes. They gently prodded their listeners – especially the white ones – towards a more generous attitude to South Africa's new realities.

The Rugby World Cup gave them plenty to talk about. For Robbie it was a dream come true, an opportunity to reconcile his two passions, rugby and racial reconciliation in South Africa. Moyane was not so sure at first. Shaking off the associations the Springboks triggered in his mind was no easier for him than it was for any other black person. He and Robbie would argue on air about rugby. Until the inaugural game against Australia.

"When I heard Nelson Mandela was going to be there I struggled to believe it," Moyane said. "But we put on the TV at home and there he was, and my wife said to me, 'Well, if Mandela is there supporting the Springboks I suppose we'll have to too. We'll have to watch this rugby!' It was an amazing thought, but it was what happened, and I believe the same conversation, or variations on it, were replayed in black households up and down the land."

Over the next month much of the morning radio show consisted of Moyane playing the naïve interrogator to Robbie's worldly-wise rugby man. One day they played "Shosholoza" on air, a version that had been recorded recently by the internationally famous all-male South African singing group Ladysmith Black Mambazo. It was beautifully done, but when Robbie asked Moyane for his opinion, he replied that, for him, the spirit of the song ought to be more raw. "It was a song of encouragement, of hope sung by men far away from their families who were working hard now but would be catching the train home soon enough." Moyane told Robbie that this was not a song designed, in his view, for heavily produced choral arrangements. "I felt it as a song to be sung with gusto, with go-for-it street passion, with heart and guts." So Robbie said, "Okay, why don't you sing it then, Dan? Show us how it's done." And Dan Moyane did. He belted out a couple of bars. "It was the first time I'd ever sung like that on air, and within seconds the telephone lines into the studio were red-hot. Both black and white people were calling in saying they'd loved it."

Soon, local music producers were calling Moyane too. Within ten days he had recorded and produced his own version of "Shosholoza" with a choir from Soweto. "Suddenly I was signing autographs in shops.

The song was a smash hit." All this was astounding enough, but nothing compared with what was to come. A week before the final, after South Africa had beaten France, the World Cup organizers invited him to lead the fans in song at Ellis Park an hour before the game against the All Blacks.

Dan Moyane did not seem, at first sight, like a natural for such a rabble-rousing occasion. Of medium height and trim build, he had soft, round features and a gentleness of manner at odds with the predominant mood and physiognomy of the average white South African rugby fan. Yet he rose to the moment as if to the manner born.

At 2 p.m., he walked out onto the field. Moyane's version of "Shosholoza" had been blaring from the sound system as fans filtered into the stadium; now they would all sing it together. Moyane walked up to the microphone and asked, "Do you hear me?"

Sixty-two thousand fans bellowed back, "YES!"

"Okay, to make sure you really are hearing me, can we have some silence now?" Ellis Park went suddenly quiet. Then the Zulu words of the song came up on the two big screens at either end of the stadium.

Into the silence, Moyane declared, "We will sing the song to drown the All Blacks out of the stadium!" and a vast cheer went up. First he read the words aloud with the crowd, and then everyone began to sing.

He led the massed ranks of Piet Retief's heirs in two full-throated renditions of the Zulu song. "All kinds of emotions and thoughts flooded through my head," Moyane said. "Images came to my mind of 1976, of my friends being jailed, people I knew who these very people – or people close to them, at any rate – had tortured and killed. But then I also thought what a gesture on these people's part! They were repaying us for letting them keep the green jersey. This was a black street song, a soccer song, a migrant workers' song, a prisoners' song. It was an amazing example of crossing the lines, of hearts changing."

. . .

And of people revving up for a big game. What came next raised the decibel levels even higher. Blame the protagonist of act two of the pre-game show, a South African Airways pilot called Laurie Kay.

Born in Johannesburg in 1945, Kay grew up entirely sheltered from the world Dan Moyane inhabited. He was one of those English-speaking white men who, by a quirk of family circumstances that had affected two million others like him, just happened to have ended up living in the southern tip of Africa. Obsessed with flying from his childhood, he joined not the South African Air Force but Britain's Royal Air Force, not out of any political conviction, but as a matter of practicality. It turned out to be easier for him to get into the RAF. "I am not proud to say it now," he said, "but the truth is that I was an utterly apolitical white person who voted Nat."

The first seedlings of a political conscience emerged within Kay shortly after Mandela's prison release. They were both on an SAA flight from Rio de Janeiro to Cape Town. It was a Boeing 747 and Kay was the captain. "It was my first and last face-to-face encounter with Nelson Mandela. I got a message that he wished to see me. So I stepped out of the cockpit and found that he was with his wife, Winnie. They were on seats 1D and 1F – I'll never forget it," said Kay. "The moment he saw me he stood up. I said, 'No, please,' but he insisted and he stood up and greeted me and shook my hand. It never, ever happened to me before or since with a passenger. For me it was transforming. The courtesy and respect of his gesture." He had floored Kobie Coetsee and Niël Barnard at first sight, as he would General Viljoen. But those men had had some political preconditioning, some notion of what to expect. With Captain Kay, he was writing on a blank page. Yet the effect, again, was automatic. "He stood up and I was in his pocket. I had reckoned he was a different kind of man. Until then he was another black face and name who may have been a threat to my way of life. I was exposed to the Afrikaans mentality, and that, while I thought little about politics, was what shaped me."

Often enough Mandela was charming for charm's sake. Quite often, too, he sought to receive something in exchange. Sometimes it was purely personal; other times it was political. This time Mandela had a specific favour to ask. "He explained that the rest of his delegation were in economy and he wished to see if they could be upgraded." Kay did not hesitate. "I immediately gave the order that they be taken upstairs to First."

Mandela had obviously manipulated him. Yet Kay's understanding that this had been the case in no way tempered his admiration, partly because, as he said, "You should see some of the cold, supercilious, arrogant types you get in first class! But it went deeper. From that day on I changed for ever. He's a magician, no doubt about it. In my mind there is an aura about certain people. Eugene Terreblanche: I walked out to an airplane alongside him once. He had an aura of evil. Mandela has an aura of goodness."

Kay's and Mandela's paths collided one more time – or they very nearly did – on the day of the Rugby World Cup final.

South African Airways had begun conversations with the rugby union a few weeks earlier to see if there was some way they might extract some marketing advantage from the big event. At first, discussions centred around the notion of getting a small radio-controlled plane with the SAA colours to fly over the stadium. But as the talks progressed the plans became more ambitious, until Kay received a call from an SAA executive asking him if he might be persuaded to fly a 747 jumbo jet on the afternoon of the final match with the words "Go Bokke" (the Afrikaans plural) painted on the plane's underbelly. Kay did not think twice about it. If Mandela had been preparing all his life for this moment, so had he. Not only was he the airline's most experienced

747 pilot, he had spent thirty years as a stunt flyer. He did air acrobatics shows and had even done a turn once in a film starring the Hong Kong martial arts actor Jackie Chan.

The difference this time was that it was not only himself he would be exposing to grave danger. Nor only the 62,000 people inside the stadium but countless more outside. For Ellis Park sat inside the Johannesburg city bowl. All around were residential buildings and office towers.

Laurie Kay spent the week before the final diligently preparing for what would be the most outrageous flyover in history. He, the civil aviation people, and the city authorities, now under the command of the new provincial premier, the charismatic former Robben Islander Tokyo Sexwale, held numerous meetings during the week before the final. "We installed a military air traffic control centre on the roof of Ellis Park and declared the sky for five nautical miles around the stadium 'sterile', meaning it was a no-fly zone, on the day of the match," Kay said. He and his colleagues at South African Airlines also had to confer with the SABC, who were broadcasting the event live around the world, to make sure that the flyover occurred at precisely the right moment for maximum TV exposure. "They said they wanted me to fly past at exactly 2.32 p.m. and 45 seconds. That was doable. But then they said I had to fly over a second time within ninety seconds. This stumped me, because I did not know if I could manoeuvre a plane so big so quickly. But I practised on the simulator and I found that, yes, I could do it."

But there was no programme on the simulator that could prepare him for the particular manoeuvre he had in mind. He had to go out and do some old-fashioned field work. "I spent a lot of time on the roof of Ellis Park and on the hills overlooking it to judge the best approach and to get a sense of what the fans would see. Ellis Park is in a depression and difficult to approach. I could see it was going to require an aggressive bit of flying."

There was something of the Wild West about South Africa at that time. With so much radical change under way, the place felt recklessly alive with possibility. It was in such a spirit that Laurie Kay approached the most perilous professional challenge of his life.

"The Civil Aviation Authority has rules for flying over built-up areas and public gatherings. I believe the minimum altitude is two thousand feet. Well, obviously, these regulations had been momentarily waived. It was up to me to decide how low to go." Kay and his co-pilot and engineer took off and headed, like a Second World War bomber crew, towards their target.

"We were three guys in the cockpit but as we prepared for our final approach I said, 'Okay, guys. I'll take full responsibility now.' Because it was no good flying on an occasion like this so high they could hardly hear you. So I came down at a low angle to make sure that the words underneath could be read by the spectators, flying at the slowest speed possible short of a stall. At 140 knots. I went slow so that we could generate maximum power to climb once we were over the stadium. So when we got there – our time over target was between two and three seconds – we revved up the engines, we really opened up to their maximum sound and thrust so as to put as much noise and as much energy into the stadium as we possibly could."

Kay flew so low he would have been jailed if the CAA hadn't agreed to suspend the rules. He flew only two hundred feet above the stadium's highest seats – the same distance as the plane's wingspan. "And we made it back in time nicely, for the second flypast, inside eighty seconds," said Kay, modestly adding, "We had factors in our favour. Visibility was terrific. No wind. But above all I wanted us to send a message down to the stadium, that we were strong and we were going to win. And so, yes, we emptied all the power we could muster into the stadium."

The first reaction of the crowd, most of whom did not see the plane coming, was sheer terror. It was as if a huge bomb had gone off inside the stadium. The impact of the Boeing 747's four screaming engines deafened every person in the stadium, making its walls vibrate. Louis Luyt was up in the presidential suite at the time, with Mandela next to him.

"How I jumped!" Luyt exclaimed. "And Mandela jumped too!" As did everyone in the stadium. "The bastard!" grinned Luyt, referring to Captain Kay. "He never told us he was going to fly that low. At two hundred feet! I got such a scare! He could so easily have touched the top of the stadium."

Surprise and shock gave way to thunderous elation. That power Captain Kay emptied into the stadium electrified every soul present, and kept the crowd purring right to the game's end. But that was nothing compared to the impact of act three of the pre-game show.

Five minutes before kick-off, Nelson Mandela stepped out onto the field to shake hands with the players. He was wearing the green Springbok cap and the green Springbok jersey, buttoned up to the top. When they caught sight of him, the crowd seemed to go dead still. "It was as if they could not believe what their eyes were seeing," said Luyt. Then a chant began, low at first, but rising quickly in volume and intensity.

Morné du Plessis caught it as he emerged out of the dressing room and down the players' tunnel onto the field. "I walked out into this bright, harsh winter sunlight and at first I could not make out what was going on, what the people were chanting, why there was so much excitement before the players had even gone out onto the field. Then I made out the words. This crowd of white people, of Afrikaners, as one man, as one nation, they were chanting, 'Nel-son! Nel-son! Nel-son!' Over and over, 'Nel-son! Nel-son!' and, well, it was just . . ." The big rugby man's eyes filled with tears as he struggled to find the words to fit the moment. "I don't think," he continued, "I don't think I'll ever experience a moment like that again. It was a moment of magic, a moment of wonder. It was the moment I realized that there really was a chance this country could work. This man was showing that he could forgive, totally, and now they – white South Africa, rugby white South Africa – they showed in that response to him that they too wanted to give back, and that was how they did it, chanting, 'Nelson! Nelson!' It was awesome. It was fairy-tale stuff! It was Sir Galahad: my strength is the strength of ten because my heart is pure.

"Then I looked at Mandela there in the green jersey, waving the cap in the air, waving and waving it, wearing that big, wide, special smile of his. He was so happy. He was the image of happiness. He laughed and he laughed and I thought, if only we have made him happy for this one moment, that is enough."

Rory Steyn, one of the members of Mandela's presidential bodyguard, also had a front-row seat. He had been deployed as head of security for the All Blacks, which meant he was down on the field with them, by their bench. "Mandela, in that single act of generosity, he carried the entire South Africa into one new nation," said Steyn, a former security policeman whose business for years had been to persecute the ANC and its allies. "The message from the black population was one we received with gratitude and relief. We share in your elation, they were saying; we forgive you for the past."

With forgiveness came atonement. That was also what the cries of "Nelson! Nelson!" meant. In paying homage to the man whose prison sentence had been a metaphor for the bondage of black South Africa, they were acknowledging their sin, uncorking their bottled-up guilt.

Linga Moonsamy, standing one step behind Mandela on the grass, drinking it all in, experienced an attack of sensory overload. On the one hand, he was tasting the dream to which he had dedicated his life as a young ANC fighter; on the other, he had a cold-eyed mission to fulfil

"There I was, stuck almost to his back, and there was this roar and the cries of 'Nelson! Nelson!' and even though I felt so emotional, more deeply moved than I had ever been in my life, I was also doing a job, I was on full alert, scanning the crowd. And then over to the right-hand corner of the ground I saw some old South African flags being waved and that caused a totally contrary response in me. The sight sent a chill down my spine. It was a sudden and alarming security alert. I knew we had to keep an eye on that sector of the crowd and I made a note of mentioning it as soon as I could to the rest of the team. Yet I was so torn, because I was absolutely blown away by the understanding of what it meant politically."

The symbolism at play was mind-boggling. For decades Mandela had stood for everything white South Africans most feared; the Springbok jersey had been the symbol, for even longer, of everything black South Africans most hated. Now suddenly, before the eyes of the whole of South Africa, and much of the world, the two negative symbols had merged to create a new one that was positive, constructive, and good. Mandela had wrought the transformation, becoming the embodiment not of hate and fear, but generosity and love.

Louis Luyt would not have known what to make of it a couple of years earlier, but now he got it too. "Mandela knew this was the political opportunity of his life and, by God, he seized it!" said Luyt. "When that crowd exploded, you could see: he was South Africa's president that day without one vote against. Yes, the presidential inauguration a year earlier was a great thing, but it was the conclusion of an election which some had won and some had lost. Here we were all on the same side. Not one vote against. He was our king that day."

That was the point. Mandela had accurately gauged the power of his gesture when he had said that wearing the jersey "would have a terrific impact on whites". He was everybody's king that day. He had already had one coronation, at the football stadium in Soweto on the day after his release. That day, he was crowned king of black South Africa. Five years later, his second coronation was taking place at Afrikanerdom's holy of holies, the national rugby stadium.

Van Zyl Slabbert, Morné du Plessis's youthful inspiration and Braam Viljoen's boss at the Pretoria think tank, was in the stadium. "You can have no idea what it meant to me to see these classic Boers all around me, with their potbellies, in their shorts and long socks, real AWB types, drinking brandy and Cokes, to see these guys, these northern Transvaal rednecks singing 'Shosholoza', led on by a young black guy, and cheering Mandela," said Slabbert, aghast at the recollection of the scene. "You would have expected him when he became president to say, 'I'm going to get you . . .!' Yet, no, he contradicts every stereotype of vengeance and retribution."

Archbishop Tutu, who as a child would tramp over to Ellis Park to watch games with his mother's sandwiches, had to live with the cruel irony of being prevented from attending the game due to a prior engagement in the United States. But he would not have missed the game for anything. He watched it, early in the morning, in a bar in San Francisco.

"Nelson Mandela has a knack of doing just the right thing and being able to carry it off with aplomb," Tutu said. "Some other political leader, head of state, if they had tried to do something like he did, they would have fallen flat on their faces. But it was just the right thing. It's not anything that you can contrive . . . I believe that that was a defining moment in the life of our country."

No one captured the sea change that Mandela had effected better than Tokyo Sexwale, who had spent thirteen years on Robben Island convicted of terrorism and conspiracy to overthrow the government; who out of prison had become the assassinated Chris Hani's closest friend; who as premier of Gauteng (previously Transvaal) Province had become one of the half dozen most prominent figures in the ANC.

"This was the moment when I understood more clearly than ever before that the liberation struggle of our people was not so much about liberating blacks from bondage," Sexwale said, picking up on the core lesson he had learned from Mandela in prison, "but more so, it was about liberating white people from fear. And there it was. 'Nelson! Nelson! Nelson!' Fear melting away."

And what of the last Doubting Thomas? What of Justice Bekebeke, the only one of the gang of eight at the Paballelo barbecue not wearing a Springbok jersey? It was a defining moment in his life too. He finally capitulated, powerless before the rushing tide of new South African sentiment that Mandela had unleashed.

"An hour before the game I was still torn and confused," he said. "But then we turned on the TV and we saw these guys singing 'Shosholoza' and then that amazing fly-past and then the old man, my president, wearing the Springbok jersey. Well, I was battling! I still could not quite shake off the old resentment and hatred, yet something was happening to me, and I realized that I was changing, I was softening, until I just had to give up, to surrender. And I said to myself, well, this is the new reality. There is no going back: the South African team is now my team, whoever they are, whatever their colour.

"This was a watershed for me. For my entire relationship with my country, with white South Africans. From that day on everything changed. Everything was redefined."

CHAPTER XVIII
BLOOD IN THE THROAT

"I couldn't sing the anthem," François Pienaar admitted. "I dared not." He had been desperate to rise to the occasion, to set an example, not to let Mandela down. He had rehearsed the scene over and over in his mind. But when the time came, when the two teams lined up on the side of the pitch before the game and the band struck up the first strains of "Nkosi Sikelele", he couldn't open his mouth.

"Because I knew that if I did, I'd fall apart. I'd just crumble, right there. I was so emotional," the Springbok captain said, "that I wanted to cry. Sean Fitzpatrick [the All Black captain] told me later that he looked over and saw a tear roll down my cheek. But that was nothing compared to what I was feeling inside. It was such a proud moment in my life and I stood there and the whole stadium was reverberating. And it was just too much. I tried to find my fiancée, to focus on her, but I couldn't find her. So I just bit my lip. I bit it so hard I felt the blood rolling down my throat."

What had brought Pienaar to the emotional brink was Mandela's visit to the Springboks' dressing room ten minutes before. Between the jumbo jet flyover and stepping out onto the field in his green jersey, Mandela had asked Louis Luyt to take him down to the bowels of the stadium to say a few words to the players.

Pienaar recalled the scene. "I had just got strapped up and there we all were, in a state of tension like we'd never known, and so much was going through my mind, knowing that this was the biggest thing ever – one shot, one opportunity to seize everything you've always wanted. And I was just thinking about all that, but at the same time with so much attention to all the details of the game, and then, suddenly, there he was. I didn't know he was coming, and even less did I know that he was going to wear the Springbok jersey. He was saying 'Good luck', and he turned around and on his back there was this number 6, and that was me . . .

"You know, the passionate supporters, they're the ones who wear the jersey of their team. So now here I am seeing him walking into the dressing room, in this moment of all moments, dressed like another passionate fan, but then I see that it is my jersey he is wearing. There are no words to describe the emotions that ran through my body."

As he had a year earlier at Silvermine, Mandela caught the Springboks by surprise. As Morné du Plessis remembered it, before he entered the room the silence was absolute. "Suddenly the players saw him and everybody was laughing, smiling, clapping. The tension just fell away." This time Mandela's speech was shorter, more familiar, and more direct than it had been on the day before the Australia game. "Look here, chaps," he said. "You are playing the All Blacks. They are one of the most powerful teams in the rugby world but you are even more powerful. And just remember that this entire crowd, both black and white, are behind you, and that I'm behind you."

Mandela then went around the room, shaking hands and sharing a few words with each player. As he walked out the door, François Pienaar called out, "Sir, I like the jersey you are wearing."

Mandela realized that his visit might raise the Springboks' blood pressure past its already dangerous level. But, he said later, his remarks "were calculated to encourage them".

His calculations were, once again, on the money. Stransky, who as fly half would arguably endure the most stress that day, confirmed that "he got the mood just right. It was so inspirational. I would have thought it was completely impossible to 'up' the feelings amongst us before the game, but Madiba did. He 'upped' us even further."

Louis Luyt, who had accompanied Mandela into the dressing room, agreed. "He charged them up with those words saying the whole country was behind them. It was a short speech but, my God, that was going to get these guys to play like hell!"

Three minutes later, as the chants of "Nelson! Nelson!" still washed around the stadium, it was the players' turn to take the stage. Now it was up to them. Responsibility for the well-being of the country passed into the players' hands. Nothing else would matter for the next hour and a half. If South Africa lost, there would still be things to salvage. There was honour in having made it to the final. The nation had come together like never before. "One Team, One Country" had ceased to be a slick marketing man's slogan. But if South Africa lost, the whole thing would end up as a limp anticlimax, as a bittersweet memory best forgotten. The great "Nelson! Nelson!" moment would live on, but without the joyous, Beethoven's Ninth, trumpet-blast associations that victory would evoke.

To seal the day, to make it eternal, the Springboks had to beat the odds and win. Which meant they had to stop Jonah Lomu. They got their first live view of him when they emerged from their dressing room into the players' tunnel in preparation for the two teams' side-by-side march onto the field. The All Blacks had a formidable team, packed with famous rugby names. But all eyes were on Lomu, as most of the Springboks' thoughts had been ever since they had seen the giant sprinter reduce the pride of England a week earlier to a rabble of bereft urchins.

"He was *so* big," Stransky said. "It was impossible not to admire him. I couldn't take my eyes off him in the tunnel. He looked like a mountain. One that we had to climb!"

A mountain that, to be more specific, James Small had to climb. "I remember seeing Jonah and thinking 'Oh, fuck!'" Small said, with characteristic concision. The whole team was aware of the weight on the "Englishman", Lomu's designated marker, who they noticed had been more than usually silent on the bus to the stadium. "It was almost the only thing on my mind. I knew that if he got a two- or three-yard start he'd be gone. But the rest of the players were really behind me, making a point of showing their willingness to back me up once Jonah got the ball." Chester Williams, whose earlier differences with Small were submerged in the solidarity of the moment, was the first to step forward to reassure him: "All you've got to do is hold him up and we'll come. Don't worry. I'll be there covering your back."

Over the previous week, the South African press had seen the emergence of a new kind of rugby expert, the Lomulogist. Everyone had their theories on how to stop him. One of them was the straightforward approach Chester Williams proposed. If Small just managed to hold him up for a second, shake him off his stride, the rest of the team would pile in on top of him. Others suggested that Lomu was not as strong in mind as he was in body. Perhaps he had something about him of Sonny Liston, the fearsome heavyweight champion whom Muhammad Ali defeated not by punishing his body, but by playing tricks with his mind, jangling his brittle self-esteem. Two days before the match the South African press had quoted amply the words of a former Australian rugby captain who said that the key to neutralizing the Lomu threat was to "to try and wreck his confidence early in the match". The idea was that Lomu became unstoppable if he believed he was unstoppable. If he lost that belief, he would crumble. The Australian said it would be helpful, for example, for Stransky to kick some high, difficult balls in his direction, pressuring him to fumble them, or, best of all, to tackle him hard to the ground once or twice in the first ten minutes. Right from the word go, the Springboks' objective had to be "confuse the big fella", "provide him with a mental setback or two".

There is evidence that Mandela tried to give Lomu a mental setback or two himself. As Linga Moonsamy later revealed, before going into the Springbok dressing room, Mandela visited the All Black one. "Jonah Lomu close up was huge," Moonsamy recalled. "But you could also see immediately that he was timid. Sort of daunted by Mandela. The New Zealand guys all had their shirts off and when Mandela stood next to Lomu, I heard Mandela say 'Wow!'" He shook hands with all the players and he wished them luck. Mandela had never been less sincere, and the All Blacks knew it. "There was one detail the New Zealanders could not avoid registering," said Moonsamy, chuckling. "He was wearing the green Springbok jersey! I really did wonder afterward if going in to see them had been his way of sending them a deliberately ambiguous message."

Fifteen minutes later, Mandela was out on the field, going down the line of New Zealand players, shaking hands with each. When he got to Lomu, Mandela greeted the man he had barely just met like a long-lost friend. "Ah, hello Jonah! How are you?" Mandela beamed. According to a TV journalist close by, "Lomu looked like he was going to shit himself!"

The last piece of pageantry before the game began was the All Blacks' traditional Haka. Teams representing New Zealand had been performing this ritual before the start of matches for more than a hundred years. It was a Maori war dance designed to instil terror in enemy ranks. The fifteen All Blacks would stand in the middle of the playing field in broad formation, each man spreading his legs wide apart in a half crouch. At a cry from the captain, the dance would begin. Amid much snarling and sticking out of tongues, great stomping, thigh-slapping, chest-puffing, and menacing gesticulation generally, the All Blacks uttered a chant that sounded far more alarming in the bellowed Maori original than it does on a page in English translation: The rousing finale went:

> *Tēnei te tangata pūhuruhuru*
> *Nāna nei i tiki mai whakawhiti te rā*
> *Ā upane, ka upane*
> *Ā upane, ka upane*
> *Whiti te rā, hī!*

This the hairy man that stands here
Who brought the sun and caused it to shine
A step upward, another step upward
A step upward, another step upward! The sun shines!

Fortunately for the All Blacks, their rivals do not usually have the translation ready at hand. What rivals tend to do is try to stare them down, or smirk with seeming contempt, or feign indifference. None of which are ever entirely convincing, so hypnotically menacing is the spectacle. On this occasion, though, there was a slight, but significant, break with protocol. Halfway through the performance, which lasts about a minute and twenty seconds, Jonah Lomu broke with the pattern of the dance and started advancing slowly but pointedly, eyes staring, towards James Small. But then something happened that few people in the stadium or watching on TV saw, but every player on the field registered. Kobus Wiese, standing next to Small, broke protocol himself and took two or three steps in Lomu's direction, cutting diagonally in front of Small. "Kobus broke the line as if to say to Lomu, 'To get to him, you have to get through me first,'" was how Pienaar remembered it. They were small gestures from two big men, infantile ones in the broader scheme of the day's events, but they had their impact. Even before the referee's whistle signalled the start of the game, it was Springboks 1, Lomu 0.

If the focus of Springbok fans was on James Small, the greater pressure was on Stransky. Because of the nature of the position he played, the kicking job, the spotlight would be more on him than on any other individual player. François Pienaar and Kobus Wiese could, to a degree, hide within the grunting hurly-burly of the scrum. If they made a mistake, few outside the team or the sphere of expert pundits would necessarily notice. The bad news was that, by the same token, they rarely received the credit they deserved. What Stransky did or did not do, on the other hand, absolutely nobody missed. His position at fly half was the most visible in the team. But he was also the player in charge of taking the kicks, and it was often on whether a kick went over that the outcome of a game turned. If the kick sailed true, you were a hero. If it did not, you ran the risk of eternal ignominy or, in the best of cases, endless self-recrimination, like a football player who misses a penalty. And, like a football player in such circumstances, so much turned on so little. The difference between glory and disaster lay in a subtle change in the direction of the wind, in almost microscopic movements of the muscles, tendons, and nerves in the ankle, the knee, the hip, the toe.

Rugby can be a spectacular game to watch, even for people not familiar with its intricacies. It combines the tactics, power, and speed of American football with the flow, expansiveness, collective effort, and individual ball talent of association football. To play the game at the highest level you have to combine the strength required in the one with the fitness required in the other. When the game is played well, with pace and skill, the spectacle is both crunchingly gladiatorial and pleasing to the eye. If the game is a close contest, even better, for then art and theatre combine.

The 1995 Rugby World Cup final produced more theatre than art. It was a grinding game. It was attrition. It was trench warfare, not pretty to watch. But in terms of sheer drama, it couldn't be beaten.

The whole of South Africa was hooked; the whole gamut of races, religions, tribes, were glued to their TV sets. From Kobie Coetsee, who found a crowded bar near his Cape Town home to watch the game, to Constand Viljoen, who saw it with friends, also in Cape Town, to Tutu who saw it with strangers in California, to Niël Barnard who watched it at his home in Pretoria with his wife and three children, to Justice Beke-beke with his old friends and comrades in Paballelo, to Judge Basson, the man who sentenced them to death, who was watching the game at his home in Kimberley. All of them were, at last, on the same team. As was Eddie von Maltitz, watching with his old Boer kommandos down on the farm, in the Orange Free State. He was now as committed to the cause of the Springboks and Nelson Mandela as he had been once to Eugene Terreblanche's AWB.

"We were praying that day, man," he said. "We were so tense. Pray-ing, praying. If we could beat that New Zealand team, we as a nation could do so much. We were so, so united, and now there was a chance we could be even more united. It was so important for South Africa to win."

So important that the streets were deserted, as only the pilot Laurie Kay and his crew members could testify. He landed the plane before the game had begun but there were no ground staff at the airport to greet them. Unless they resorted to an extreme measure like deploying the emergency slide, they were trapped. Finally, their driver came along, found some stairs, and rolled them up to the plane. "There was no one at all on the streets. It was like something from that post-apocalyptic novel *On the Beach*. I made it home in ten minutes flat." Which meant he must have been going faster on the road than he had in the air over Ellis Park.

But the game itself was a more sluggish affair. It never flowed, partly because South Africa simply did not let Jonah Lomu do his stuff. James Small need not have worried; the whole team took charge of Lomu. If the first tackle did not bring him down, the second, or third, or fourth would. There were moments in the game when Lomu looked like a buffalo under attack from a pride of lions. Before the gang tackle had been perfected there were a couple of acts of individual valour. The very first time Lomu received the ball, one of the lightest South African players, the scrum half Joost van der Westhuizen, brought him crashing down with a low tackle just below the knees. ("*That* set the tone for the game," Pienaar said.) A little later, when it seemed Lomu might have found the space and time to build up a head of steam, he was brought down with similar aplomb by Japie Mulder, the center three quarter paired with Hennie le Roux. As the big man was getting up, Mulder – a pygmy next to him – pushed his face into the Ellis Park turf.

"It was rather ungraceful of Japie to have done that," said Morné du Plessis, without a hint of disapproval. "But it was a message he was conveying to Lomu and to the All Blacks. No one's going to get through us today."

And no one did. The All Blacks had got drunk on try-scoring during the tournament – but they managed not one against the Springboks. John Robbie, the former rugby-playing radio host, summed it up well. "The Springboks closed the game down, fought for every inch of ground and tackled like hell. Against this team, that was the only way they stood any chance of winning."

The problem was that the South Africans did not score any tries either. The All Black line held as firm as the Springbok one. It really was the sporting equivalent of the First World War – no breakthroughs, lines doggedly held, shells lobbed from one side to the other. It was a game decided by kicks. Penalty kicks and dropkicks accounted for all the day's scoring.

By halftime Joel Stransky had bisected the posts with his boot three times, while Andrew Mehrtens, the All Blacks' fly half, had done so twice. The score at half time was 9–6 to South Africa. But Mehrtens equalized in the second half and at full time, in a mood of excruciating tension, in which everything could have gone one way or the other at any moment, the scores were level at 9–9. For the first time in a Rugby World Cup, the game had to go into extra time, two halves of ten minutes each. No player on the field had ever crossed this threshold. Physically and mentally they were exhausted. But the fans were suffering more, Mandela not least, even if – in common with most of the fresh black converts around the country – he missed some of the finer points of the action. "He did not know that much about the game, but enough to follow it," recalled gruff Louis Luyt, sitting next to him. "He would ask me questions, 'That penalty kick, what was it for?' But, boy, was he tense! Tense as hell! On a knife edge!"

Mandela did not hesitate to corroborate Luyt's impression of how he was feeling. "You don't know what I went through that day! You don't know!" he said, speaking for all of his compatriots. "I'd never seen a rugby match where there was no try scored. All penalties, or dropkicks. I had never seen a thing like this. But when they decided, now, to give us ten more minutes, I felt like fainting. Honestly, I have never been so tense."

Morné du Plessis, himself a veteran of a hundred rugby battles, felt like fainting too as he imagined himself in the players' shoes. "This was far more than a rugby game, remember, and they all knew it – it was like sending a group of soldiers who have just been through the trauma of the battlefield, and then sending them immediately back in again, straight to the front line."

Pienaar, the twenty-eight-year-old general, reminded his teammates of their higher purpose in the interval before play resumed. "Look around you," he told his weary troops. "See those flags? Play for those people. This is one chance. We have to do this for South Africa. Let's be world champions."

But his eloquence did not stop the All Blacks from going ahead with a Mehrtens kick just one minute into the restart. New Zealand were 12–9 ahead, but as the tenth minute approached, just as the halftime whistle was about to blow, Stransky popped another penalty kick high and straight between the posts. It was 12–12. The whistle blew for half-time, and five minutes later, the leaden-legged players resumed battle, for one last time. The ten final minutes of the game.

"A few days before the final, Kitch Christie [the team coach] had said to me, 'Don't forget about drop goals,'" Joel Stransky recalled. "And that made me practise drop goals for the couple of days leading up to the big game. Lucky I did.

"I can only remember three of the five kicks I kicked that day. The last kick was one of them. Seven minutes to go, the score still at 12–12. We had a scrum twenty-five yards out from their line. François called for a back-row move. One that we had practised over and over."

That meant the forwards trying to make a rush through the dense All Black lines for a try. "But Joel cancelled my call," said Pienaar. "He said he wanted the ball immediately." So that was what they did. As Wiese recalled, "Joel needed a specific kind of scrum, we had to wheel in a particular direction, to do his drop-goal. We were very tired, but we tried it and it worked."

The ball emerged from the human thicket of the scrum and Joost van der Westhuizen, the scrum half, whipped the ball to Stransky. He had had thirty seconds between making his call and receiving the ball to ponder the terrifying knowledge that this could be the biggest moment of his life, and of lots of other people's lives. The mental pressure, the towering responsibility, in combination with the physical difficulty of dropping the ball and catching it cleanly with the foot the instant it touches the ground in such a way as to make it sail high and straight, in the full understanding that two or three extremely large men are racing towards you, with murder in their minds . . . Stransky had volunteered for some of the most hazardous duty possible in any sport.

"I received the ball, clean and true, and I kicked that ball so, so sweetly," said Stransky, reliving his life's sweetest moment. "It was holding its line. It was spinning truly and it didn't veer at all. And I didn't even watch to see if it would go over. I knew, as it went off my boot, that it was too sweet to miss. And I felt absolute jubilation."

As did every South African watching: Justice Bekebeke, Constand Viljoen, Arnold Stofile, Niël Barnard, Walter Sisulu, Kobie Coetsee, Tokyo Sexwale, Eddie von Maltitz, Nelson Mandela – the lot. But there were still six minutes to go. And Lomu was still there. And so were the other fourteen All Blacks, in the words of the London *Daily Telegraph* "the most astonishingly talented" rugby side anybody could remember.

The word from Pienaar to his men was to hold on, to hold on and to do everything necessary to try to keep the ball in the New Zealand half, pin them down, not give them the slightest glimpse of daylight.

"When Joel Stransky had that drop kick there was a British chap near me who said, 'I'm sure that's the decider,'" Mandela said. "But I could not allow myself to quite believe it. And the tension, oh, the tension! I tell you, it was the longest six minutes of my life! I kept looking down at my watch, all the time, and thinking, 'When is this final whistle being blown, man?'"

The six minutes passed, the Springboks held the line, and the whistle blew. François Pienaar exploded out of a scrum and leapt high with his hands in the air. Suddenly he went down on one knee and put his face in his fist, and the other players got down on their knees around him. For a moment they prayed, then they got up and they jumped in the air and they hugged, which was what everyone else in the stadium was doing, including Nelson Mandela, who was not usually the hugging type.

"He was on top of the world," said Moonsamy. "I was with Nelson Mandela for five years, the whole of his presidency, and I never saw him happier. He was so thrilled, so ecstatic. When the final whistle blew the whole suite erupted. If people think we bodyguards are robots, well, they should have seen us when the final whistle went. We too were hugging, and some of us were crying."

Mandela laughed so hard as he recaptured the moment that he could barely get his words out. "When the whistle blew, Luyt," he said, "Louis Luyt and I . . . we just suddenly find ourselves . . . embracing! Yes, embracing!" Luyt confirmed it. "When the final whistle went and the players dropped to their knees, we hugged. And he said, 'We got it, man! We got it!' We hugged so hard – he probably didn't mention this part – that I lifted him off his feet!"

Up in the stands, 62,000 jubilant fans once again took up the cry: "Nel-son! Nel-son!" The thrill of victory made their chant louder, more visceral than before. Down on the field, engulfed in the crowd's ecstasy and his teammates' and his own, Kobus Wiese was gulping down the mighty significance of the moment. "I was so aware of the fact that only a chosen few will ever have this feeling and be part of this. And I cried tears of joy. I think we all cried. You just suck up the emotion of those moments after victory and you don't talk. You just hug each other and nobody has to say anything. We realized there on that field, emotional as we all were, that we were part of history now."

"It was impossible to say anything that could express what we felt. We all just jumped and jumped, and smiled and smiled," said Joel Stransky, smiling. "I smiled for a whole week. I've never stopped smiling."

CHAPTER XIX

LOVE THINE ENEMY

"When the game ended," Morné du Plessis said, "I turned and started running towards the tunnel and there was Edward Griffiths, who had invented the 'One Team, One Country' slogan, and he said to me, 'Things are never going to be the same again.' And I agreed instantly, because I knew right there that the best was behind, that life could offer nothing better. I said to him 'We've seen it all today.'"

But Du Plessis was wrong. There was more. There was Mandela going down onto the pitch, with his jersey on, with his cap on his head to hand over the cup to his friend François. And there was the crowd again – "Nelson! Nelson! Nelson!" – enraptured, as Mandela appeared at the touchline, smiling from ear to ear, waving to the crowd, as he prepared to walk towards a little podium that had been placed on the field where he would hand the World Cup trophy to François Pienaar.

Van Zyl Slabbert, the liberal Afrikaner surrounded in the stadium – as he put it – by beer-bellied AWB types, was amazed at the new South African passion of his born-again compatriots. "You should have seen the faces of these Boers all around me. I remember looking at one of them and there were tears rolling down his face and he kept saying, in Afrikaans, 'That's my president . . . That's my president . . .'"

And they applauded with still more tears when Pienaar offered what would be the first of two memorable moments of impromptu eloquence. A reporter from SABC television approached him on the field and asked, "What did it feel like to have 62,000 fans supporting you here in the stadium?"

Without missing a beat, he replied, "We didn't have 62,000 fans behind us. We had 43 million South Africans."

Linga Moonsamy, walking onto the field one step behind Mandela, looked up at the crowd, at the old enemy screaming his leader's name, and he battled to remember that he was working today, that while all those around him were losing their heads, he had to keep his. But he preserved enough professional sangfroid to remember that before the game began he had seen in the right-hand corner of the stadium those old South African flags. So he shot a glance toward that area again. "But no," he said, "those flags were gone now. There were only new South African flags. And the people in that sector of the crowd were crying and hugging, like everybody else. So I let go a little and allowed myself to think how huge this moment was for the country, how I myself had done what I had done when I was younger, had taken risks, had fought for this, never imagining it would express itself on such a scale."

Tokyo Sexwale, who was there in the stadium, shared Moonsamy's sentiments. "You sit there and you know that it was worthwhile. All the years in the underground, in the trenches, self-denial, away from home, prison, it was worth it. This was all we wanted to see. And then again, 'Nelson! Nelson! Nelson!' We stood there, and we didn't know what to say. I was proud to be standing next to this man with whom I had spent time in prison. Look how high he is now! And you are just proud, so proud, to have supped with the gods . . ."

The gods at that moment were Mandela and Pienaar, the old man in green, crowned king of all South Africa, handing the cup to Pienaar, the young man in green, anointed that day as the spiritual head of born-again Afrikanerdom.

As the captain held the cup, Mandela put his left hand on his right shoulder, fixed him with a fond gaze, shook his right hand and said, "François, thank you very much for what you have done for our country."

Pienaar, meeting Mandela's eyes, replied, "No, Mr. President. Thank *you* for what you have done for our country."

Had he been preparing for this moment all his life, he could not have struck a truer chord. As Desmond Tutu said, "That response was made in heaven. We human beings do our best, but those words at that moment, well . . . you couldn't have scripted it."

Maybe a Hollywood scriptwriter would have had them giving each other a hug. It was an impulse Pienaar confessed later that he only barely restrained. Instead the two just looked at each other and laughed. Morné du Plessis, standing close by, looked at Mandela and the Afrikaner prodigal together, he saw Pienaar raise the cup high above his shoulders as Mandela, laughing, pumped his fists in the air, and he struggled to believe what his eyes were seeing. "I've never seen such complete joy," Du Plessis said. "He is looking at François and just, sort of, keeps laughing . . . and Francois is looking at Mandela and . . . the bond between them!"

It was all too much for the tough-minded Slabbert, hard-nosed veteran of a thousand political battles. "When François Pienaar said that into the microphone, with Mandela there listening, laughing and waving to the crowd and raising his cap to them, well," said Slabbert, "*everybody* was weeping. There wasn't a dry eye in the house."

There wasn't a dry eye in the country. The groot krokodil's old minister of justice and prisons, down in his crowded bar in Cape Town, was sobbing like a child. Kobie Coetsee could not stop thinking back to his first meeting with Mandela ten years earlier. "It went beyond everything else that had been accomplished. It was the moment my people, his adversaries, embraced Mandela. It was a moment comparable, I felt then, to the creation of the American nation. It was Mandela's greatest achievement. I saw him and Pienaar there and I wept. I said to myself, 'Now it was worth it. All the pain, anything that I have experienced, it was worth it. This endorses the miracle.' That's how I felt."

Far away in dusty Paballelo, Justice Bekebeke felt the same. Five years earlier he had been sitting on Death Row, sent there by one of Coetsee's judges, but that suddenly seemed very remote now. "I was in heaven!" he said.

"When Joel Stransky scored the drop goal the rest of the guys were celebrating and shouting their heads off and so was this Doubting Thomas. I felt 100 per cent South African, more South African than I ever had done before. I was as euphoric as everyone else in the room. We were all going absolutely nuts. And after the final whistle blew, after Mandela handed Pienaar the cup, we were running in the streets. So was everybody else in Paballelo. Horns were blaring and the whole township was out dancing, singing, celebrating."

These were the same streets where Bekebeke had killed the policeman who had opened fire on a child; where the riot cops had gone berserk the night before the death sentences were passed on the Upington 14, clubbing everyone in sight, sending twenty people to the hospital.

"It was unreal. And to imagine that these scenes were being repeated all over black South Africa only five years since Nelson Mandela's release, two since Chris Hani's assassination. To have imagined then that I'd be celebrating a victory of the Springboks would have been the most unlikely thing in the world. Yet, looking back, I cannot believe my indifference on that morning of the final, that I did not care. Because there was only one way to describe my feelings now: extreme euphoria."

In Paballelo, in Soweto, in Sharpeville, and a thousand other town-ships, groups of youths were charging up and down the treeless streets performing their own Haka, the old war dance, the Toi Toi. But they weren't defiant now; they were seized by multicoloured national pride, celebrating the victory of the AmaBokoBoko.

Reports washed in from the affluent suburbs of Cape Town, Dur-ban, Port Elizabeth, and Johannesburg that white matrons were shed-ding generations of prejudice and restraint and hugging their black housekeepers, dancing with them on the leafy streets of prim neigh-bourhoods like Houghton. For the first time, the parallel apartheid worlds had merged, the two halves had been made whole, but nowhere more manifestly so than in Johannesburg itself, and especially around Ellis Park, where the Rio carnival met the liberation of Paris in a riot of Springbok green. One old black man stood in the middle of the road outside the stadium waving a South African flag, shouting over and over again, "South Africa is now free. The Boks have made us free, and proud."

Across the road from Ellis Park were the offices of the black Sun-day newspaper, *City Press*. Khulu Sibiya, the paper's editor, was agog at the spectacle he beheld from his window. "I have never seen so many black people celebrating on the streets. Never. In fact, our stories the next day had more about the amazing fact of black people celebrating than about Pienaar and the cup itself. It was amazing."

Archbishop Tutu, who also had a keen nose for news, agreed. The black celebrations *were* the story. "What we saw that day was a revolu-tion," said Tutu, joyous that he had lived to see his country give birth to a new model of revolution, one in which the enemy was not eliminated, he was brought into the fold; that instead of dividing a people, uniting them. "If you had predicted just a year – just months – earlier that people would be dancing in the streets of Soweto to celebrate a Spring-bok victory, most people would have said, 'You have been sitting in the

South African sun too long, and it's affected your brain,'" said Tutu. "That match did for us what speeches of politicians or archbishops could not do. It galvanized us, it made us realize that it was actually possible for us to be on the same side. It said it is actually possible for us to become one nation."

The inevitable patriotic hysteria in the South African papers next morning, the sense that the country had changed for ever, was summarized in the eight-column front-page headline of a newspaper that had the good fortune to be born that very day, the *Sunday Independent*. "Triumph of the Rainbow Warriors," the newspaper's very first issue screamed. The foreign press got in on the act too, with even the sportswriters almost forgetting to write about the game itself, like the rugby reporter from the *Sydney Morning Herald* who began his story, "South Africa emphatically became 'one team, one country' yesterday as the rainbow nation went into raptures." Adding, in a reference to the end of the Second World War, "It was like a re-enactment of VE Day, involving similar waves of passion, and the feeling that something momentous and unforgettable had just occurred."

Van Zyl Slabbert, a big man, every inch a Boer, found himself in the thick of the post-match hysteria. "I went out into the streets, which were awash with dancing black people, and I had to find my way home, so I got on a black taxi." A "black taxi" is a half-bus, half-traditional taxi, a vehicle that one hails down but plies a regular route and carries around a dozen people. It is "black" because in South Africa it was always a form of transport used by black people: whites almost invariably owned their own cars. What Slabbert did, to hail and jump on one, was almost unheard of, especially for inhabitants of the posh northern suburb, not far from Houghton, where he lived. "I got in, and people were cheering and shouting and carrying on with as much passion as the Boers inside Ellis Park. I said to the driver that he could drop me off at the Civic Centre, there in town, but he asked me what my final destination was going to be. I said my home in the northern suburbs but I said that the Civic Centre would be fine, guessing it would probably be on his route. But the driver was very insistent. He said no, he would take me all the way home, which was about half an hour out of his way, and with the traffic and mayhem that day, probably more. Then I said, okay, but what about all these other people in the taxi, which was completely full. They all shouted that no, it was no problem at all. They would enjoy the ride. They were so happy, they said, that nothing else mattered. Eventually we arrived home, and as I got out I asked the driver, 'How much?' He smiled at me and said, 'No. Today nobody pays.'"

No one on that taxi, Slabbert reckoned, had anything more than a dim understanding of rugby, but that did not temper the general celebration in Johannesburg any more than it did five hundred miles away in Paballelo. "In my township, among my people, there was not a single rugby lover," said Bekebeke, "Yet on that day . . . even my mother was ululating in celebration. We were celebrating as South Africans, as one nation. And we knew, deep down, that the Springboks had won because we had willed them to win. It was a phenomenal day! Such a young, infant democracy and there was the symbol of our transformation, Mandela. When he hoisted that cup, that was our victory. We knew at last that we were a winner nation."

Arrie Rossouw, the Afrikaner journalist who met Mandela in Soweto on the day after his release, echoed that point, but with even more feeling because he, as a white South African, had felt himself a loser, a pariah, in the judgment of the world. "We were no longer the baddies anymore," Rossouw said. "Not only did we win, the world actually wanted us to win. Do you realize what that meant to us? What joy? What enormous relief?"

Tokyo Sexwale said that Mandela had liberated white people from fear. That was true, but it went deeper than that. He set them free in a larger sense. He redeemed them, in their own eyes and the eyes of the world.

And then he made them world champions. Kobus Wiese, François Pienaar, Hennie le Roux, Chester Williams, James Small: they all agreed, the Mandela factor had been decisive. They had won the game for him, and through him. "The players knew that the country had a face and a name," as Le Roux put it. "We were playing for South Africa but we were also playing not to let the old man down, which came to the same thing."

"It all came perfectly together: our willingness to be the nation's team and his desire to make the team the national team," said Morné du Plessis. "It came at just the right moment. And I am convinced it was the reason we won the World Cup."

Even Louis Luyt agreed. "We could not have won it without Mandela! When I went down with him to see the players in the dressing room before the game – I saw it, he lifted them a hundred per cent up! They won it for him as much as anything."

Morné du Plessis felt it was going to be South Africa's day the moment he saw Mandela on the edge of the field in the Springbok jersey receiving the crowd's acclaim. "I say this with no disrespect to a truly memorable All Black team, but the enormity of the man we had behind us, and the power that emanated from him and through him, struck me as a little unfair." Sean Fitzpatrick, the formidable All Black captain, admitted much later that Du Plessis had a point, that he did experience a certain awe on hearing the crowd's response to Mandela. "We heard them shouting his name," said Fitzpatrick, "and we thought, 'How are we going to beat these buggers?'"

Too late, Fitzpatrick understood that his team might have Jonah Lomu, but the others were playing with a one-man advantage; they had a secret weapon against which the best rugby team in history had no answer. Joel Stransky could have taken credit for the triumph, but handed it instead to the Springboks' sixteenth man. "The impact he had on the players was immeasurable. That day was a fairy tale come true, with Mandela at the heart of it. He won it for us."

And that day, he revelled in it. The ride home from the stadium took three times longer than expected, but, as Moonsamy said, it could have taken six times longer and Mandela would have asked for more. "All our best-laid plans went out the window. Our route was absolutely clogged. The whole city was transformed into a giant street party. But Madiba was loving every minute of it."

Moonsamy remained alert, but the notion that someone might now wish to assassinate Mandela seemed outlandish even to him. When the four-car convoy finally made it back to Houghton, a small crowd was standing outside his home celebrating. When Mandela got out of his Mercedes to greet them, an elderly lady came up to him. Moonsamy stood aghast as she made a little speech to Mandela declaring that until that afternoon she had been an AWB member, but now, she told him, "I renounce my membership."

It was dusk now, around 6:30 in the evening. Mandela set his body-guards free. "Chaps," he said, "go out and enjoy yourselves."

They took him at his word. "I got home, through the baying crowds," Moonsamy said, "and then my brother-in-law and his wife and kids and me and my family, we went down to Randburg Waterfront where the crowds were gathering to celebrate, and there I saw South Africa become one. Whites and blacks hugging and laughing and crying, late, late into the night."

Mandela opted for a quiet night in. "I came back from the rugby and I stayed here at home, happy and reflecting" – and following his inviolable routines. He watched the TV news in English at 7 p.m., then again in Xhosa at seven-thirty. At ten to eight he sat down for his habitual light dinner – chicken leg on the bone with the skin on, sweet potato, and carrots. Nothing more. Before going to bed, one hour later, he sat down in his living room alone to take stock, as he would do in his prison cell every evening before falling asleep. What surprised and gratified him was the degree to which he had ended up being the focus of attention. For he understood that behind that spontaneous clamour from the white Ellis Park crowd – that "Nelson! Nelson!" – lay eloquent and convincing evidence that his hard toil had paid off. In paying homage to him, they were rendering tribute to the high value of "non-racialism" for which he had endured twenty-seven years of prison. They were crying out for forgiveness and they were accepting his, and through him, black South Africa's generous embrace. It had begun with Kobie Coetsee that day in the hospital in November 1985, the first of his enemies whose heart and mind he conquered. Then Niël Barnard, then P. W. Botha, then the Afrikaans media, De Klerk and his ministers, the high command of the SADF, Constand Viljoen and his fellow bitter-ender generals in the Afrikaner Volksfront, Eddie von Maltitz, John Reinders and the rest of the staff at the Union Buildings, Morné du Plessis, Kobus Wiese, François Pienaar: one after another succumbed as he widened and widened his embrace until the day of the rugby final when he embraced them all.

John Reinders understood it perfectly. "The Rugby World Cup final was him at his best; that was him all over," he said. "That was the day that the man we had seen in private the whole country now saw in public. It was the day that everybody, especially white South Africa, got to see him as he really was."

"It was a day to remember," Mandela said, with a smile that lit up the very living room where he had sat and tasted victory that night of June 24, 1995. "I never imagined that the winning of the World Cup would have such an impact directed towards an individual. I never expected that. And all that I was doing was continuing my work of mobilizing South Africans to support rugby and to influence the Afrikaners, especially towards nation-building."

"Influencing" was one way of putting it. The great task of his presidency, securing the foundations of the new nation, "making South Africans", had been accomplished in not five years but one. At a stroke, he had killed the right-wing threat. South Africa was more politically stable now than at any point since the arrival of the first white settlers in 1652.

Die Burger summed it up well. Noting that "sports isolation was one of the main pressures that precipitated political change", the newspaper said, "Isn't it ironic that rugby should be such a uniting force when for so long it served to isolate us from the world? For there is no longer any doubt that the Springbok team has united the land more than anything else since the birth of the new South Africa."

John Robbie, who had warlike right-wingers calling his radio show every day, put it more simply: "From that day on we knew everything was going to be all right."

So, more to the point, did Constand Viljoen. Those worries that had tormented him, the thought that he had been wrong to choose elections instead of a Boer freedom war, or that a war might yet start without him, were all gone now. "This rugby event convinced me that I was right in my decision," he said. General Viljoen's relief emanated from the understanding that, when the rugby hordes chanted "Nelson! Nelson!" a huge responsibility had been lifted from his shoulders. In that gesture the Afrikaner people were transferring the responsibility from the general to themselves, making his devotion to Mandela their own.

"To see him, the icon of the black people, being so jubilant wearing that Springbok jersey, to me was deeply reassuring. It had been very difficult for me to make my decision and I never imagined I would see myself justified in a manner that was so spectacular."

In this sentiment, his brother Braam, the "good" twin, found common ground with Constand at last. "I have been exposed to the wrath of Afrikaner politics all my life and that this could have happened is, to me, a miracle," he reflected. "The charisma of that man! The leadership of Mandela! He took my brother's arm, and he did not let it go."

Did Mandela have any flaws? Sisulu knew him better than anyone. His answer was that his old friend had a tendency to trust people too much, to take their good intentions too quickly at face value. "He develops too much confidence in a person sometimes," he said. "When he trusts a person, he goes all out." But then Sisulu thought for a moment about what he had said and added, "But perhaps it is not a failing . . . Because the truth is that he has not let us down on account of that confidence he has in people."

Mandela's weakness was his greatest strength. He succeeded because he chose to see good in people who ninety-nine people out of a hundred would have judged to have been beyond redemption. If the United Nations deemed apartheid to be a crime against humanity, then what greater criminals were there than apartheid's minister of justice, apartheid's chief of intelligence, apartheid's top military commander, apartheid's head of state? Yet Mandela zeroed in on that hidden kernel where their better angels lurked and drew out the goodness that is inside all people. Not only Coetsee, Barnard, Viljoen, and P. W. Botha, but apartheid's ignorant henchmen — the prison guards, Badenhorst, Reinders — and its heedless accomplices — Pienaar, Wiese, Luyt. By appealing to and eliciting what was best in them, and in every single white South African watching the rugby game that day, he offered them the priceless gift of making them feel like better people, in some cases transforming them into heroes.

His secret weapon was that he assumed not only that he would like the people he met; he assumed also that they would like him. That vast self-confidence of his coupled with that frank confidence he had in others made for a combination that was as irresistible as it was disarming.

It was a weapon so powerful that it brought about a new kind of revolution. Instead of eliminating the enemy and starting from zero, the enemy was incorporated into a new order deliberately built on the foundations of the old. Conceiving of his revolution not primarily as the destruction of apartheid but, more enduringly, as the unification and reconciliation of all South Africans, Mandela broke the historical mould.

Yet, as his reaction to the crowd's response to him at Ellis Park showed, he surprised himself along the way. He underestimated the strength of his charm.

One Sunday a few weeks after the Springboks' victory, Nelson Mandela visited a church in Pretoria. This church was Dutch Reformed, the denomination that had once sought to provide biblical justification for apartheid; that had persuaded Constand Viljoen there would be separate heavens for blacks and whites; that had exiled his brother Braam for calling the new doctrine a heresy. "That was the occasion," Mandela said, his eyes sparkling, "when I saw that the impact of the rugby match was going to last, that the attitude of the Afrikaners towards me really had changed completely." During the service he addressed the faithful in Afrikaans, and afterwards they surrounded him outside the church door, pressing in around him like a scrum. This was exactly what had happened to him at a hundred ANC rallies in townships up and down the land. Everywhere he went the black people treated him as if he were a cross between Michael Jordan, Evita Perón, and Jesus Christ. Now here the whites were doing the same. "From the crowd, hands reached out wanting to shake my hand. And the women – they wanted to kiss my cheek! They were so spontaneous, so enthusiastic. They were falling over each other, and as for me, I was bounced from pillar to post. And I lost a shoe. Would you believe it? I lost a shoe!"

Mandela was almost doubled over with laughter as he recounted the story. He laughed because it was funny, but also because he was describing the consummation of his life's dream, the moment he understood that South Africa was one country at last.

EPILOGUE

Twelve years after the Rugby World Cup final, in August 2007, a bronze statue of Nelson Mandela was unveiled in London's Parliament Square alongside ones of Abraham Lincoln and Winston Churchill. Reporting on the event, one British national newspaper described Mandela as a "black leader". No offence was meant, presumably, but it still felt vaguely insulting to see him described in such terms. As it would have been to see Lincoln or Churchill described merely as "white leaders".

To identify Mandela by his race is to diminish him and to miss the point. Tony Benn, a veteran British parliamentarian, was closer to the mark when he described Mandela at the unveiling ceremony as "the president of humanity".

But it is also to miss the point to imagine that Mandela, then eighty-nine years old, was some kind of an aberration of nature. As he said when his turn came to speak, frail but with steady voice, "Though this statue is of one man, it should in actual fact symbolize all those who have resisted oppression, especially in my country."

Mandela's modesty could be affected sometimes, but this time it was not. He was the expression of the best his country had to offer. I saw it myself time and again during the six years I was based in South Africa, between 1989 and 1995, a time when, amid all the hopeful forward movement, terrible violence was unleashed in the black townships, especially those around Johannesburg, where I lived. The best thing about South Africa was not Mandela, but that the country was awash with mini-Mandelas, with people like Justice Bekebeke, his girlfriend, Selina, or "Terror" Lekota, the premier of the Orange Free State who invited Eddie von Maltitz to his birthday party.

The first time I interviewed Mandela, early in 1993, I asked him how it was that the ANC's message of "non-racialism" had captured black South Africa's imagination at the expense of the rival PAC's vengeful "one settler, one bullet". He replied that history had shown his people to be warm, kind, and generous, even in dealing with their enemies. "Bitterness does not enter the picture," he said, "even when we fought against something we regard as being wrong." The message of the African National Congress, he said, had "merely consolidated that historical pattern".

The truth of that was borne out by my experience, but it was not the whole truth. A different kind of ANC leader could have elected the easier option of tapping into the indignity and hurt black South Africa had endured and channelled it towards violent confrontation. It took a rare wisdom for Mandela to say to his people, as he paraphrased it for me in that same interview, "I understand your anger. But if you are building a new South Africa you ought to be prepared to work with people you don't like."

His generous pragmatism was all the more unlikely given the historical pattern of his own life. Albert Camus wrote this in his book *The Rebel*: "Twenty-seven years in prison do not, in fact, produce a very conciliatory form of intelligence. Such a lengthy confinement makes a man either a weakling or a killer – or sometimes both." In defence of the French philosopher, he died in 1960, before Mandela had even been jailed. Few would have disputed the logic of what Camus wrote when he wrote it. Mandela was a first, and quite possibly a last. He was to South Africa what George Washington had been to the United States, the indispensable man. As Archbishop Tutu remarked to me, "We couldn't have done it without him, you know."

Mandela stopped a war from happening but that did not mean that he bequeathed to South Africa a state of perfect peace and harmony, any more than Washington did in the United States. After apartheid South Africa shed its global singularity, it ceased to be the paragon of injustice and the (entirely merited) scapegoat for humanity's incapacity to overcome its racial, tribal, nationalistic, ideological, and religious antagonisms. It became a country that had the same challenges as others in similar economic circumstances: how to deliver housing for the poor, how to combat violent crime, how to fight AIDS. And there was corruption, there were unsavoury examples of political patronage, there were doubts as to the ANC's efficiency in government. And humanity's eternal bane, the regressive problem of skin colour, did not magically disappear either, though by the start of the twenty-first century the transformation was such that there were not too many countries whose black and white citizens engaged as naturally as they did in South Africa.

It was also true that the political fundamentals remained as sound as Mandela had left them at the end of his five-year presidential term: the country remained a model of democratic stability and the rule of law remained firm.

Whether this would remain the case for ever, who could possibly know? What would endure was Mandela's example, and that glimpse of Utopia his people saw from the mountaintop to which he led them on June 24, 1995. When I asked Tutu what the lasting value of that day would be, he replied, "It's simple. A friend in New York gave the answer when he said to me, 'You know what? The great thing about everything good that has happened is that it can happen again.' Simple as that."

WHERE ARE THEY NOW?

NIËL BARNARD: held a senior National Party position in Mandela's power-sharing government until his retirement from the post in August 1996, when Mandela hosted a farewell banquet at his official residence in Pretoria to honour his contribution to peaceful change. Today he works as a consultant, using his "experience and expertise", as he puts it, advising African leaders throughout the continent "on governing and governance".

JUSTICE BEKEBEKE: became chief electoral officer for the Northern Cape Province of South Africa and in 2004 formed part of a team of independent international monitors that travelled to the United States to help certify that the presidential elections that year were free and fair.

P. W. BOTHA: died of a heart attack aged ninety in 2006. Mandela sent his condolences to Botha's family and said, "While to many Mr Botha will remain a symbol of apartheid, we also remember him for the steps he took to pave the way towards the eventual peacefully negotiated settlement in our country."

CHRISTO BRAND: runs the official tourist shop on Robben Island. His son Riaan, the one Mandela secretly cradled in prison when he was eight months old, died in a car crash in 2005. Mandela, whose own son died at a similar age in a car accident while Mandela was on Robben Island, flew down to Cape Town to comfort his old jailer.

KOBIE COETSEE: died of a heart attack aged sixty-nine in 2000. Mandela said, "We shall always cherish and hold dear the memory of Kobie Coetsee as one of the major architects of transformation towards a democratic South Africa. It saddens us that he passed away before we, and the country, could adequately pay our tribute to this quiet and unassuming man for his pioneering contributions we are now experiencing the fruits of."

NICHOLAS HAYSOM: worked for the United Nations in conflict resolution and nation-building in Lebanon, Nigeria, Indonesia, the Philippines, East Timor, Sudan, Somalia, Sri Lanka, Lesotho, Colombia, Congo, Tanzania, Zimbabwe, Kenya, Nepal, Myanmar, and Iraq before being appointed director for political affairs in the Executive Office of the UN Secretary-General.

NELSON MANDELA: a few weeks short of his eighty-sixth birthday, in June 2004, he called a news conference to announce his retirement, at the end of which he said, "Thank you very much for your attention, and thank you for being kind to an old man – allowing him to take a rest, even if many of you may feel that after loafing somewhere on an island and other places for twenty-seven years the rest is not really deserved." Since then he has dedicated himself to his three personal charities: the Mandela Rhodes Foundation, the Nelson Mandela Foundation, and the Nelson Mandela Children's Fund, dedicated respectively to promoting education, fighting poverty, and combating HIV/AIDS.

LINGA MOONSAMY: is chief of corporate security for South African Airways, but remains close to Mandela. He is married to a niece of Mandela's wife, Graça Machel, and is often over at Mandela's home for Sunday lunch.

EDDIE VON MALTITZ: still lives on his farm in the Orange Free State, still wears military camouflage gear, still carries a gun, and still phones South African radio stations to denounce perceived wrongs.

MORNÉ DU PLESSIS: runs the Sports Science Institute of South Africa and is a member of the World Sports Academy, a body of former sporting greats that includes Jack Nicklaus, Dan Marino, Martina Navratilova, and Sir Bobby Charlton. Each year they gather to select the winners of the Laureus World Sports Awards, sports's closest equivalent to the Hollywood Oscars.

CONSTAND VILJOEN: runs a farm peacefully in what is now called Mpumalanga Province (it was the Eastern Transvaal when he grew up there) and takes occasional holidays in Cape Town, staying with his wife at a seashore house available to retired servicemen called "el Alamein".

BRAAM VILJOEN: devotes his working hours to his farm north of Pretoria. He and his brother are closer than at any time since their childhoods. They enjoy talking politics.

FRANÇOIS PIENAAR: works as a senior executive for First National Bank in Cape Town. Mandela, who is the godfather to his eldest son, Jean, has invited him, his wife, Nerine, and their children to his home on several occasions. Mandela nicknamed Pienaar's younger son, Stephane, "Gora", which means "Brave One" in Xhosa.

TOKYO SEXWALE: a philanthropist and multimillionaire businessman, with interests in diamonds and platinum, remains a leading force in the ANC.

EUGENE TERREBLANCHE: the leader of the far-right Afrikaner Resistance Movement (AWB) was jailed in 1997 for grievous bodily harm and attempted murder, both offences involving defenceless black men. He was released in 2004 and now delivers sermons preaching repentance and redemption.

AWB: an editorial in the organization's newsletter, *Storm*, published in 2002, said, "Since the 1994 election, patriotic Afrikaner organisations have been debilitated by the uncertainty existing among their supporters about whether they should vote or not. The unity which existed prior to the 1994 election has been destroyed. Our people are disappointed that the ANC has taken over power, and a feeling of powerlessness has overtaken us. Since then the attitude is one of 'Every man for himself' and all interest in politics has disappeared."

THE SPRINGBOKS: they won the Rugby World Cup again in 2007, beating England in the final, still wearing the green and gold jersey. Yet again, the whole country exploded in celebration, black and white and all shades in between.

ACKNOWLEDGMENTS

First of all, a thousand thanks to the many players in the South African drama who took the trouble to talk to me for this book.

Thank you to Pearlie Joubert, for fixing for me to see them, and just for being so great.

Thank you to Stephen Glover, as well as Andreas Whittam Smith, for appointing me South Africa bureau chief of the London *Independent*. Had they not showed such faith in me way back in 1989, this book would never have happened.

And thank you to Javier Moreno, my present boss at *El País*, for indulging me with the time necessary to write it.

A warm thanks to my private editor in Barcelona, Elena Ramírez, whose blend of rigour, intelligence, and support have made an immeasurable contribution.

Zelda la Grange (along with Pearlie, a strong contender for the title of greatest living female South African) was very kind. So too were Moegsien Williams and Kathy Macfarlane at the Johannesburg *Star*, and Amanda Oosthuizen at *Die Burger*. As was Marietta Van Wyk.

Indra Delanerolle, David Fanning, Sara Blecher, Sharon Cort, Cliff Bestall, Lindy Wilson, and the rest of the gang on the TV documentary we made on Mandela: much thanks to all.

Friends and acquaintances who prodded and suggested and encouraged, and to whom much gratitude is due, include (those I have omitted, please forgive me) Daniel Tanzer, James Lemoyne, Peter Ettedgui, Mark Phillips, Wim Trengrove, Stephen Robinson, Jorge Valdano, Jeremy Thompson, Tony O'Reilly, Teresa Rioné, Morgan Freeman, Sebastian Spear, Jayendra Naidoo, and Tony Peckham.

Special thanks to Lauren Jacobson and Keith Coleman, Michael Shipster, Joaquín Villalobos and Kobus Jordaan, fine friends so very generous with their time and knowledge and sharpness of mind.

Gail Behrman did a terrific job pulling together the photographs for this book. Sue Edelstein's advice and sensibility and encouragement and kindness were a huge boost, every step of the way.

Anne Edelstein (no relation), my Barcelona and New York-based agent, was decisive. The idea for this book had been stewing in my mind for years. Without the enthusiastic impulse she provided it might never have happened – and it certainly would not have happened now. Her devotion to the enterprise, both as a book and as a cause, has been invaluable and inspirational.

Thanks to Anne, I found my editor, Eamon Dolan. He (and Anne) provide confirmation of a long-standing belief that the best Americans are the finest of people. If this book has any value, a big chunk of the credit must go to Eamon – a brilliant, exhaustive, passionate wordsmith. I still cannot believe my luck.

Thanks also to my very fine editor at Atlantic, Ravi Mirchandani, and his magnificent slip-fielder, Mark Handsley.

Finally, thank you to South Africa for having shared its secrets and its genius with me. Thank you to Nelson Mandela and the thousand less famous Mandelas, of all shades, whom I had the immense good fortune to meet in my time there, whose generous spirit infuses the best this book has to offer. I think of Justice Bekebeke, I think of Walter Sisulu and Ahmed Kathrada, I think of my old pal Mandla Mthembu (who saved my life at least once), I think of Kader Asmal, Terror Lekota, John Battersby, Dudu Chili, Cyril Ramaphosa, Shaun Johnson, Ronnie Kasrils, Jacques Pauw, Gill Marcus, Debora Patta, Carl Niehaus, Max du Preez, Henrietta Mqokomiso, Halton Cheadle, Aziz Pahad, Ali Bacher, Anton Lubowski, Andy Durbach, Brian Currin, Desmond Tutu, Tim Smith, John Allen, Helen Suzman, and I think of the late, great Bheki Mkhize, the kindest, bravest, noblest man with the biggest heart I ever met, anywhere. He lit up South Africa for me like the sun.

A NOTE ON SOURCES

Practically all the material for this book is based on interviews I did either specifically for the book, between 2000 and 2007, or in the course of my general journalistic work after I went to live in South Africa in 1989. One project I was closely involved in, a TV documentary on Mandela: broadcast on PBS (*The Long Walk of Nelson Mandela*) and SABC (*The First Accused*) and elsewhere in 1999, was especially valuable. Some books proved very helpful too, among them: Nelson Mandela's autobiography, *Long Walk to Freedom*; Anthony Sampson's *Mandela: The Authorized Biography*; François Pienaar's *Rainbow Warrior*; *Days of the Generals* by Hilton Hamann; *One Team, One Country* by Edward Griffiths; *Anatomy of a Miracle* by Patti Waldmeir; *One Step Behind Mandela* by Rory Steyn and Debora Patta; *Apartheid: The Lighter Side* by Ben Maclennan; *The Other Side of History* by Frederik van Zyl Slabbert; and *A Common Purpose: The Story of the Upington 25* by Andrea Durbach.

INDEX